MY LIFE AS A MOUNTAINEER

MY LIFE
AS A MOUNTAINEER

by

ANDERL HECKMAIR

Translated by
GEOFFREY SUTTON

LONDON
VICTOR GOLLANCZ LTD
1978

First published in Germany under the title
Mein Leben als Bergsteiger
© Nymphenburger Verlagshandlung GmbH., München, 1972

English translation © Victor Gollancz Ltd, 1975

First published March 1975
Second impression June 1978

ISBN 0 575 01930 1

Printed in Great Britain at
The Camelot Press Ltd, Southampton

CONTENTS

LIST OF ILLUSTRATIONS

CHAPTER I

In the Beginning

As an undernourished orphan during the First World War I had the luck to be sent to Switzerland for the summer holidays in order to recuperate. There were 40 of us, with two nuns in charge who took us for walks in the neighbourhood of Stans. Hand in little hand as befitted orphans, we walked up the paths leading to the Bürgenstock, where the sister clapped her hands and said: "Now, children, you may run around and play." Immediately, we tore off up a steep gully interrupted here and there with short vertical rock steps, scrabbling off loose stones without a thought for those who were following behind. Before long there came a scream of terror; someone had been hit by a stone and had fallen down the gully. Nobody was allowed to move until one by one we were escorted down by some local inhabitants. The boy who had been hit was lying dead in the grass. Until help came I had to remain beside him with one of the sisters. It was my first impression of the seriousness of the mountains. I found it quite natural, and it in no way prevented all my thoughts and desires from inclining towards mountaineering.

Nobody is born a mountain climber. Upon leaving the orphanage I was apprenticed to the respectable calling of gardener. During these years, between the ages of fourteen and eighteen, despite the heavy physical labour of gardening, I went in for all kinds of sport, gymnastics, athletics and the like. My older brother was my example; each time I attained his level and began to surpass him, he would change to a different sport and I would feel bound to change too. Then a stroke of destiny took me to Stuttgart.

One day while I was there I received a postcard from my brother who was up in the mountains. Immediately, my old longing flamed up. I could think of nothing but how to get up there again. By chance I was offered a grant to attend the Advanced Horticultural College at Weihenstephan bei Freising, and grabbed at the opportunity. How I managed to study, to live and to spend almost every weekend in the mountains on 30 marks a month is nowadays a puzzle to myself.

It was not long before I found a circle of friends. As it was wintertime, one of them dug out a pair of skis for me and took me up to a hut. I had never worn skis before and knew about them only from hearsay. It was also the first time I had experienced the atmosphere of a mountain hut, and I felt proud and happy to be there. We had carried the skis up an icy goat-track in the dark; long, ugly looking things with a comical binding of leather thongs. Early next morning we strapped them on, together with some kind of sealskins, and set off up the Brünstein. The uphill plodding and trail-breaking came as a real pleasure to me, and I grasped the idea of kick-turning at once, so that I was always a couple of hundred metres ahead of the others. I reached the summit in great shape and without the least care for the descent. Presumably it would be just like a standing sleigh ride. There seemed no point in hanging about, so I attacked straight away. Aha, so that was how one did it! All one needed to do was to pick out a spot to head for and land on in a heap. I found it great and continued by this technique all the way down to Bayrischzell. Suddenly I felt so exhausted that I could not even eat, and the others, who at least had some idea of how to do a snow plough turn, did not seem to be much better off. This in no way impaired our enthusiasm, since at that time nobody really knew how to ski anyway. Many winters were to go by before I picked up the technique by trial and error. When at last in 1932 I took my ski-instructor's test, an onlooker remarked pointedly: "Never seen so many bad skiers on one slope all at the same time."

All my thoughts and desires were of the mountains. Passion lies deep in the soul and is not to be explained. It can lead to supreme heights but also to ruin.

While I sat there on the school bench, my brother had in my eyes developed into a real mountain climber. Knowing my uncontrollable nature, he had no intention of letting me come with him. However, I knew that next weekend he and his companions would be going up to the Meilerhütte in the Wettersteingebirge above Garmisch. In the secret hope that he would ask me along I accompanied him to the station, but the thought never entered his head. Sadly I slouched home. It was true that there remained one more train to Garmisch,

although it did not get there until 11.30 p.m. But after all . . .
why not? No sooner thought than done. I groped my way up
through the darkness as best I could, and in the dawn twilight
slumped down on the bench in front of the hut. The first to
appear through the door were my brother and his friend.
"How the hell did you get there?" they asked. However, they
could not very well chase me away, so instead they took me
along with them to the Musterstein.

By the time the next weekend came around they knew that
there was no point in not taking me along, so I was able to
join in the trip to the Kopftörlgrat in the Wilden Kaiser.
Modest and well-behaved, I trotted behind them on the way up
from Hinterbärenbad to the Törl, and the end of the rope
was passed over to me with the words: "There! That's so
that you can become a great mountain climber." I thought to
myself: "They're a bit crazy, but I suppose it must be a
custom." Astonished and slightly apprehensive I followed my
leaders as they worked their way panting and snorting up the
chimneys and grooves. When it was my turn to climb I simply
thought "Why do they need to make such a lot of noise about
it?", but said nothing and kept my thoughts to myself until
we reached the summit, where I asked: "Is that all there is to
it?" Upon this, my brother Hans, who always took great
interest in my upbringing, gave me a resounding box on the
ears.

That same year my brother and his friends arranged to
meet at the Stripsenjochhaus in the Kaisergebirge. As it was
pouring with rain, Hans suggested that if I took his place he
would pay my fare. In this way he avoided making a journey
in vain and at the same time did not let his friends down. That
was all right by me, and I did not care two hoots about the
weather. As far as Hinterbärenbad I knew the way already,
but at that point it began to grow dark. Naturally I had no
torch. Night and cloud combined to create a darkness, as impenetrable as the legendary Stygian gloom, so that I literally
could not see my hand held up before my eyes. There seemed
nothing for it but to sit it out until morning. The rain continued, and presently I grew so wet and cold that I had to
move at all costs. I groped my way up the path backwards in
a sitting position, but even then I was none too sure if I was
still on the right track. After I had been sliding around in the

wet on my backside for hours it began to grow lighter at last, and I was able to rise to my feet. By the time I reached the hut, the rain had turned to snow. Not really expecting anyone to open the door, I knocked half-heartedly and had already picked out a half-dry spot to lie down on when suddenly the hinges turned and a sleepy but kindly girl ushered me into the warm inner room. She brought me some dry clothes and I curled up on the bench before the stove, rejoicing in the marvellous change. I woke at about 6 a.m. as the first climbers began to appear out of the dormitories. Outside, everything was powdered white and the sky a radiant blue. I waited for my brother's friends to appear, but they seemed not to be there.

A climber sat down next to me and began to sort out his pitons and karabiners. I had heard of these things. Fascinated, I looked on respectfully. Presently he asked: "Are you alone too? If you like, we could do something together." I would have gone with him on any face without another thought. He suggested the north spur of the Predigstuhl and I agreed with enthusiasm.

The gullies and grooves leading up to the foot of the climb were wet and icy. The first pitch begins with a traverse. I watched piously to see how he would tackle it. After he had slipped a couple of times he announced: "It's no good, it won't go today." I asked him to let me have a try, and somewhat derisively he agreed. I stepped down, used the hold on which he had been standing as a handhold, and suddenly there I was in the cracks above, so I continued and finished the pitch. When his turn came to follow he was most complimentary and took over the lead until the next difficult pitch, where it was up to me again. So it went on until we came to the final tower.

Failing to find the normal route (the Opelband) we climbed straight on. That was when it happened. I was on a small but good stance, belaying over a spike of rock, when he skidded off an admittedly icy slab and swung to and fro below me on the rope, wailing "Slack! Slack!" in the most alarming manner. Centimetre by centimetre, so that the rope should not run out too fast, I lowered him down to a ledge where he could stand again. What was I to do next? He had the hammer and all our pegs and karabiners on him. "Abseil down to me!" he called. "Yes? How?" I had absolutely no idea how one went about such a manœuvre, and anyway I wanted to go up, not down.

After a prolonged exchange he hit upon the idea of tying the ironmongery to the rope, and I hauled it up. I then drove in the first piton of my life, though not without a few powerful blows on my own fingers. Luckily he was no more than ten metres below me, so I was able to lower the rope doubled. One strand I fixed so that he could climb on it while I pulled him on the other. By the time he finally reached me he was as white as a cottage cheese; there could be no question of going on. Back then. I had to tell him exactly where to go, like a little child. As afternoon dimmed into twilight he wanted to call for help, but that was not at all to my taste and for a moment we almost came to blows. Somehow or other we reached the foot of the spur in total darkness. As for groping our way back to the hut, I had had plenty of practice. After depositing him I found my way down to Kufstein alone, so as at least to catch the first train back to Munich in the morning. At the station in Munich I ran into my brother, all gripped up. I felt positively touched.

The climbing bug now really bit me for the first time. The holidays had arrived, and in order to earn some pocket-money I took a job in Munich. Each evening after work I cycled up the Isar valley to the training crag, where the experts were to be seen swinging from hold to hold like monkeys. To climb like that became a goal. For the time being I contented myself with the fingertip traverse, which is close to the ground. After a few evenings it began to go better, and soon I began to strike up friendships with others of about the same standard. The great men paid no attention to us beginners. For our part we observed them closely to see how to tie on and above all how to distribute one's weight so as to climb and abseil cleanly.

As yet I did not possess a rope of my own, but a pair of proper kletterschuhe* were my pride and joy.

Somehow we tend to associate with those neither much richer nor much poorer than ourselves, and so it was that I teamed up with another climber who possessed nothing at all,

* *Translator's note*: A light boot for rock climbing only. Nowadays rubber-soled, in those days they were usually shod with felt. The German name is used by English and American climbers.

not even a rope. Regardless, we resolved to try the east face of the Lamsenspitz in the Karwendel. In spite of my dubious success on the north spur of the Predigstuhl I had gained greatly in self-assurance, feeling myself already in the position of leader although ropeless. Anywhere my companion found himself in difficulty I lowered him my anorak, and he pulled up on it. It seemed the most natural thing in the world. We cycled home feeling extremely pleased with our success.

A week later my friend fell to his death on the east face of the Watzmann, which he was trying with other companions. That is a risk that climbers take, but it ought not to have happened so soon. Just one week later, another friend from the training crag fell off and was killed in the Karwendel. It began to dawn on me that mere rock-climbing technique is not all that a mountaineer needs. Nevertheless, this did not inhibit me from trying to climb one of the more notorious faces, the east face of the Fleischbank in the Kaisergebirge. Once again my partner was an acquaintance from the practice crag, this time a dentist's son who possessed a rope.

My brother had by now grasped the fact that he was not going to keep up with my development as a climber—he was always the more reasonable of the two—but nevertheless wanted to be somewhere around and therefore teamed up with Hans Ertl to do the west face of the Predigstuhl, right opposite the Fleischbank. We climbed quickly, having already learnt and practised the various tricks for getting up the harder bits and doing tension traverses at the training crag. Now I wanted to see what really severe pitches were like, but even those that were so graded seemed no harder than what I had already done elsewhere, and certainly far from extreme. The play of balance that gives the marvellous feeling of freedom came naturally to me, and as I was never extravagant in my demands I was quite happy to make do with small holds. Nevertheless, the death of my two comrades was a wholesome and painful recall to realities. Even if one is lucky enough to have a kind of sixth sense it still needs to be exercised, developed and sharpened. The early, impetuous years are the most dangerous, and in those days far more so than now.

Our cheerful shouts echoed backwards and forwards across the crags, then suddenly there was a curious noise and the other party became very quiet. Not until we were sitting together on the Stripsenjoch after successfully completing our respective climbs did we learn that a solo climber who was following us had fallen off and been killed. The faces of Hans Ertl and my brother, who had had a clear view of the fall, still bore signs of the shock.

Later the same year, my companion on the Fleischbank also fell off on the Vajolet Towers, so I teamed up with Hans Ertl and climbed a number of fine routes in the Kaisergebirge, the Karwendel and the Wetterstein. One of them remains in my memory particularly because through no wish of my own it was my first first ascent. Hans wanted to do the east face of the Oberreintalturm. However, we could not even find the start. "If we just climb straight up," I said, "we're bound to reach the summit." No sooner said than done. Hans was not all that keen on the idea, but when he emerged on the top, covered in blood as a result of my dropping a stone on his head shortly before, his pride over the first ascent was hardly to be restrained. To me this seemed rather incomprehensible, since I was embarrassed at having to admit that we had failed to find the proper route. However, I first felt really badly about the whole thing when, as a result of the inadequate description we had given him, Franz Singer, a most likeable member of our circle and an excellent climber, fell off and was killed trying to make the second ascent.

This eventful year of 1928 ended with our finding favour in the eyes of the tigers whom we had admired at the training crag, and we were elected members of a ginger group called the Hochempor. The qualifications were to have done a number of extreme climbs and to be able to play Schafkopf, as at the weekly gathering each member would give an account of the route he had done the previous weekend and then everyone got down to playing cards. Anyone who could not play did not belong. For us, membership represented not only a great honour but also a great advantage, as the club had two huts for its roughly 30 members, the Bockhütte in the Wetterstein and a ski hut on the Spitzing. The latter was particularly interesting at this time, as I wanted at all costs to improve my miserable abilities on skis. All the other members were already hot skiers and racers without much understanding for my problems as a beginner.

In Bayrischzell there was always a ski-jumping competition

at New Year. One of the participants, Leo Rittler, broke a leg while training, only one day before the event. "You'll just have to take his place," I was informed; and when I objected "But I don't even know how to ski yet," nobody was interested. Leo's jumping skis were passed over to me, and we hung on behind a car from Neuhaus to Bayrischzell, arriving safely just in time for the competition. My knees were still knocking from the ski jöring, and after a look at the ramp I began to shake inwardly as well. Suddenly it was my turn, or at least the turn of my number, as I was jumping for Leo. Well, if I made a mess of it, he was the one who would get the blame. The thought comforted me and gave me confidence. As I jumped an appalling gulf yawned before me, then the next moment I thudded on to the steep landing slope. Applause broke out, but nobody was quite so surprised as myself at my success. Feeling quite the star, I climbed back up the tower. This time I fell heavily, but that was the usual thing. Successful jumps were infrequent. That was just a little artistic licence, I thought, this time I'll show them. Show them I did: I landed so heavily that pieces of ski flew in all directions and I had to be carried off on a stretcher. My grateful public took a collection, which proved so generous that I was able to replace Leo's old skis and buy a pair of jumping skis for myself.

By spring my broken leg was healed. Not only could I ski again, but I wanted to try out my new jumping skis. There was still snow on the Hochalm above Garmisch, so we spent a whole day whizzing down a home-made ramp and rushing back up again. Admittedly I could still only ski in a straight line, but for ski jumping nothing more is required. I smiled pityingly at the others as they practised their turns, feeling immeasurably superior until suddenly I planted my tips and had to be carried down again. As I was brought into the same clinic in Munich that I had only just left, the doctor stared at me. I comforted him with the thought that the leg he had just healed had stood up perfectly to the strain, and that this time it was only a knee. It turned out to be the meniscus, and by the time they could let me go the spring was over.

That summer I finished my studies. My report turned out better than I could have dreamed, so that on the strength of it I got a job in the Munich municipal gardens. They had no idea what they were taking on. On Sundays I would do a difficult climb and often help to carry down the victim of an accident. On Monday and Tuesday I would be tired, on Wednesday I would have to go to the funeral, which they could not very well refuse, and on Friday and Saturday I would be saving my energy for next Sunday's climb. So it went on week after week, month after month, throughout the summer. Small wonder that my superiors looked on me with disfavour. To me, my mountaineering achievements were of far more importance. Before concentrating on first ascents I wanted to climb all the classics within reach, since I had already evolved my philosophy, namely to climb for my own pleasure and not to impress others.

That summer of 1929 brought me wonderful experiences. With various companions I climbed all the hardest faces in the Kaisergebirge, the Wetterstein and the Karwendel one after another. Nowadays, these climbs count as nothing very special, but at that time they had been done less than a dozen times. Few people were interested in them, and those who climbed them tended to be exaggeratedly praised or condemned. Either way, we did not care; we had disputes of our own. For example, the south-east face of the Fleischbank, climbed a few years earlier by Wiessner and Rossi, had still had very few ascents. The weekend before our turn came, Leo Rittler and Peter Aschenbrenner had climbed it, and during the week a party came rushing down with the tale that all the pitons had been removed. So what? Those who had made the first ascent had got along without them. We decided to go anyway. My companion was Wiggerl Gramminger, whom I shall often have occasion to mention in this book. We climbed the face, found enough pitons for our purposes, and took out as many of them as we could.

The following weekend found us on the Laliderer Wand in the Karwendel. I had already walked along the foot of this gloomy north face in the course of a solitary expedition as a boy. I had gone up to the Karwendelhaus, got a place in the attic dormitory and overslept in the morning because the shutters were closed. Furious and therefore all the quicker I had clambered up the Birkkarspitze and along the west ridge to the Kaltwasserkarspitze, then down a very steep gully that turned into a chimney, then uphill again to the Halleranger-haus—at this distance in time I cannot remember the whole route exactly. On one narrow ledge, however, I came round a corner to find myself suddenly face to face with an outsize mountain goat. I do not know which of us was the more startled. When the goat began to back away I thought it was in order to charge, but in fact it was only to turn around and dash away with a clatter of stones. In the evening I reached the Falkenhütte. Never again has any face impressed me so much as that incredible wall, not even, strange as it may sound, the north faces of the Grandes Jorasses and the Eiger. The awed impression of youth remains the most profound.

Now, however, we stood at the foot of the wall well-equipped, as we had a description of the route from Dr Wilo Welzenbach, who had carefully warned us about all the traps and dangers. Of the two of us, Wiggerl Gramminger, was the more experienced mountaineer, but, as leading is what brings the most pleasure, he unselfishly let me go ahead. Nevertheless, I felt as though it were really I who was being led, as he directed me upwards metre by metre. By early afternoon the wall lay below us. While we were on the way down the Spindler gully a storm broke, and in order to avoid being hit by stonefall we had to climb back up again.

Now began a twelve-hour march along the Rossloch towards Scharnitz, then over past the Karwendelhaus to the Falkenhütte, which we reached in the half-light of dawn. After a little reviver we carried on down to the place where we had left our bicycles and pedalled back to Munich. Passing through Grünwald it occurred to us that it would be fun to play around for a while on the training crag. We were going to miss work that day anyway. On the crag we ran into friends who greeted us excitedly with the words: "The mountain rescue (which we belonged to) is just sending out a search party for you." Somebody had the idea of telephoning from the nearest café to say that they had found us on the training crag. Instead of praise we got a good telling off.

We had made the mistake that beginners often make, whatever their age, because they are simply unable to imagine that others are worrying about them. But that was not the only charge that we had brought upon our guilty heads. The same weekend, another party had set out to do the south-east face of the Fleischbank and found very few pegs, some of which were, moreover, badly knocked about. Forced to retreat, they blamed their failure on us. Our fellow climbers treated us like outlaws. However, I did not care too much about that. My view was and is that if someone feels himself man enough to tackle a particular climb, he should not expect to have it prepared for him by others. Wiggerl Gramminger did not agree, and felt that we should make up for what we had done and at the same time demonstrate that we ourselves could climb the route without *in situ* pitons. So back we went and replaced the more necessary pegs. Honour was satisfied, at least in our own imagination.

What I personally failed to understand was why climbers were so often judged according to nothing but the severity of the climbs they undertook, when there were so many other beautiful things to experience in the mountains. In this respect I owed a lot to my work, that had given me an eye and a taste for geology and botany. Even the roughest among us were sensitive to all these beauties of nature. I am convinced that it has always been so and always will be.

CHAPTER II

Out of Work

DURING THE COMING winter I was determined to learn to ski properly. I had had enough of jumping, and since I mightily enjoyed the whole business of seal-skinning, breaking the trail and running down through the deep snow—even if only in a straight line—I was now much keener on touring.

One day, however, it happened that there was a cross-country race, and some of my friends, knowing my powers of endurance, insisted that I should take part. At least it would be safer than jumping. A further minor incentive was that the start and finish were in Bayrischzell, where my brother had settled down as a goldsmith and photographer. He lent me his cross-country skis, and shortly before the start took me into a field and showed me how to use them. With a warning not to wear myself out at the start he tied on my number bib, and after the count-down "Three, two, one, go!" away I went. In view of his warning I walked rather than ran, and was therefore naturally overtaken. I thought to myself: "Just wait a while. When I cut loose I'll eat the lot of you." It was the eighteen-kilometre race counting for the Munich championship, and when after ten kilometres I decided that the time had come to accelerate, I found I was too tired and just plodded on. I was deeply ashamed to find myself last on the list.

Not long afterwards came the Bavarian cross-country championships, also at Bayrischzell. This time I wanted to redeem myself in my own eyes and therefore set out from the beginning to race until I dropped. Putting the plan into practice I did not drop at all, and even overtook some very well-known racers. Just before the finish I passed the person who had started ten places before me. He was a good sort, since he stared at me in an astonished way, shook my hand and congratulated me. Much later I was to learn that this was Wiggerl Vörg, who was to play such an important part in my life. This time I was satisfied with myself, and did not care what place

I had obtained. When the finishing list appeared, however, Vörg, whom I had overtaken, was credited with a time superior to mine by several minutes. Wiggerl could not swallow this and immediately lodged a protest, only to be shot down in flames. A judge never makes a mistake! Well, if it was like that they could stuff their races. I preferred touring anyway. But I never forgot Vörg's sportsmanship and sense of justice.

I really wanted nothing more to do with racing. It was true that I had slightly improved my technique, but I was well aware how little I still knew. Perhaps the others had not noticed, as they challenged me to join them for a relay race. Apparently they thought I was the ideal man for the first lap from the Rotwand to the Spitzingsee. Personally, I had strong doubts about this, but I could not let my friends down, so I duly plodded up to the Rotwandhaus where the starting line had been fixed.

It was cold, the snow was being driven along by the wind, and a lot of strong racers were waiting for their turn to start. I knew this descent, I could feel the apprehension in my guts, and now I had to race down it. This kind of thing tends to affect our insides, and shortly before my number was due to come up I felt a powerful call of nature. The "place" was a privy above a trench. No sooner had I sat down than there was an explosion, presumably caused by the gas under the frozen crust, which blew me right off the seat and covered me with stinking muck. At least I was only plastered from behind: another person who had just opened the door to go into the next compartment got the lot in his face. Once the initial fright was over there was a great roar of laughter that put me into a towering rage. I stripped off my underpants, wiped myself down with them, hurled them away and dressed again as best I could. As soon as I re-emerged my number was called. I was happy to get away from the guffaws and grinning, and also to get ahead of my own stink, so that on the climb up to the col I overtook two men whom I would never normally have caught up. On the descent I hurled myself downhill with such fury that all slopes seemed flat and I lost all sense of speed. The inevitable happened. Shortly before the end of the lap, where the next lot of racers were waiting to take over the batons, an almost invisible stone stuck out of the snow. I crashed into it heavily. On getting to hospital I was given a good bath, for which I felt positively grateful to my broken coccyx.

The joys of racing were definitely not for me any more. That my employers at the city gardens should regard my ambitions without enthusiasm seemed natural enough, and I was in no way surprised to receive my notice. Widespread unemployment was beginning. So long as I remained in hospital, however, I could not be dismissed. My wages were paid, I received sickness benefit, and also got something from an insurance policy, so that by the time I was let out I had 1000 marks. I had never been so rich, and decided to stay up in the mountains as long as the money should hold out. Companions were soon found. Hans Brehm did not need to be asked twice, and Hans Ertl promised to follow us with somebody else. We fancied a trip to the Dolomites. At the headquarters of the Bavarian section of the Deutscher Alpenverein we heard a famous climber, Walter Stösser, giving a talk on the fourth ascent of the north-west face of the Civetta. In the course of his lecture he mentioned: "The number of ascents may be limited, as the hand-traverse with which the climb begins is crumbling away and when it goes there will be no way of getting on to the face." We believed this quite literally—presumably he did too—and suddenly we felt drawn to the Civetta.

Our only means of getting there was by bicycle, and to solve the luggage problem we built ourselves "the gig", a little trailer that could be loaded with our voluminous rucksacks and towed behind a bike. As far as the top of the Brenner everything went well, but from there to Bolzano the roads were all torn up for reconstruction. The trailer was useless on such ground, so we ended up carrying not only the rucksacks but the trailer as well. Days of pushing over the Karer and Pordoi passes did not worry us too much. There was hardly any motor traffic. After a few days we reached Alleghe, where for the first time we were able to take a refreshing bathe in the lake before going up to the Coldai hut. The sacks were lashed to the gig, but we did not get far with it and before long we had to shoulder both the sacks and the infernal gig again. To cap everything we were caught by a storm on a col below the hut, so we quickly pitched the tent and crawled into shelter.

It was still very early in the year, and the mountain was

plastered in ice and snow. However, this did not stop us starting up it next morning. The initial hand-traverse was indeed earthy and brittle, but only about half as bad as we had imagined from the description. It appeared that even the accounts of famous mountaineers were to be taken with a pinch of salt. The wall was in fact tricky, but we advanced quickly until we came to another traverse. By the time I had got across this it was 10 a.m. Hans Brehm fell off after a few moves and swung at least ten metres until he was hanging below me. Haul and tug as I would, I could not shift him, and finally had to let him down a couple of metres to a place where he could stand. There was nothing for it but to abseil down to him.

With hanging heads we sat there and thought of giving up. "Let's just try once again." I fixed a rope across the traverse, and this time it went. At 2 p.m. we stood on the same stance that I had reached four hours earlier—and this on the biggest and hardest face we had ever tried to climb. We did not even have a bivouac sack with us. The only solution was to go fast. We managed to keep up our speed and reached the summit at eight o'clock that evening. It was still light enough to climb down if only we could have found the way. Thick cloud had built up from the side of the ridge. There was no alternative but to sit down behind a stone and wait for clearer weather. However, we were in such high spirits after our efforts on the face that neither the wet nor the cold bothered us in the least. During the night the cloud thinned out and it came on to rain. By dawn it was really pouring, but we could see and discovered the way into the gully. Here we found a track and began to argue whether we should go left or right. I insisted, though inwardly I was far from sure. For hours we followed it to and fro from one gully into another. Thick fog closed down on us again as the path vanished into a grassy pasture. "Now you're in the clag," grumbled Hans. Suddenly we heard something. We were standing 20 metres from the Coldai hut.

We celebrated our victory with a plate of pasta and a quarter-litre of wine, then carried on down to our tent where we found Hans Ertl with Mungo Herzog, brother of the famous Otto, known among climbers as "Rambo".

Every climber has his own life style. When I am not actively doing something I tend to be lazy, and could not be induced to stir from our marvellous camp site for the next week. Hans Ertl, who was an excellent cook, mollycoddled us until we recovered some drive.

Our next route was the east face of the Sass Maor, climbed by Solleder and Kummer in 1926 and still awaiting its second ascent. We had been starting to think of ourselves as the lords of the mountains, but at the sight of these 1100 metres of yellow crag our knees began to tremble. All our expectations and fears were duly fulfilled, as knowing nothing about étriers and such like aids we had to climb everything free.

However, we were already using double-rope techniques. We hit on this idea for a very simple reason. In those days the only ropes we had were of hemp 12 and 13 mm thick. As they had to be 40 metres long for the climbs we were doing, they were just too heavy. Even so, on an occasion when the leader of another party fell off I saw the rope snap. Probably it was an old one. Anyway, the incident decided us to start using two thinner, lighter ropes, thus giving each of us a lesser burden to carry. The idea that this would lead to a development of climbing technique never entered our minds at first. We only thought that if one rope broke in the event of a fall the other would hold. However, we soon found that overhangs were much easier to climb if one of the ropes was clipped to a piton with a karabiner and then held in tension while the leader leant back, hammered in another piton, clipped the other rope into it, and then took tension on this second rope while the first one was left slack. In this way we managed to climb quite considerable overhangs.

This ascent of the Sass Maor was the subject of my first article. I sent it to an Alpine review which printed it at once. When a fee eventually came I was astonished at first, and then I thought: "What a small fee for such a big climb. They ought to be ashamed!"

As a "dessert" the day after the Sass Maor we were tempted by the Schleierkante, which was to remain my favourite climb in the future.

After this I gave way to laziness and set off for home instead of going on climbing. In spite of the state of the roads, without the gig I made it from Bolzano to Bayrischzell in a day.

I wanted to bring a present home for my brother, and had

therefore packed Italian cheese, sausage, bread, fruit and chocolate into the rucksack. At eleven o'clock at night, three kilometres before Bayrischzell, I was suddenly seized with such ravenous hunger that I sat down on a wood-pile and gobbled the lot. Once started, I was simply unable to stop. A few minutes later, with empty hands and troubled conscience, I reached the house where my brother lived. He was out. There were not all that many taverns, and it did not take me long to find him. He was in the process of celebrating his victory in a chess tournament. I joined in with a will, and neither of us ever knew how we got home.

The summer of 1930 was not over yet, and to give my brother a treat I took him up the west face of the Totenkirchl. This trip turned out to have a decisive effect on my mountaineering future, as up at the hut I met Gustl Kröner from Traunstein. He had just been doing some difficult ice climbs in the western Alps.

I could not hear enough about his adventures in the high western ranges. He told me about the Grandes Jorasses and the north faces of the Eiger and the Matterhorn, all of which he had already at least seen. If we teamed up together, he said, we could try one of these faces. I thought he was crazy, as I had never climbed on ice. "That doesn't matter at all," he said. "Anyone who can climb rock like you can manage on ice." Moreover, we did not necessarily have to attack the face right away; we might just look at it and then perhaps do something else. That made sense to me, but the question was which one to look at. The Mont Blanc range offered the most possibilities, and besides I liked the name of the Grandes Jorasses best. By the time we quit each other's company it was definitely decided that we would visit the Mont Blanc area together the following year.

But all that was still a long way off. First, I had to get through the winter. In the meantime I had indeed registered as unemployed, but it was hardly possible to survive on the relief, let alone go climbing. Other members of the Hochempor Club were in a similar position. We therefore decided to go without the inadequate dole and moved up to our ski hut at Spitzing. Those who still had jobs brought us so much food at the weekends that we could always get through the following week somehow.

I became particularly close friends with Bartl Hütt, with whom I had already done some climbs in the Kaisergebirge. Now that hard times had thrown us together, we noticed to what a remarkable extent we complemented one another. Bartl was as strong as a bear and rather silent. He was an infinitely better skier than I and took some trouble to teach me what I needed to know for ski touring. This was exactly what I wanted, as I had had quite enough of any kind of racing.

We stayed up in the hut until spring, at which point he first came out with a plan, namely to tour in the central Alps. My objection that I could not ski well enough was simply brushed aside. As for thoughts of money, he just said: "If we wait for money, we'll never get out of here." That seemed clear enough, and our preparations did not take long. On 1 March 1931 we set off. Each of us carried two rucksacks, one in front and one behind, stuffed full of food. We had 30 marks between us. Thus equipped, we left Garmisch station with the intention of reaching the Ötztal somehow. We chose not to follow the road over the Fernpass, but humped our four rucksacks up the track from Lermoos to the Wolfrats-hauser hut, having conceived the crazy idea of running down to the Fernpass from Grubigstein. Moreover, we intended flitting from hut to hut, since the rules of the Alpenverein guaranteed us an overnight hut-fee of 40 pfennig in case of emergency, and that was the utmost we could afford. And somehow or other we did succeed in getting down to the Fernpass, though I hurtled over a little cliff in the process. I was able to hold on to the precious rucksacks, but broke a ski stick. Once we reached the road we built a sledge with the skis, loaded the rucksacks on to it, and sped off down the pass.

Bartl had been on the road once before, and knew how to get a night's lodging at a monastery. With piously raised eyes he asked the brother porter at the little fortified cloister below the pass for alms and a spot to curl up in for the night. Both were accorded to us in exchange for a prayer for the poor. We then spent the night in the straw of the pigsty with one of the brothers.

Next day we tramped on into the Ötztal. A heavy truck gave us a lift as far as Zwieselstein, at which point the driver noticed with horror that he had lost one of our ski sticks.

With many apologies he bought me another pair. I could not trust myself to protest.

For weeks we wandered through the Ötztal range, making ourselves useful in huts, now and again guiding a few tourists, and constantly under the impression that each tour would be the last and that we should be asked to leave the country within 24 hours. Yet miraculously it went on and on, and for the time being we had more money in our pockets than when we set out.

Gathering confidence, we crossed over via the Gepatschtal to the Silvretta. Above Compatsch we reached the Heidelberger hut without realizing that we had passed through Swiss territory. Again we moved on from hut to hut, making our situation known on arrival and asking for odd jobs. We chopped wood, fetched post and provisions, folded blankets and swept dormitories: no task was beneath us. Most of the hut wardens were reluctant to see us move on, but we did not want to get bogged down. There were many ups and downs, not only on the mountains, but also with tourists, hut wardens and guides.

It is still a mystery to me how our inadequate equipment survived weeks and months of tough, unrelenting use. Never once did we really get stuck on account of it. With the steel edges, however, we waged unremitting war, until finally we nailed them right through the skis and hammered the points over. Every single summit within reach was climbed. When new snow fell we nearly always broke the trail, and the tourists and even the guides behind us were so grateful that they would stand us a meal and a drink in the hut afterwards. We also humped rucksacks from hut to hut for tourists. Our original idea of carrying two sacks of our own had soon been given up, so we generally had room for a tourist's sack on our chests. Bartl frequently even went so far as to carry three, but I preferred to do the trip twice.

By the time we reached a new hut we had generally been talked about by tourists and were thus expected. At the Wiesbadener hut the warden even greeted us with the words: "Ah, there you are at last. Go into the kitchen and have a bite to eat, then ski down to Galtür, spend the night there at my expense, and tomorrow bring up everything written on this list." We were a little bit astonished at being disposed of in this way. However, it was Easter, and when we saw the hordes that were staying in the hut we understood well enough. Moreover, it turned out to be in no way to our disadvantage: when we got back to the hut with the post for the guests, they had a gigantic Easter dinner waiting for us.

Our campaign had now lasted six weeks. On reaching the Tübinger hut we sat down and counted up our wealth, which came to precisely two schillings. "What should we do," asked one, "head for home or slip over the border into Switzerland?" "We can't get home on two schillings anyway, so Switzerland it is."

Down in Klosters it was already spring. Our first thought was to try building-sites to see if we could earn something. Everywhere they would have been glad to have us, but it was against the regulations. Next we tried in a nursery garden. Naturally, I had no testimonials with me, and the boss was mistrustful at first. However, when I was able to reel off the names of all the plants in a hot-house, and he began to credit my claim to know something about laying out gardens, he became most enthusiastic, found us rooms, and said he would soon fix everything up. In the meantime we were to go around to his house and get a meal from his wife. Having gone hungry for a week, we did not need to be told twice. It was nearly supper-time. The good lady placed an enormous bowl of noodles and sauce on the table and told us to tuck in without waiting for the others. That was her mistake. Our hunger was so overpowering that we were unable to master it. Bartl normally ate enough for two men anyway, and now he ate for four while I ate for two of the absent homecomers. In a few moments the bowl was clean. When the boss and the others came in and found nothing left his eyes bulged and his wife was properly horrified to think that we had devoured the lot in such a short time. However, the Swiss cannot be accused of inhospitality. As the others made do with coffee we again kept up with them powerfully.

After we had worked for a week the local policeman appeared and told us to leave the country. The boss gave us some money and told us to disappear up to a hut, during which time he would get work permits for us. Nothing could have suited us better. We went up to the Parsenn hut and spent our time enjoying the fabulous ski runs, the fame of which we never suspected, until the boss came to fetch us. He had succeeded in obtaining permits, but after a few days the policeman came around and withdrew them again because we had previously worked illegally. In darkness and fog we set out, provided, nevertheless, with food and generous pocket-money. The boss had tears in his eyes at having to lose us. We were supposed to leave the country at once, but instead trekked over via the Vereina hut to the Engadine and went up into the Bernina range.

At the Boval hut we ran across two well-known climbers from Vienna, Dobiasch and Vaitl, who next day guided some tourists up Piz Palü. Really we had intended to have a rest-day, but the fine weather and ready-made tracks were too tempting. We set out late in the morning and caught up with the others on the summit. Far from being praised for our speed, however, we got told off for taking advantage of the track. One would have expected such great men to be above all that. Next morning we got up at three o'clock and made the trail all the way up to the Piz Bernina. This time Messrs Dobiasch and Vaitl did not disdain to follow in our track, about which they were most complimentary afterwards. Vaitl stared hard at my anorak with a hood, an article of clothing completely unknown in those days. "Where did you get that?" he asked. I explained that I had found it at the foot of the Civetta. "Then it's mine," he said. "I brought it back from Lapland and left it lying at the foot of the Civetta." Such things happen. A friendship was struck up, and we had no more need to worry about food supplies or hut fees.

After this we sampled the grazing around the Coaz hut. In particular, I remember skiing down from the Fuorcla della Sella at sunset as one of the most beautiful moments of my life. It was now the end of May, and gradually we began to think of home.

Our skis and everything else we did not immediately need were sent off by rail from St Moritz. We ourselves set out on Shanks's pony, rather annoyed at having forgotten to forward the rope, which we took to be an unnecessary piece of ballast. In this we were very much mistaken. Just before reaching Zuoz we spent the night in a haystack only to be turfed out in the grey light of dawn by a farmer whose language in his Romansh dialect was truly terrible to hear. Since he had woken

us up quite unnecessarily, it seemed to me that it was ourselves who ought to be cursing. As he showed no sign of ever
leaving off, I suddenly said to Bartl: "Get him!" That was all
Bartl had been waiting for. Next moment the farmer took a
short but unwilling flight head-first into the hay, then ran off
towards the town. As our night's rest was now disturbed
anyway, we pulled on our shoes and naïvely started to walk
in the same direction. In the middle of the town our way was
suddenly barred by three men, one of whom was our farmer
and another the policeman, although not in uniform. It was
the most critical moment of the entire trip. One false word and
there would have been an almighty punch-up.

Bartl was already in an attitude of joyous readiness. The
policeman said soothingly: "Don't do anything silly. We just
want to know who you are and whether you're on the wanted
list." That sounded reasonable enough, and we went meekly
along with them. They led us to a house and up a steep staircase, politely stood back to let us enter a room first, slammed the
door behind us and locked it. It hardly seemed elegant to have
lured us into a trap like that. On peering out of the window
we saw that our prison was a turret room, and that below
the window was a smooth wall ten or twelve metres high
descending into a garden. What were we carrying the rope
for? A couple of minutes later we were standing in the garden.
It is definitely a mistake to imprison mountain climbers in
towers.

A forced march through steep forest brought us across the
border to Ehrwald, from where we had enough money to
catch the train to Pasing, a suburb of Munich. The kindly
ticket-seller paid the extra out of his own pocket so that we
could go on through to the main station. No such good Samari-
tan appeared to help us with the tram out to Giesing, our
destination, so we just had to pound along through the city
on our blisters.

The blisters soon went away, the bad moments of the adventure were quickly forgotten. What remained was an experience
that the thickest wallet in the world could not have purchased.
And already the next adventure was beckoning.

CHAPTER III

Attempts on the Grandes Jorasses

BARTL HAD TO report back to the labour exchange in order to survive. For my part, I still had an arrangement to visit the Grandes Jorasses with Gustl Kröner, and it was now high time for us to make the necessary contacts. He had meanwhile been preparing everything, so that just four weeks after my return from Switzerland we set off for Chamonix on our bicycles in company with Leo Rittler and Hans Brehm, who had their sights on the north face of the Matterhorn. As far as Lucerne our roads lay together, and our parting was coarse and uproarious. It would have been more emotional had I known that I was not to see them alive again.

We set up our headquarters at the Leschaux hut below the Grandes Jorasses, carrying our loads up from Chamonix via Montenvers. Financial considerations ruled out the mountain railway, so each trip took five or six hours. Our undertaking was financed partly by the Bavarian section of the German Alpenverein in the strictest confidentiality, and partly privately. In particular Gustl Kröner himself, who though not exactly rich was not poor either, sank his entire savings into our venture. I had nothing to offer but my companionship and drive. As long as the latter did not become too excessive, Gustl was in agreement.

In the hut was a two-burner cooker. We soon learnt how to deal with it; so well, in fact, that it would not go unless we wanted it to. Whenever we saw a party coming up the glacier to the hut—we could spot them a good two hours in advance—we would switch it to "out of order". After watching them fiddle around with it for some time we would do our rescuing angel act, thus earning their gratitude. In bad weather we would have a brew of hot tea waiting for them, so that our relations with all visitors were of the best.

It was mid-July when we made our first cautious approach to the face. It disappointed us from every angle, and from the foot it looked as though we could climb it in a couple of

hours without any trouble. My powers of judgement were
untroubled by any experience whatsoever. Gustl merely
grinned. Putting on crampons was quite a little ceremony; I
had never had such things on my feet before. The bergschrunds
were soon crossed, and after a couple of pitches on steep ice
Gustl let me do some leading so that I could get the feel of
it. And indeed, I felt at home straight away. "It's great," I
shouted down. "You don't have to hang around looking for
holds." The steepness did not bother me in the slightest. The

With Gustl Kröner on the Grandes Jorasses

treacherousness of ice was something I only learnt about
much later in very disagreeable circumstances. Gustl, however,
was careful, hammering in ice-pitons at stances and as running
belays, and thus in my estimation wasting far too much time.
He cut his way upwards step by step. When my turn came,
although a complete beginner on ice, I did without steps and
just walked straight up on my ten-point crampons. After that
he would not let me lead any more. This was undoubtedly a
piece of luck, as we were only half-way up the ice slope when a

storm gathered from the west and imposed a rapid retreat. As
we abseiled down I noticed for the first time how steep the ice
was. We were hardly across the bergschrund when the storm
broke. It did not last long, but already stones and avalanches
were whizzing down the gully up which we had been intending
to climb. That such a little storm could produce so great an
effect! Was it possible therefore that the gully might not be
the safest way up? With this revelation we walked back to the
hut and celebrated the fact that we were still alive.

The weather was unusually bad all that summer of 1931.
There were never more than two or three fine days before
another bad period set in. So it was now, and it was nearly a
week before we were able to get back on to the face. Wise from
our experience, we avoided the gully and climbed diagonally
towards a buttress on the right. Even here we came under fire,
and a stone the size of my fist knocked the axe out of my hand
and half cut through the rope. By some miracle I was unhurt,
but we had had a shock and beat a hasty retreat.

Our third attempt was on a line up the Walker spur, later
to become famous. But the time was simply not yet ripe for
the north face of the Grandes Jorasses. Today I realize that
what we thought of as bad luck was in fact a colossal stroke of
good fortune, since drive and rock-climbing ability are not
enough in themselves. The requisite equipment and experience
for such an ascent did not yet exist. Far greater mountaineers
than ourselves, with whom we could not even be compared, had
had no better luck. Some years earlier Welzenbach and Merkl
had also been repulsed.

After a while it began to seem stupid to be always just
starting up the same face and turning back without having
achieved anything, so we amused ourselves with other projects.
On our return from the Mer de Glace face of the Grépon we
found Welzenbach and Merkl at the Leschaux hut. They told
us about their attempt on the north face of the Charmoz and
how a storm had forced them to traverse out to the right from
the top of the big ice slope. Naïvely and not very tactfully we
announced that we would go up and do the first direct ascent
of the face. Apparently this idea did not suit them too well, as
a couple of days later they again set out from Montenvers to
finish the climb. Once more a storm caught them high up, and
they remained stuck in the same spot for three days. The

newspapers were already blowing the affair up into a drama and for good measure reported us missing also, while we sat in the warm hut frying flapjacks. When the flour finally ran out we went down to Chamonix and there learnt of our disappearance. However, we were seriously worried about Welzenbach and Merkl, and went back up so as to be ready to look for them next day. It seemed as well to find out at Montenvers where they had last been seen. At four o'clock in the morning, to our amazement, the window of their room stood open. As we stood there wondering what it might mean, a form appeared. It was Welzenbach. They had traversed eastwards across the face through continuing bad weather, passed over the summit, and finally got back to Montenvers at midnight, five days after starting out. As though they had not been getting enough fresh air in the course of three bivouacs, they had been sleeping with the window wide open and thus had heard our muttered conversation. Naturally they asked us to come up to their room, where at that unearthly hour we drank a bottle of wine to celebrate their return.

Meanwhile dawn had come, and as we had all our climbing gear with us it seemed best to make the most of the day. We therefore walked up the Mer de Glace to climb the Dent du Requin. Another storm surprised us in an icy chimney just below the summit. This time we had really had enough. "Requin" meant shark, we remembered, and decided to head for where the real ones swam around—it would certainly be warmer. We descended to Chamonix, got on our bikes and pedalled off towards Marseilles. On the way we saw a signpost which said 250 kilometres to Nice. That was no part of our plans, but if it was practically on our way like that, after all, why not? So we turned left towards Nice. Twenty kilometres before reaching it we freewheeled down out of the mountains, and as we finally arrived we dashed into the waves with happy shouts.

Next we wandered along the whole Riviera to Marseilles. The Tour de France was on, and despite our rucksacks we were often taken for strayed racers and appropriately treated. There seemed no reason to disillusion anybody.

In the old port at Marseilles we ran across other Germans who offered to find us work on the docks. With a view to replenishing our purses we accepted gladly. All we had to do was carry 100 kg sacks. Gustl, who was even weaklier than I, refused at once. However, I had been observing an aged, emaciated Arab trotting down the gang-plank with one sack after another. Ambition seized me, and I signed on. The first sack almost crushed me, then I seemed to get the hang of it, but after a couple of hours suddenly I was whacked. My knees buckled. Gustl, who had in the meantime been rolling barrels, was watching me mockingly. Quickly he came over and helped me back to my feet. All my "colleagues" were extremely kindly and sympathetic.

I was mightily ashamed, but the ready cash we were paid was a powerful and comforting remedy. We immediately invested in an enormous lunch. As for accommodation, we were recommended to try the poorhouse, where one paid nothing and got a bowl of hot broth. You had to be there at 6 p.m. and were let out again at 6 a.m. We were not all that keen to bed down among negroes and Arabs, and anyway we wanted to see something more of the sinful city, for which there was more than one opportunity in the area of the old port. But not without money. We were ready for any adventure, but as "they" generally demanded payment in advance and we had nothing to pay, we always got shown the door. Nevertheless, we had good fun until one o'clock in the morning. As there seemed to be nothing doing, we got on our bikes again and headed for Chamonix, which we reached after two and a half days and went straight on up to the Leschaux hut.

As we passed under the north face of the Grands Charmoz it looked so inviting that we suddenly said: "Let's do it now!" Sensibly, however, we decided to have a good sleep, a rest and a meal, and then to go for it. Towards lunchtime next day we were satisfied and could feel no more trace of fatigue, so we decided to bivouac at the foot of the face. By three o'clock we were there. It seemed much too early to bivouac. We were sure to find a good site higher up.

So up we went. The first part of the face, a kind of pedestal some 600 metres high, contained no difficulties worth speaking of. It was indeed loose, icy and streaming with water, but at the speed we were going we had no time to think about such things. By six o'clock we were at the foot of the main ice slope. That seemed to be about enough for the day, so we

We did not always have to push our bicycles—sometimes we had to carry them. On the way to the Bernese Oberland (1931)

Crossing the Brenner with the gig (1930)

Cross-country with
the gig

started to arrange a bivouac in the crevasse between the rock and the ice. At this moment the whole snowcover of the ice slope suddenly slid off and went thundering down over the pedestal. We were doubly lucky not to be still on the pedestal and to be out to one side of the slope. After this our little bivouac site somehow seemed less attractive; who knew if there might not be something more to come? It seemed more prudent to go up at least as far as the upper edge of the ice slope.

Never again have I experienced such curious conditions. The surface of the ice was hard, but as soon as one cut a step the meltwater came pouring out of it like a spring. I felt like Moses smiting the rock, only I had no one to provide for. There was so much water that it began to fill up our boots. Without steps then! We had no twelve-point crampons, as they had not yet been invented. Stamping all my ten points hard into the slope, I ran out a whole pitch as fast as possible, then cut a stance, hammered in an ice-peg, and let the water spray over my feet. Using risky methods like this it was scarcely surprising that we made rapid progress and soon reached the upper edge of the icefield.

Unfortunately, the angle here was so steep and the ice so rotten that there could be no question of a bivouac. Which way had Welzenbach and Merkl gone? We would have been glad to find any way off, but only succeeded in reaching the ice gully leading to the summit. Before long it began to grow dark; down at Montenvers the lights came on. We still had enough light to see that a bivouac here was impossible. The beginning of the gully looked almost vertical. However, in the bordering rock wall there was a crack parallel with the slope just the right width for jamming the hands and the right distance from the ice so that one could continue to walk up on crampons. It went excellently, only I could find nowhere to stop. Gustl did not relish this piece of gymnastics, but just had to climb at the same time. At last I reached a break, there was snow again in the bed of the gully and I could stand in it. It was high time, as the crack in the rock wall had petered out and it was now almost totally dark. The exit was not far off, though garnished with a giant cornice. I did not trust the monstrous structure at all and directed Gustl out of the line of fire to a place where he was even able to belay. It was just as well, as I had hardly begun to dig my way through when the entire wave of snow broke over my head and carried me down with it. Gustl hung on like iron and I found myself panting on the end of the rope. But not for long. Clambering up again, I found no difficulty now that the cornice was gone. After a few more rocks we reached the summit together just as the full moon rose. Transported with happiness, we fell on one another's necks and yodelled our joy.

The word "wet" does not describe the state we were in, but there was nothing we could do about it. The careful Gustl had brought a sleeping bag along with him. Though it was only designed for one man, we managed to insinuate ourselves into it. He also had a handful of rice. What more could anyone desire? We had moonlight although we were wet, the most wonderful view imaginable although we were cold, and when all was said and done there was no wind and in due course morning came again.

Such things, combined with the feeling of danger surmounted and inner satisfaction at one's own performance, are the reward of the mountaineer. Any external recognition would have felt quite alien at the time, and when we got down to Montenvers next morning we celebrated with a small glass of beer as we sat and gazed up at the north face we had climbed. Every phase of the fight came back to us, accompanied with the feeling of danger. We had challenged fate to such an extent that we almost felt shamefaced to be alive. Now, however, we were able to enjoy a well-earned rest at the hut. Gustl looked after the inner man while I revelled in an orgy of botany and geology, filling the hut with flowers and crystals. We had no difficulty in finding customers for the latter in Chamonix, and were thus able to carry plenty of goodies back up with us.

For the north face of the Grandes Jorasses we were acquiring an ever-growing respect. With our inadequate equipment it was clear that we would never survive bad conditions, and there seemed no likelihood of getting as much as a week's fine weather.

Another spectacular storm chased us back to the hut from the traverse of the Dru. This expedition took us nineteen hours, and as we stumbled back up the Leschaux glacier with only the dazzling lightning to show us the way we were close to exhaustion. For lack of anything better we put some potatoes on to boil, then lay down for a rest until they should be ready. By the time one of us woke up the hut was full of blue smoke and an odd smell. It was still dark. Then we discovered that it was not still dark, but dark again: we had slept for a whole day, and the potatoes in the saucepan looked like shrivelled lumps of coal.

We owed our miscalculation on the Dru to presumption. A couple of days earlier on the Rochefort ridge good conditions had made everything seem so easy that we had jumped to the conclusion that where the guidebook said two hours we could count 20 minutes. We had therefore reckoned six hours for the Dru and in fact required nineteen. It came as a real blow to our morale, and our formerly overweening pride was reduced to nothing. Hence our hesitations concerning the Jorasses.

However, we did not remain idle for long. Moving over to Courmayeur, we walked up to the Gamba hut with a view to climbing the Peuterey ridge, only to run into storms once more. By the time we got back to the valley it was fine, so up we went again to the Torino hut—all this naturally on foot, as there was no cable car in those days—then down the Mer de Glace, reaching the Leschaux in a snowstorm.

The hut was shut on the outside as usual, but inside reigned the disorder typical of a hurried departure. Suddenly it hit me: "Leo Rittler and Hans Brehm have been here!" We had indeed heard at the Torino hut that the north face of the Matterhorn had been climbed, not by Leo and Hans but by the brothers Franz and Toni Schmid. We did not begrudge them their victory; on the contrary, it gave us great pleasure, as they belonged to our own circle of friends. But how would Leo and Hans feel about it? A suspicion had formed itself in my mind: perhaps they would come over to Chamonix to join in our fight for the Grandes Jorasses. Now the suspicion had become a certainty. I reached into the pocket of a jacket hanging on the wall and found Hans Brehm's passport in my hand.

There could be no further doubt. Outside the storm raged with unimaginable power, and our friends were up on the face. Of course it was also possible that they were down in

Chamonix buying provisions, but I did not believe it. I knew Leo and Hans too well. In their disappointment over the north face of the Matterhorn they had certainly gone straight up to the Grandes Jorasses. There was also a chance that they would turn back; it was still only early afternoon. Just in case, we brewed some tea. The clouds seemed to be thinning—there, almost at the foot of the face, something was moving! I rushed out and shouted. There was no reply. I had imagined the movement. It was just a rock, not so far away, with the cloud blowing over it. We could drink the tea ourselves. As night fell hope began to fade. Next morning the weather was still bad. "Why don't we check down in Chamonix? Maybe we'll run into them down there," Gustl suggested. In Chamonix we met a lot of climbers, but no Leo and Hans. With hanging heads we went back up to the hut, not looking at the people we passed on the way. What did they know of our struggles and worries? Towards evening the weather cleared slightly as we neared the hut, and hope revived for a moment. But again there was nothing. There could be no further doubt that they were on the face. Not being quite so close to them as I, Gustl was able to be a little more optimistic, although he understood and shared my disquiet.

Next morning dawned fine at last. Immediately we trekked up to the bergschrund with the firm intention of climbing the face until we should find out what had happened to Leo and Hans. However, there was no need to go any farther. At the lower bergschrund I saw a hand sticking out of the snow. We found our friends stiff in the new snow, still roped together. The sun was now touching the summit of the mountain and the face was coming to life. It was no time to hang around; we stood exactly in the fall-line below the central gully. We dragged the bodies out of the danger zone, buried them again in the snow, marked the spot, and hurried down to report what had happened. On the way we ran into climbing friends who took over the task, and before long the stretcher party arrived. Now we were no more than onlookers, and for the first time I was overcome with grief. Many important personalities came to the funeral in Chamonix. Where they had come from and why they came I did not really understand. All of a sudden our presence was no longer required, and we followed at the tail of the procession. Our home-made wreath of pine and heather was the last to be laid upon the graves.

For that year we were sick of the Grandes Jorasses and the whole range of Mont Blanc, but before setting off home we went up once more to the foot of the face and swore to return.

CHAPTER IV

A Ski Tour in Spring

AFTER THE LONG journey home from Chamonix, it was time to come to terms again with the problems of everyday existence. For Gustl this presented no great difficulty, as his father had a flourishing painter's and decorator's business in Traunstein; but for me it was a real headache. Timidly I reported to the Munich labour exchange, partly hoping, partly fearing to be offered a job. And indeed, an amiable young woman informed me: "Someone has been inquiring for qualified gardeners in the Rhineland." Travel expenses would be paid to Opan. A tremor of panic ran through my limbs, not at the prospect of work of any kind, but at the thought of having to move. There was no obligation to take any job offered, but my refusal meant that I could draw no unemployment benefit.

When times are hard it is best to keep out of the way of people we know, especially if our problems are of our own making. I therefore found it downright disagreeable when a delivery van stopped beside me and a childhood playmate jumped out and greeted me affectionately with "How are you? What are you doing these days?" and so on. When I told him that all I had in the world was a rumbling stomach he suggested I become his partner. He made his living buying fruit and vegetables in the city markets and selling them in the country, and urgently needed someone to help. I accepted with enthusiasm. The van, however, was temperamental. It was a Model T Ford and looked more like a hearse than a delivery van. We had to get up at 3 a.m. in order to light a small fire under the engine and then crank it by hand for half an hour before it would consent to start.

The goods were bought at the central market and sold to country shops for 100 per cent profit. We needed this margin because the old vehicle not only had an enormous petrol consumption but also swallowed up three litres of oil per 100 kilometres. In addition, as we had no spare wheel, we would have to stop and patch a tyre three or four times per trip. Wheel off, tyre off hub, tube out, clean puncture with petrol, apply prepared patch, put it all together again and give 600 strokes with the hand pump, then drive on until it happened again. In time it became almost automatic and hardly bothered us any more. The only drawback was that we could never be punctual and the customers would get grey hairs. We carried on like this all winter, until one day near Pasing as I was driving home there was a terrible noise and the peevish old truck refused to move another millimetre. It steamed like a locomotive, while at the same time brown icicles hung from the radiator—it was always leaky, and we used to plug the radiator with chicory coffee-powder.

Like an idiot I peered under the bonnet, knowing already what had happened. The crankshaft had broken.

A policeman strolled up and remarked that the van seemed to be on its last legs. "They've just given way," I replied. "What should I do?" After intense cerebration the policeman advised me to take off the number plates, since everything must be dealt with in the proper order and I would need to hand them in. The van could be left standing where it was and would be towed away in due course. My friend and partner was most upset, but there was nothing he could do. We therefore divided our takings, and I went off to see Bartl to ask him if he would not like to do another little ski tour.

This time we decided to go somewhat farther afield to the Bernese Oberland and, if we could make it, on to the Valais. Having a happy experience of bicycling, we sent off our equipment and skis by rail to Gletsch, hopped on to our bikes and pedalled off towards the Rhône valley. The start of our tour was not very encouraging. It was 3 a.m. on 1 April 1932 when I went around to rout out Bartl, and a snowstorm was in full swing. At Pasing we had to go into the station waiting-room in order to warm and dry ourselves. However, we were not too put out. The snow stopped, it got light, and we set out on our journey in good spirits, reaching Kaufbeuren the first day.

Like the temperamental April weather, our mood changed from light-hearted optimism to utter despondency. Was the adventure feasible at all? This time we had 50 marks between us. Anyhow, we were on our way, and in due course we somehow reached our first objective. On inquiring about our sacks at Brig we learnt that there was indeed a station at Gletsch, but no trains, as the line was closed for the winter. A kindly railway clerk telephoned half Switzerland before finding out where our sacks had got to. It would take at least two days for them to arrive. Seeing what a pair of poor devils we were he offered us his hospitality, and sheltered and fed us until our kit arrived. In the course of our conversation, he wondered what had impelled us to set out on such an adventurous journey. When we replied that rather than fritter away the time waiting for work and living on charity we preferred to accept effort, hardship and hunger if by doing so we could live fully, he understood. The mountains were our ideal, we explained. Up there we felt no social distinctions, and what we needed would always turn up. Out of his honest heart he wished us good luck and loaded us up with as much food as we could carry. Travelling thus, we met people and certainly got to know them better than one who goes first class with a bulging wallet.

Our next move was to push our heavily laden bicycles up to Fiesch, where we stayed in the youth hostel.

Two days of climbing took us up to the Concordia hut, which we pronounced our headquarters. No summit in the vicinity was safe from our attentions. Every time we thought we were running out of food or money for wood—every stick of wood we burned had to be paid for—a party of tourists would arrive with excess supplies. It was astonishing to see how many tried to get away without paying the hut and wood dues. We watched them like hawks, and nobody fancied actually coming to blows with Bartl. On one such occasion when it got quite tense, we were silently observed by a couple of Swiss. As we triumphantly put the carefully reckoned dues in the safe, they came forward, introduced themselves as officials of the Swiss Alpine Club section to which the hut belonged, and presented us with a free pass to all their huts.

By the time we decided to go down to Fiesch again the whole of April had gone by. An army unit had occupied the hut. On the coat-hooks in the vestibule hung salami sausages. As we went out the temptation was too much: we stuffed one hurriedly into a rucksack, then headed out into the wide open spaces of the Aletsch glacier. White-out conditions prevailed, and we were unable to find the way through the maze of crevasses to the notch by the Märjelensee. The decision whether to bivouac or to return to the hut was trying in the circumstances, but in the end common sense won out. After all, we thought, even if they have noticed the missing sausage, they can't very well just put us straight up against a wall. In fact all that they had noticed was that we had gone; they even seemed glad that we had got back before dark, as the weather had taken a turn for the worse. We hung the sausage back in its place, and spiritually relieved took our place in their circle. Before long we were telling them about the tours we had done and our projects in the Valais. We were taken for veritable prodigies, and next morning there was no more need to pinch sausages; they loaded us up with as much of their rations as we could carry.

We had now been up in the mountains for over three weeks. In the youth hostel where we had left the bikes an atmosphere of panic reigned. They had already reported us missing to Bern. It was difficult to grasp that we mattered enough for anyone to worry about us. Finally, we were sent off with the admonition to give news of ourselves now and again when we wanted to be away for long.

Down the hill to Brig we spun, along to Visp and then up past St. Niklaus to Zermatt. On the last stretch there was no road, only a path up which we often not only needed to push the bikes, but to carry them. Our first impressions of Zermatt were given by three days of unrelenting rain. We set up house in a hay barn. Our provisions were better suited to staying in a hut than in the valley; the staple was polenta, supplemented with fat, salt and sugar. The small remaining quantity of sausage we wanted to preserve for special occasions. In his own special brand of black humour Bartl chanted fervently: "Our father, who art in heaven, send us this day some money so we can get enough daily bread to make the table bend, then let us get on up the mountain!" However, our heavenly father did not take pity on us, and there was nothing for it but to walk up to the Monte Rosa hut with empty stomachs, where for the first time we allowed ourselves to make real inroads into the polenta. This gave us enough drive to tackle Monte Rosa, which, being in good training, we were able to do easily enough in the day. On the upper slopes there was powder, then a short zone of breakable crust, and on the moraines such perfect firn that at every turn the snow spray spurted over the outcropping rocks. The joy in our faces found an echo on those of a group who had been observing our descent from the hut. It must be admitted that at first we were not so overjoyed to see them, as it is always pleasantest to have a hut to oneself. Our moroseness was, however, rapidly dissolved by their friendly reception. The guides Friedrich Schneider and Toni Matt had tea ready waiting for us, and were horrified when we wanted to make do with our polenta alone.

Next day the group attempted to find a way up the tortuous Zwillingsgletscher to the summit of Castor. Meanwhile we went up the Grenzgletscher and climbed the Lyskamm. The double-corniced ridge gave us a lot of trouble as it has many another party, and more than once the cornice collapsed under one of us, forcing the other to jump down the other side of the ridge. This did not cause us any particular comment, as we had already had occasion to practise the technique on the Grünhorn in the Bernese Oberland. We reached the summit about midday and got back to the hut late in the afternoon.

Soon afterwards Matt and Schneider arrived back with their party, having failed to find any way through the labyrinth of crevasses on the Zwillingsgletscher. "How far did you get?" they asked. "To the summit." "Go and tell that to the marines." They took it as a big line and left us alone with our polenta.

Next day we exchanged objectives. Naturally we did not try to get through where the others had failed, but where it looked possible to us. We struck lucky and reached the summit. By following our trail the others also reached their summit without too much difficulty, and that evening were profuse in their apologies for their mistrust and incredulity. Good terms were once again established. As the conversation came around to the Civetta, the Grandes Jorasses and the Charmoz, their respect knew no bounds. Thus it was natural that they—then the best skiers in the world; in those days there was as yet no distinction between skiers and mountaineers—should invite us to accompany them up Castor. Admittedly the weather turned bad, but it gave us a lot of fun. The conditions forced us to set such a pace that Toni Matt could only just keep up, while the others were obliged to wait on the col for our return. We all skied down together, Bartl and I out in front without ropes, since we found they spoiled our pleasure, the others carefully roped up behind. This went on until Schneider snarled at us: "I don't care what you may have done, now you're going to rope up. I can't stand this recklessness any longer!" Bartl replied: "But there's enough of you to haul us out of anything we fall into!" Nevertheless, we obeyed the well-meant injunction.

After doing a few more tours together we parted the greatest friends. They too left us all their surplus provisions and paid our hut fees and wood taxes, so that in a roundabout way our heavenly father seemed to have helped us after all. We stayed up at the hut until the last crumb was consumed.

An attempt to climb the wintry Matterhorn did not succeed; in fact we failed to reach even the Hörnli hut, and with this reminder that the mountain is always stronger than the mountaineer we set off for home.

CHAPTER V

Morocco

BARTL GOT HIMSELF fixed up with another job. In my case it was not even worth asking, as in the meantime something quite different had cropped up through the intermediary of Gustl Kröner. Somehow the idea of an expedition to the Atlas mountains had grown up in the Bavarian section of the German Alpenverein, and Gustl had been invited to go along as a junior member. He immediately made it a condition that I should be asked too. Some were in favour, others strongly against. While awaiting the decision, I went back up to our club hut at Spitzing. Even there, however, I needed something to live on, and as I had not a bean in the world I decided to go over the Rotwand to Bayrischzell in order to stay with my brother. It was a reluctant decision. Thus I was happy to accept the invitation of a Bavarian friend up at the Kleine Tiefentalalm. "Anderl!" he called. "Come in and drink a cup of tea." I stayed with him for two months.

In the meantime our expedition had been abandoned on account of financial difficulties. We made up our minds to go anyway on our bicycles. Strictly on the condition that we should make up a team of at least four, we were offered some support. The companion who had invited me to tea up at the Kleine Tiefentalalm was Arwed Möhn, famous for having traversed the Alps from Vienna to Chamonix on ski, and he suggested his brother Felix as fourth man. Indeed, we had no other choice.

In the meantime something happened which was to have a decisive effect on the course of my life. Here I must go back to the year 1930, when Leo Rittler had set out to climb the west face of the central summit of the Predigstuhl with Karl Brendl. In the course of the ascent Brendl, who had made the first ascent of the south ridge of the Aiguille Noire de Peuterey and was reckoned one of the best climbers of his day, fell off and was killed. In the attempt to hold him Leo burnt his hands on the rope. Immediately thereafter he had an

engagement to guide an American who was especially keen
on difficult routes. In view of the state of his hands Leo did
not trust himself to lead the south face of the Scharnitz in the
Wettersteingebirge, and invited me along for the purpose.
Thus indirectly I obtained my first guiding job. After Leo was
killed on the Grandes Jorasses the American, whose name
was Edwards, remained faithful to me and engaged me as his
guide—although I had not yet become one—in the Gesäuse
and the Dolomites.

Two years later we climbed again in the Kaisergebirge.
With us was Hans Steger, a friend of mine from Bolzano and
at that time one of the best mountaineers in the Alps. We
took our American client up the south-east face of the Fleischbank, and were mightily proud to have done it in two and a
half hours despite being a party of three. Not so the American;
he was even rather annoyed. "I want value for my money,"
he said, "and that means at least a ten-hour climb. We'll go
back and do it again tomorrow." Such a point of view was
not only foreign to our conceptions, but at the time absolutely
incomprehensible. However, next day we obediently went
back to the face, wondering what to do to fill in the time. We
practised climbing up and down the cracks, did all the rope
traverses two or three times and sunbathed on the ledges. In
the end we found it all such fun that we decided that Mr
Edwards' approach was really the only way to get the maximum
pleasure out of a climb.

Mr Edwards next insisted on climbing the Schleierkante
in the Dolomites. I was restless and impatient, as I had arranged
to set out for Africa with my friends in the middle of July.
When we got back from the Schleierkante, however, Mr
Edwards put his car and chauffeur at my disposal. I had
myself driven out to Bayrischzell, where I had just one hour
to get my kit together, say goodbye and head back to Munich,
where the others had already been waiting the whole day with
freshly greased bicycles. It was 4 p.m. when I arrived and we
set off at once in the direction of Africa, stopping, however, in
a beer garden for a last tankard, since we would not be having
another for a long time.

Our road lay through Switzerland, then down the Rhône
valley past Nîmes, Montpellier, Sète, Port Bou, and so over
the frontier into Spain. In these motorized times such a journey

is no problem, but on bicycles and with road conditions as they were then it may be regarded as something of a feat. We surprised ourselves by reaching Barcelona in a week. There we discovered that a group ticket on the train would work out far cheaper than the slow journey by bicycle, and all the more so as Felix's visa was not in order and we had to go via Madrid. Getting the visa fixed up at the consulate caused no particular difficulties; these first arose when we tried to get a night's rest on the lawn in front of the imposing post-office building. There appeared to be some kind of a baby revolution going on, and a number of fugitives went sprinting past with the police at their heels. As they were unable to catch up the fugitives they arrested us instead. It was clear to them that our ice-axes were highly suspicious instruments of death and destruction. We were clapped straight into a cell, where to our profound satisfaction we discovered quite passable bunks. However, hardly had we made ourselves comfortable than we were hauled out again for interrogation. There was an interpreter to do the translating, but they had only the haziest notion of mountaineering. Nevertheless, the atmosphere began to thaw.

Presently a climber was found who could speak German, and the tone of the meeting became positively hearty. They offered us coffee and cigarettes, and we had to explain exactly how to use ice-axes, ropes and pitons. Our nailed climbing boots were particularly admired; they had never seen anything like them. Finally they decided to let us go. However, as we had nowhere to go to, and as sleeping in the open seemed to be too dangerous, they allowed us to stay in the cell. Next morning we were escorted to the station. This turned out to be an unexpected advantage, as the station was thronged and in tumult. The trains were so crammed that without our escort we would never have got on.

From Algeciras the ferry took us across past the Rock of Gibraltar to Ceuta. The first bathe on the African coast was something of a disappointment. Despite the midsummer heat a cold wind was blowing; the rocks were not exactly beautiful and were covered in sea urchins on which we promptly stepped. Next a couple of jellyfish stung us on the hands, which burnt worse than nettles. Thus served we retreated to dry land where, however, our ordeal was not over. A pack of

Arab urchins attached themselves to us, screaming with joy whenever our nailed boots slid on the up-and-down streets, polished by the bare feet of generations of Arabs, so that we sat down hard. In the end we took off our boots and went barefoot too.

A short trip by rail brought us to Tetuán, whence we had to cross the Rif mountains to Larache by bus. There were classy buses for Europeans, but they cost too much for us and we preferred to travel on the Arab one. It was supposed to leave the market square at eight o'clock in the morning. Like good Germans we were on the spot punctually, but there was no bus to be seen. We were assured from all sides that it would be coming presently, so we did the same as the Arabs and sat down in the dust to wait resignedly. The bus made it about noon and was stormed in a general uproar. We found a place for ourselves and our baggage on the roof, where there was fresh air, the welcome wind caused by our speed, and a wonderful view. We sat there feeling pleased about it all until, as dusk drew down over the mountains, shots rang out. The driver drove full tilt down the steep dirt road, so that we were hard put to it not to roll off.

The following evening we reached the Atlantic coast just as the sun set in splendour. The journey went on past Rabat and Casablanca to Marrakesh. Here we were as close to our first goal, the High Atlas, as Munich to the Schliersee. Nevertheless there was nothing to be seen of the mountains, and all the more understandably because Marrakesh is a big city built over a former oasis, with a European and an Arab quarter. In between lies a fine park full of palm trees where we settled down to make ourselves at home. Once again unexpected difficulties arose. It was not so long since the area had been, as they say, "pacified". The region we wanted to visit lay beyond the demarcation line. In order to obtain authorization to cross this line we had to leave a deposit which we did not possess. Instead we had letters of recommendation from the German Alpenverein and the Swiss Alpine Club. These had to be verified, and telegrams flashed to and fro. All of this took several days, which Gustl and I at least wanted to put to good profit.

Our explorations into the Arab medina went farther and farther, and we soon discovered that life really began at

sunset. The market place was thronged, and story tellers
and snake charmers found their audiences. In between were
stalls laden with every variety of sweetmeats. As we were
nibbling some of these we noticed two deeply veiled Arab
ladies gazing at us with lightning in their eyes. The lightning
struck. Taking them by the arm, we indicated that we would
like to go home with them. It seemed as though they understood and were not averse to the idea. So that everything should
go with a swing we purchased a bottle of wine and followed
them full of happy anticipation. The districts through which we
made our way became progressively gloomier and shadier.
Finally one of the women knocked on a gate which was
forthwith opened. A romantic-looking inner courtyard appeared, lit by several dim paraffin lamps. A lot of Arabs lay
sprawled out in all directions sleeping or dozing on mats. They
took not the slightest notice of us. At the back of the courtyard a
completely unromantic iron staircase led up to a row of
cubicles on the first floor. Our two beauties led us into one of
these cubicles where we settled back expectantly on leather
hassocks. In the nature of things we could not make much
light conversation and were thus all the readier to make a
grab. In order to brighten the atmosphere we drank a toast
and, big-hearted as we were, passed the bottle over to our
pair of charmers. At this moment Gustl was inspired to find
out just what we had taken on and whipped the veil off one
of them. We saw a flattened nose; projecting, over-rouged
lips; and a face no longer of the youngest. Horrified, we
sprang to our feet. The two ladies began to scream as though
they had been impaled. Grabbing our bottle of wine, we
bolted along the passage and stormed down the iron staircase
with our iron-shod boots striking a shower of sparks. My foot
landed on the belly of a sleeping man, but by now there was
such an uproar that nobody knew what was happening. The
gate opened as though by a miracle and we tumbled head-
first into the street. Still rolling in the dirt, I called out:
"Gustl, are you all right?" "Nothing missing. Still with you."
At that moment a Foreign Legion patrol came down the
alley, and an astonished voice rang out: "Germans, are you?
Well, you're in luck." At the sight of the legionaries the Arabs
recoiled, the gate slammed shut and we got to our feet.

"What are you doing here?" asked our rescuers. "We're

German too, serving in the Foreign Legion. Come with us and we'll get you out of here. This is a dangerous district."

We had really been lucky. After questioning us as to where we came from and what our plans were, they sat us down in a café with instructions to wait until they should come back. When they did, they were in civilian clothes. It was no ordinary café, but more of a cabaret where exotic beauties danced breast and belly dances. Compared with the adventure we had just been through we found it tame, and we were glad when our new-found friends appeared again. They paid our bill and said: "Come on, now we'll show you Marrakesh." We were tense with anticipation. In the event they led us straight to a brothel where the inmates sat around in scanty clothing and made eyes at us. One by one our companions disappeared with the ladies of their choice, and Gustl too picked one out. Finally only I sat there with pounding heart, feeling exactly what Karl Valentin so classically formulated as: "I would have gladly, but did not trust myself to dare." As we left the "free" house, the pitying glances of the legionaries plainly enough expressed the thought that there was nothing to be done with a character like me. They led us through tortuous alleys to a quarter where Arabs who had come in from the desert left their wives and children while they went on to do business in Casablanca. The district was closely guarded and was out of bounds for the legionaries, but as tourists, once we had given proof of our identity, we were allowed in. We remained for three days and nights. Money did not come into it, but my innocence was a thing of the past. When we emerged and went back to Arwed and Felix, who had been told by the legionaries where we were, they greeted us like prodigals. In the meantime permission had arrived for us to continue with our journey.

The mountains of the High Atlas were indeed interesting, but not at all imposing. We sought out the most interesting ways up rocky ridges and precipitous faces, also climbing the highest peak, the 4100 metre Toubkal, from which we had a fascinating view southwards into the desert. The desire one day to penetrate into those unending wastes began to germinate in my mind, though at the time I did not dream that eventually it would be fulfilled. We climbed numerous summits, but what do such "first ascents" mean? It was great fun, but after four weeks we had had enough.

The journey home was no less adventurous than the outward one. In Barcelona we recovered our bikes, happy not to be bound to schedules and timetables any longer. We travelled along the south coast of France to Marseilles, but this time without stopping, then on past Genoa, along the valley of the Po and back over the Brenner. As there were still a few lire left in our pockets we quickly changed them into schillings so that we could spend a week in the Kaiser, a perfect way to wind up our mountaineering and other experiences.

CHAPTER VI

A Man has to Eat

BACK AT HOME I found myself faced with my usual problem of how to live. I had already given up my room in Munich, so I went up to my brother's place at Bayrischzell. However, I could not go on sponging off him forever.

"Give a lecture on your experiences!" he suggested. I was far from keen, but spurred on by my need I knocked together a lecture on "Severe climbs on rock and ice" which I gave for the first time in Bayrischzell, reading from the manuscript. To my astonishment everyone was enthusiastic. Most of all I was impressed by the appreciation of a millionaire who lived in the village. "I have been everywhere in the world," he said, shaking me by the hand, "but I envy you your experiences." A millionaire had said that to me! I was paid ten marks for the lecture, which seemed a considerable sum to me at the time. Several clubs and sections in Munich also showed an interest in my lecture, and soon I was receiving from 20 to 40 marks a time.

I used the money to buy food and retreated up to our club hut at Spitzing, which I made my quarters for the whole winter. A lecture a month gave me enough to live on. During this time I put together another lecture on our Morocco trip. The "première" in Bayrischzell was as successful as before. Among the audience were visitors taking the cure at the spa; one of them who belonged to the Alpenverein invited me to give a lecture to the Hamburg section.

Thus it was that I travelled off to what seemed to me the remotest north. An elegant, chauffeur-driven car met me at the station and drove me to a distinguished-looking villa on the Alster, where I was entrusted to the particular care of the son and the grown-up daughter of the house. I was so well looked after that I almost forgot my lecture.

I still do not quite know how, all alone and clad in a ready-made suit, I inquired my way through to the lecture hall in time. It was an enormous building. Before the door stood a uniformed commissionaire who refused to let me enter until somebody from the Alpenverein arrived and piloted me in. When I saw the inside I was no little alarmed. Despite the fact that it could hold an audience of 2000 it was packed full and positively radiated carefully fostered atmosphere. And that was where I was supposed to speak! Somebody sat me down at a table and comforted me with a glass of wine. I surrendered my box of slides, arranged my script on the lectern and waited for developments.

At last everything was ready. After someone had introduced me I stepped up to the microphones, picked up my script— and suddenly went rigid. The pictures were of Africa, but the text was that of "Severe climbs on rock and ice". It rendered me speechless. Throughout the hall there reigned a breathless silence. There was not even a mousehole into which I could disappear. I had to do something. Suddenly a wave of anger swept over me and I banged my fist down on the accursed manuscript. Magnified by the microphones, the noise thundered through the hall. I simply said: "I'm terribly sorry, but I've brought the slides for one lecture and the script for another. As you only half understand my dialect anyway, you may as well at least look at the pictures." There was a great roar of laughter throughout the hall, but nothing could shake me any more. So it was that I came to give the first lecture of my life without notes or script. It was a tremendous success, and I never used a script again.

At this time a thought had been preoccupying me for some time. Leo Rittler had applied to become a mountain guide. As we had had about the same Alpine experience, why should I not take his place at the examination? I went around to ask Dr Wilo Welzenbach's advice and he promised to see what could be done. Welzenbach had great influence; in June 1933 I was invited to attend the guides' training course and examination at Innsbruck.

The course lasted six weeks. Four of these were spent at the university studying theory, followed by two weeks' practice up at a hut and then the examination. Thanks to my training at the school of gardening and all the practice I had already had on rock and ice it did not seem too difficult, and I was therefore not too swollen with pride at coming first.

The Grandes Jorasses were far from being forgotten. Gustl

was inciting me to a new attempt, but it was precisely on his account that I felt scruples. He had in the meantime got engaged, his father had a business employing ten men which would eventually become his, and he himself had artistic talent and to spare. He had studied at the Munich Art School, and *Die Mappe*, the leading review of applied art, had brought out a special issue on his work. Wherever he went, his sketching pad was always to hand so that he could capture any image that struck him; thus on the north face of the Grands Charmoz he had recorded scenes in places where it was impossible to take photographs. My view was that with so many advantages on his side he ought not to run the sort of risks that we were envisaging. We almost quarrelled over it. He would not listen to my arguments, and instead joined forces with a no less fanatical climber from Pforzheim, Walter Stösser. He was killed by stonefall while trying to make the second ascent of the north face of the Matterhorn. I was deeply upset by the death of my friend.

The news reached me in the Dolomites, where I had also just done a climb which was dangerous on account of stone-fall. Steel helmets from the First World War lay all over the place, and I decided to take one home to test its effectiveness as a means of protection against falling rocks. With the object of finding out how it felt to receive a violent blow, I donned the helmet and challenged my brother to beat me over the head with an iron bar. The helmet stood up to the shock very well, but my neck was so painful for the following week that I had to go to the doctor.

As mountain guiding was too slack for me to live off it, I signed on as a tourist guide with a travel agency for which I had worked as a ski instructor in winter. The first trip lay through the Bavarian Oberland. I was astonished to find out how much more I knew than was in the supplied programme. Mountain climbing can also be a form of education. The next journey was to the Dolomites, then I had one to Venice and three to the western Alps. On one occasion my party was unlucky with me, or I with it. A group of Swabian school-teachers had hired the entire coach. Right from the outset I was looked at askance, and while we were still in the town somebody decided to test me out by asking about some monument. "I'm sorry," I replied, "but I am a mountain guide and have only been assigned to this trip in order to help out because it goes through mountain country." After that I got some peace until we saw our first mountains. Immediately somebody piped up: "What mountains are those?" They were the Myths,* but as I did not know them I just said: "Foot-hills." Only a schoolmaster can deliver the kind of dressing down I thereupon received.

Finally we came to Zermatt. To my secret amusement it rained continuously for two days, but during the night preceding the last of our three days it cleared up suddenly. At three o'clock in the morning, clad in his nightgown and holding a candle in his hand like the Darmolmann,† one of the teachers patrolled through the corridors of the hotel intoning loudly for the benefit of all who cared or did not care to hear: "The Matterhorn is clear! The Matterhorn is clear!" In no time several of them were rattling at my door with the urgent request that I should reserve the first train up to the Gornergrat for the group. This I succeeded in doing, and once up there I was surprised myself by the radiance of the day. Everything was thickly powdered with new snow, the sky startlingly blue. I stood on a rock and pointed out the mountains around, giving the dates of the first ascents and recounting a few of the victories and tragedies that had taken place on them. My audience grew and began to include bystanders who applauded enthusiastically. Not so a little runt out of my own flock who followed my discourse with map and guidebook. "You called that mountain by the wrong name!" he yapped. Probably he was looking in the wrong direction. "And you've missed this mountain out entirely." That was because it did not seem to me very important. Suddenly I was overcome with rage. Leaping down from my rock, I told him what I thought of him in no uncertain terms. For this he brought an action against me which, however, was rejected in Germany and treated as trivial in Switzerland.

I had had enough of being a tourist guide. When I reached home, however, the next group was already waiting. It consisted of teachers from the same association who wanted to make the same trip. The agency implored me to take on the

* *Translator's note:* a range in eastern Switzerland.

† *Translator's note:* a figure in advertisements advertising a product called "Darmol".

job: what else could I do? This time the atmosphere turned
out to be exactly the opposite. Everything went off in perfect
harmony. It taught me that the mass of mankind simply
follows along behind a minority whether for better or worse,
and that a collective judgement is the most perverted thing in
the world. It was a useful lesson to have learnt at a time when
nationalism was beginning to run wild.

With this second group I again spent three days in Zermatt,
this time to my great satisfaction in fine weather. As I was
due for a day off, I wanted to climb the Matterhorn. Having
neither suitable clothing nor equipment I was, so to speak, in
civvies, so that I did not take my own project altogether
seriously. Nevertheless, I had a quick job of nailing done on
my walking shoes—Vibram soles did not yet exist—and bought
a pair of stockings and a pullover.

Thus provided for, I stole out of the hotel at four o'clock
in the morning with a lunch packet under my arm. The
essentials were quickly stuffed into my pockets and the rest
heaved into the rapidly rolling Visp for the fish to enjoy. By
half-past seven I had reached the Hörnli, where I was recognized by an Austrian guide who immediately greeted me with:
"You're going up the mountain, aren't you?" "Well, only
as far as it seems easy and safe." "At least take my ice-axe with
you." So I did, and hurried on, overtaking the first party
near the Solvay hut. I had no intention of racing or breaking
any records, but I had slipped into a rapid rhythm and there
was no one to hold me back. Up near the shoulder, nevertheless,
I had to wait for a party descending one of the fixed ropes.
After five minutes I became impatient and looked for a way
around. Above the steep section I was able to traverse back on
to the normal route along the line of junction between rock
and ice. A guide was sitting there, safeguarding his tourists;
as he saw me he started as though confronted with a ghost
or a lunatic. One could scarcely blame him, as despite the
cold weather I was clad in flannel trousers and pullover, not
to mention my walking shoes, and in order to keep my hands
warm I had stuck them in my pockets and was carrying the
ice-axe under one arm. Finally he got his voice back and
asked: "Where have you sprung from?" Tickled by the comic
aspect of the situation, I could not forbear answering: "Out
of the mountains." At that he got angry and began to curse,

informing me that I was provoking fate. Inwardly I had to admit that he was right, but before he could curse again I pointed out a fault in his technique. In his astonishment he had forgotten his party, who were climbing down all unaware of my presence. The rope was just running out free. "What would you do if your client fell off now?" I asked. Hastily he grabbed at the coils and I went on my way at once, having neither time nor inclination for further exchanges. After overtaking a couple more parties I reached the top. I was alone. The air was so still that as I lit a cigarette the match-flame did not flicker. Later I was often to visit this summit, but never again experienced such conditions.

As soon as the last party I had overtaken arrived I started down. I had no desire to speak to anybody, as nobody would have understood me. It was positively embarrassing to have to overtake all the parties again on the way down, and I deliberately wandered out on to the east face. The same guide with whom I had had the entanglement called out to me: "The route is much farther left on the ridge." I thanked him and thereafter stuck to the route like a good boy.

By five o'clock I was back in the hotel for tea. No one believed that I had been to the top. It did not matter to me. I had had my fun and, to be honest, my inner satisfaction, and these were worth more to me than any recognition on the part of others. The only one who never doubted me for an instant was the Austrian guide. When I brought him back his axe, he said: "I knew right away you were going up. However you camouflaged yourself, you couldn't fool me."

He had indeed eyes in his head. I proved to be less clear sighted that summer of 1933 as on my way up from Ellmau to the Gaudeamus hut I ran into Hans Steger guiding two pleasantly curvaceous ladies. Why on earth would anyone want to take something like that up into the mountains, I thought to myself, and struck off to the side. Up at the hut, however, we naturally met again. For the next few days bad weather set in, so we whiled away the time in our usual way, which was uproarious and not always particularly polite. The two ladies sat in the corner and obviously enjoyed the fun. When we sat down to our simple—but at Mother Maria's always abundant— meals, there would invariably be wine on the table. The ice melted and out of gratitude for the many flasks of wine we

With Hermann Köllensperger at the Grandes Jorasses hut after the Walker spur (1951)

With Gustl Kröner in the Kaisergebirge (1930)

The Totenkirchl in the Kaisergebirge

invited them to join in our games. When the weather cleared up we did a couple of climbs together, and they proved not bad at all.

The one to whom I had been paying particular attention invited me to spend the winter in St Moritz as ski instructor to her club. For me this was a dream come true. A friendly relationship developed which led to my friend's husband, who was a film producer, bringing a whole team to the Kaiser to make a film with our collaboration. Its title was *La croix des cimes*.* When the time came for synchronization we all had to go back to Paris, and there I learnt about a completely different side of life. Unforgotten Memy....

Occasionally in my life I have come to places where the way divided. Always I have chosen the one that led back into the mountains, even when a woman stood in the other road. Had I chosen otherwise, the whole course of my life would have been different. Perhaps I might have become a playboy, perhaps the foster son of a charming, influential French family. Perhaps....

* Summit crosses.

CHAPTER VII

An Old Fuddy-Duddy Already?

I HAD HAD enough of being a tourist guide, I had some money in my pocket; altogether, there seemed nothing to keep me from the mountains any longer. In Munich I had a friend called Martl Maier who was one of the best climbers and whom I knew to be keen on the Grandes Jorasses. As soon as I told him about my plans he was all for them. We agreed on the essentials and parted for the time being.

At this point I got a guiding commission in the Dolomites. Before leaving I went back to Munich to settle further details with Martl, but he was nowhere to be found. All I could find out was that he had gone. Where and with whom, nobody knew. Deeply disappointed, I slouched off through the streets of Munich. Turning a corner I bumped into another climbing friend, Ludwig Steinauer.

"Weren't you interested in the Grandes Jorasses too?" I asked.

"With you I'd go any time. When are we off?"

"First I have to go to the Dolomites, but I can get to the Leschaux hut by 1 August. I'll need axe, crampons and this and that."

"Agreed. I'll be there with the kit."

Thus it was that I travelled off to the Dolomites in a happy mood, guided my clients, and reached Courmayeur on 1 August. Next day I wanted to walk up to the Col du Géant and down the Vallée Blanche to the Leschaux hut, but did not feel so keen on crossing the glacier on my own. The idea of engaging a guide never came into my head. As I wandered around, I came across a tent in a field: perhaps it might be climbers also wanting to cross over to Chamonix? They turned out not to be climbers but some young Danes who did indeed wish to visit Chamonix. "Then you're in luck. I'm a mountain guide and I'll take you over the mountains," I announced. They had been going to walk peacefully over the Little St Bernard pass. At 6 a.m. they stood ready to go, and by noon we had reached the Torino hut on the col. After quite a short rest we were able to continue; despite their heavy packs they had really gone well. I did not allow the fact that they only had shorts and thoroughly unsuitable shoes to bother me too much. Before setting foot on the glacier I roped them on and gave them the necessary instructions. We had not gone 500 metres before the one in front fell into a crevasse. Before long we had him out, looking a trifle pale. "Don't worry about a little matter like that," I reassured them. "That kind of thing happens on glaciers all the time. That's why you're tied on." Secretly I was relieved to be tied on too. Despite several more little excursions into crevasses I piloted them on towards the Requin hut.

Another group came towards us, with a single walker about 100 metres away from them. As they came nearer I recognized Martl. We rushed towards each other with howls of joy.

"Why didn't you leave word for me in Munich?" I asked.

"But I did leave you a letter!"

"Well, I never got it, so I made an appointment to meet Steinauer at the Leschaux hut. He'll be there today or tomorrow with all my kit. There's nothing we can do about it. We'll just have to climb as a rope of three."

Martl was not particularly enthusiastic about this idea, but I tied him on close in front of me anyway and let the Danes go ahead without paying much attention while we chatted. Presently we became aware that we had wandered into a fearful maze of crevasses. There was nothing for it but to abseil into a wide crevasse and climb up the other side, which was more or less feasible. The poor Danes, who had never seen anything of the kind before, were absolutely exhausted by the time we reached the Requin hut. From here on, the path to Montenvers was quite safe, so we left them there to spend the night and hurried on towards the Leschaux hut, where Steinauer was duly waiting. The greeting between him and Martl was somewhat frosty, but he too had to accept the state of affairs.

First of all we had to spend a couple of days establishing good relations and preparing for the climb. The hut was in the process of being renovated, so we found a convenient shelterstone some 100 metres above. Then competition appeared on the scene in the form of two other Munich climbers,

Peters and Harringer, who pitched a tent 100 metres below the hut on a slab of rock. Each party kept an eye on the other. I made an attempt to establish diplomatic relations by undiplomatically suggesting that they should wait and see how we got on. Peters commented that he had his own ideas as to what he should do, and I withdrew in a huff. In any case the weather was so bad that with the best will in the world it was impossible to try anything at all. One day it got so unpleasant that the workmen invited us to leave our grotto and join them in the hut. We accepted gladly, and they suggested that we should also bring up our friends from the tent. I scrambled down and called out: "Don't be stubborn. The workmen are letting us use the hut. Come on up, all your gear is soaking." Harringer responded, but not so Peters, who remained sulking in the tent. For this breach of good manners we begged the pardon of the kindly French workers. They believed that we must have had a ferocious quarrel.

The storm roared around the hut as it only can in the mountains. We were happy to have a dry corner and could not understand Peters' attitude. Suddenly flames flared up below the hut; Peters' petrol cooker had exploded and the tent had caught fire. We ran down and helped him to stamp out the blaze.

"Now you'll come up and join us at last?"

"Why on earth? I can sleep in the bushes. I still have a sleeping bag, and I don't care a damn about the wet."

I doubted his sanity, but he held out and remained in excellent humour even though the storm continued for several days.

There was another job that I wanted to see to, and as the face would take a good week or ten days to get into condition after such a period of bad weather I suggested to my friends that they should take a look at it without me. They were not particularly pleased, but had to admit that my arguments were logical.

While I was away, Steinauer and Maier seized the first opportunity to attack the face, so that Peters and Harringer should not get in before them. They bivouacked on the top of the first buttress to the right of the central gully. During the night Martl got hungry and tucked into the provisions, thus provoking dreadful reproaches from Ludwig in the morning. They quarrelled so violently that there could be no question of going on. As soon as they got down Steinauer left, but Martl remained in the hope of joining forces with Peters and Harringer. This idea formed no part of Peters' plans, so he left Martl where he was and attacked the face with Harringer. Conditions were still bad, and on the third day they were obliged to turn back. As they were preparing their bivouac, Harringer, who was unbelayed, slipped and fell soundlessly to his death, bearing with him the rucksack containing the bivouac equipment.

Peters passed a terrible night, and next day continued to abseil down with the remaining section of rope. As time went on he became snowblind. In this state he reached the big ice slope, where he was observed by climbers at the Leschaux hut who hastened to his rescue, among them Martl Maier. Now for the first time Peters was willing to join forces with Maier and took him on his pillion back to Munich. In the summer of 1935 they succeeded in making the first ascent of the face together.

That year bad luck continued to dog me. I nurtured no grudge over Maier and Peters teaming up together; all that mattered to me was to find a new companion and to get in ahead of the competition. The companion was soon found in the person of Hans Lucke from Kufstein, a climber of unshakeable good humour with whom I had already done many climbs in the Kaisergebirge and who was always ready for any adventure. We had plenty of time ahead of us to get into training and organize our finances. I earned my money working as a ski instructor in Switzerland for the travel agency which had employed me as a tourist guide. Every mark, every franc I earned went into my savings, as we could not hope for any kind of grant. I had, indeed, connections with very wealthy people, but was unwilling to saddle them with feelings of moral responsibility in the event of something happening to us.

It was mid-June when we left for Courmayeur, this time by train. On the way up to the Col du Géant we ran into snow even below the level of the Pavillon de Mont Fréty. It was so soupy that we decided to bivouac and go on in the morning. In the morning, however, there was breakable crust over the soup, which was even worse, so we waited for another day. The

c

weather turned bad into the bargain. "You know what?" I said. "We're three or four weeks too early. Let's go down and catch a train to Portofino. I know some people who have a little house there. We can stay there until conditions improve." Hans was all for it, so we travelled away towards Genoa and Portofino, where our skis, ice-axes and nailed boots excited no little attention.

We were welcomed with open arms. Our hosts believed that they could talk us out of our foolhardy project, but we were happy to let them spoil us and passed three marvellous weeks swimming, walking and even climbing, as we found some excellent rocks in hidden creeks where we could train in complete privacy.

Having fixed the day of our return to the range of Mont Blanc, we dashed down to our private crags the afternoon before out of sheer high spirits. It happened that at one point I had to jump down, and in doing so broke some bones in one foot. The disappointment was bitter. Instead of Courmayeur it was back to Munich after ten days with my leg in plaster. I had written to a friend in Munich to tell him of my misfortune. He met me at the station with a slightly anxious smile and under his arm a newspaper with blazing headlines: "Grandes Jorasses north face climbed by Peters and Maier." So they had done it! My friend tried to comfort me. "Don't let it get you down," he said. "Who knows, your bad luck may have been a blessing in disguise. In any case, you'll soon be thirty. It's time to join the ranks of the fuddy-duddies. Find yourself a steady job and give up all this frantic competition." His blunt words were meant kindly, but they hit me very hard.

The next few weeks were spent in hospital until my foot was all right again. I was not very talkative but lay all day in self-examination, staring at the ceiling. Was I a failure? Was my place really among the fuddy-duddies? Well, if so, there was nothing I could do about it. I would just go on being a mountain guide, living in the mountains and doing the climbs I enjoyed, and leave off vexing myself with ambitious projects. As time went on I became cheerful again and got over not only my broken leg but also my spiritual wounds, of which the doctor knew nothing.

Soon after being released from the hospital I was engaged by a lady schoolteacher to do some climbs in the Dolomites.

On our way up to the hut below the Tre Cime di Lavaredo we encountered a couple of friends from Nuremberg, radiant with joy at having done the fifteenth ascent of the Cima Grande. Originally climbed by Comici, in those days it was reckoned to be the hardest route of all. Instantly I began to feel twinges of that very ambition which I had so solemnly renounced while in hospital. When she was not looking I began to size up my schoolteacher, wondering whether I could talk her into trying the face. But no, it would have been too insane. I put away the thought and steeled my will to be a staunch, honest guide who would never encourage a client to attempt anything beyond his or her ability.

The hut was not too full, and I noticed a lanky, pleasant-looking young man tucking down a triple-sized evening meal with evident relish. Drifting over in his direction, I asked: "Was it good?" He glanced at me in surprise and simply nodded. I tried another approach. "Did you get your appetite doing a hard route?" Now at last he deigned me an answer: "My friends have left. I had another day's holiday left and was just using up my remaining lire." As soon as he spoke I detected his Nuremberg accent. He had been with my friends and was rather put out at missing the north face. "Then we could go and do it together," I exclaimed. He accepted with joy, and my client was quite glad to have the chance of a day or two's rest.

I was bursting with enthusiasm and could hardly wait for the next day. But next morning the rain was drumming on the roof of our attic dormitory. Paradoxical as it may sound, mountain climbers in general like their comforts and are often even lazy, qualities of which I have my fair share. If bad weather ruled out a climb, I could always sleep through the whole day with pleasure and a clear conscience. On this occasion, however, I was so annoyed that I could not sleep another wink. Towards seven o'clock the rain stopped, and an hour later nothing worse than cold, damp clouds drifted around the mountains.

My companion, whose name was Theo Erpenbeck—we had finally got around to introducing ourselves—had already packed his sack to go down to the valley, remarking: "You can't do a climb of that calibre in this kind of weather, and anyway it's much too late." I begged him just to walk up to the foot of the face and do the first two or three pitches with me, after which I would feel satisfied and we could abseil off. Thus it was that at 9.30 a.m. we stood at the start of a climb that had never been done without a bivouac. As we tied on to the rope above the first easy rocks I reassured him that I would only do two or three pitches before packing in. There was no need for me to place any pitons; there were too many already for my taste. I wasted no time trying to take any of them out, but simply did not bother to clip in to all of them. In any case, I did not have enough karabiners. After three pitches I had no more intention of turning back. Theo had no time to say anything about it; no sooner had he reached the stance than I whipped off the belay and climbed on.

Only once, after climbing at least fifteen metres without seeing any pitons, did I feel that anything had gone wrong. At this point I noticed a row of pegs running up a slightly overhanging corner about five metres off to one side. Without any pitons for security the traverse across to the corner was far from easy, but if I had hammered any in my companion would also have been obliged to deviate from the proper route. As I reached the stance and shouted to him to come on, I heard a reproachful voice saying: "Have you given up clipping in at all?"

Shortly before coming to the corner in the upper part of the face we reached a roof overhang* about half a metre across. I had heard that at this point most people hung a loop of rope off the piton to stand in. As I had no slings I leant out backwards as far as I could and found a fantastic hold, big enough to get both hands on while I lay back in tension on the rope. On the command "slack" my legs swung clear of the rock. It was lucky that I had been a good gymnast in my youth. A quick mantelshelf† and I was up. In the gully above I would gladly have taken off the rope, but as poor Theo's arms had no more feeling left in them he did not agree. Nevertheless, now that the real difficulties were over, there was no more talk of turning back. By three o'clock in the afternoon we were sitting on the summit. Out of his sack Theo

* *Translator's note:* an abrupt horizontal overhang as opposed to a leaning wall.

† *Translator's note:* a pull-up leading into a push-up so that the feet arrive at the level of the hands.

pulled a thermos of red-wine tea that he had only intended to take up as far as the foot of the face. I have hardly ever tasted anything so delicious.

By now we were thoroughly tuned up, so we fairly bombed on down to the hut, where we were greeted with the question: "Where did you turn back?" Once again I was stared at with patent suspicion as I replied: "We've climbed the whole face, and we can't help it if we're back already." My peace of mind was restored; I knew now that I did not belong among the old fuddy-duddies, and could lead my schoolmistress patiently up all the routes she chose. Theo left for home the next day, and I first saw him again several decades later, after he had recovered from a severe illness. He wanted nothing more to do with climbs of this order, but my own appetite was only aroused.

One face remained unconquered. Now that I had got back my self-confidence, I concentrated all my thoughts and all my will on the north face of the Eiger.

CHAPTER VIII

The Eigerwand—Prehistory and First Attempt

YEARS WENT BY, but nobody cared to attempt the Eiger-wand until 1935. I followed the events with interest, knowing from my experiences on the Grandes Jorasses that such a face does not yield to the first attack. It was one thing for it to happen on the north face of the Matterhorn, a very different matter on the Jorasses, and quite impossible on the Eiger.

The first to try this murderous wall were Max Sedlmayer and Karl Mehringer. Max's brother Heini was a good friend of mine, but was more of a skier than a mountain climber. Although both climbers came from Munich I knew nothing about either, but they certainly made an all-out attempt. The climbing of the first rock-step after the initial pedestal still compels our highest respect. They reached the third icefield, although not until the fourth day. Then the weather broke and they lost their lives. That was the first round in the struggle for the Eigerwand.

The excitement among the so-called experts was enormous. While some lyrically applauded the daring and spirit of sacrifice displayed by the protagonists, others bitterly con-demned their foolhardiness and fanaticism. In Switzerland feeling ran so high that a law was passed forbidding attempts on the face, but this was later repealed following protests by leading Swiss mountaineers who rightly asked where the limit lay. For some people, they pointed out, a simple Alpine walk might already be dangerous, while for others even the Eigerwand might be just another climb, albeit a difficult one. The future was to show that they had spoken no more than the truth.

Probably this prohibition would not have bothered us much, as the first ascent would have been worth more than a couple of weeks in prison. But a lot was to happen before that.

Throughout the winter of 1935–36 I worked as a ski instructor at Arosa, Davos and St Moritz, and when summer came I did more climbing in a professional than in a private capacity. An operation on a meniscus held me up a good deal, but in the end it healed and I soon got fit again.

During the summer of 1936 there was a lot of activity on the Eigerwand. Independently of one another, three parties arrived at the foot of the face with the same objectives. These were the Munich climbers Herbst and Teufel; Andreas Hinterstoisser from Bad Reichenhall and Toni Kurz from Berchtesgaden; and the Innsbruckers Edi Rainer and Willy Angerer. At first there was absolutely no thought of joining forces. On the contrary, they avoided one another so far as possible. It was still too early in the season for a serious attack on the wall, so as a training climb Herbst and Teufel, who did not want to sit around doing nothing, made the first ascent of the north face of the Schneehorn in the Jungfrau group. As they were climbing down the ice bulges of the Jungfrau glacier Teufel slipped and pulled his companion after him. Teufel was killed instantaneously, while Herbst was badly injured and had to be rescued by Swiss guides. Although the latter received some compensation, it was nothing in proportion to the effort and danger involved, and it was natural enough that they should have nothing good to say about the so-called candidates for the Eigerwand. What if something should happen to them up on the face? And precisely as the guides feared, something did happen.

Under the effect of the accident, the two other parties decided to pool their resources. At 2 a.m. on 18 July they set out on their doomed attempt.

The leader was Anderl Hinterstoisser. After they had surmounted the pedestal, he turned the overhanging zone on the right, climbing the pitch below the Rote Fluh now known as "the difficult crack". After a relatively easy stretch he then made a tension traverse on the rope across to the first icefield, a pitch which has ever since been renowned as "the Hinterstoisser traverse". Yet it was this very pitch which was to prove their undoing when the onset of bad weather later forced them to retreat. In icy conditions it proved impossible to reverse, and they were obliged to take the fateful decision to seek safety by a series of free abseils. In the course of these Hinterstoisser fell, Rainer and Angerer were killed by falling stones, and only Toni Kurz remained. His shouts for help were heard in the valley, and immediately three guides volunteered to rescue him despite the official declaration that "Guides shall not be required to intervene when an accident occurs on the Eigerwand".

The Jungfraujoch railway made a special train available to take the rescuers up to a gallery opening from the tunnel on to the face. From here they had only to traverse a few hundred metres before making verbal contact with Toni Kurz, but they were unable to reach the spot where he was hanging. Kurz explained that Hinterstoisser had fallen off and that the other two were hanging on the rope below him. The guides advised him to cut the rope retaining the bodies, to unlay the remaining rope and tie the strands together, then lower the resulting cord weighted with a stone. All this took hours to accomplish, and in the meantime it grew dark. The guides were forced to retreat to the gallery, leaving Kurz suspended over the cliffs like a condemned prisoner. By dawn they were back again. To their surprise, he still sounded reasonably fresh as he answered their questions. The unlaid rope was lowered, and to it they attached two new ropes, pitons and food, all of which was then hauled up. At last the ends of the new ropes were thrown down and Kurz came sliding along them. He reached the level of the guides, but was still too far out from the overhanging wall. At this point something unforeseen occurred: a knot would not go through the karabiner with which he was abseiling. He mumbled something incomprehensible. The guides tried to give him advice, but he had reached the end of his strength. Suddenly he tipped over and hung dead on the rope. Not until a week later was it possible to cut down the body with a knife bound on the end of a pole, and as there had been no way of tying him on he vanished over the cliffs, not to be seen again until found a year later in the course of a search party for the remains of some Italian climbers.

Deeply as I personally regretted the fate of these four climbers, it was quite clear to me that they had been mistaken about the nature of the face. To undertake climbs of this order in the western Alps one needs high mountain experience, and they had none. One cannot rely entirely on luck, and especially not on the Eigerwand.

I was by now so obsessed with the thought of climbing the face that nothing would make me abandon the project.

Nevertheless, I was fully aware that it was not just a question of catching a train, wandering up the climb and coming home with the laurels. One might just have a lucky break, but I had no desire to rely on that. It should be possible to learn a great deal by observing the face for a period of some weeks and perhaps climbing a certain distance up it with the prior intention of turning back.

Such were my ideas, and when Theo Lösch and I set off on our bicycles to lay siege to the face in 1937, I stuck to them. Secrecy was more essential than ever, less on account of rivals than of public opinion. Nobody likes to be regarded as a fanatical lunatic so goaded by ambition as to be willing to face certain death. Things had reached a pitch where it was bad form among mountaineers to speak of the face at all.

So it came about that in the spring of 1937 I did a number of difficult climbs in the Kaisergebirge with Hias Rebitsch with the object of getting in training for the Eigerwand. I had the darkest suspicions that Hias was nurturing the same plans, but neither of us spoke a word about it to the other. Perhaps everything would have worked out very differently if we had not both kept so rigidly to the unspoken code. However, the underlying reason for our reticence was probably that neither of us absolutely needed the other in order to realize his plans. Each of us found another companion, and in July I pedalled away towards Switzerland with Theo Lösch.

Intent that no one should see us in Grindelwald, we hired a beach cabin at Interlaken from the attendant, who was a friend of mine. It was there we learnt of the ban on attempting the north face of the Eiger. Taking every precaution not to reveal ourselves as "candidates" we cycled to Grindelwald without rucksacks and walked up to Alpiglen, where the Alpenhorn player offered us a hide-out and kept our secret. As soon as anyone approached he would warn us with a blast on the horn. Bit by bit we assembled our equipment up there and reconnoitred the foot of the face. When the weather was unfavourable we went down to Interlaken and mingled harmlessly with the bathers.

In spite of all our precautions we were scented by two journalists who had disguised themselves as walkers and involved us in conversation. Our suspicions were first aroused when they began to take snapshots of us. And indeed, two days later our photographs appeared in the papers over the caption: "Two incognito Eigerwand candidates who were unwilling to give their names." Luckily we had at least avoided that mistake. Not that we really cared in the last resort, but as we were no longer totally unknown in climbing circles it would have caused a certain amount of sensation.

Unfortunately, there were other parties that really courted publicity, telling everybody about their intentions whether they wanted to listen or not. In full view of observers whom they had invited they climbed around the foot of the face, let people stand them drinks in Grindelwald and generally tasted the fruits of victory in advance wherever they could find them. To our embarrassment they were also from Munich, and the local guides were quite right to be annoyed. It is comforting to report that they duly got the thumping they deserved and were finally expelled from Switzerland for their misdeeds. We became more cautious than ever and trusted no one.

The day came when all was ready for a serious attempt. The plan was to start at 2 a.m., but when we awoke the sun was shining into the tent. We had properly overslept, but did not worry too much about it and lay back again lazily. As one of us remarked: "What the hell, it's bound to stay fine for more than one day."

Perhaps this was a stroke of fate, as towards midday a black wall of cloud gathered about the mountain and a terrible storm broke. That was all we had been lacking. We had now been hanging around for six weeks and our pockets were almost empty. During the past few days we had even been going without one meal a day in order to spin out the money. We could not go on starving much longer, and even if we did we would be in no physical condition to stand up to the massive efforts that the climb would require. We therefore took the difficult but only right decision to raise the siege for the time being and return without fail the following year.

Once the decision was taken, there was no point in waiting any longer. We packed up our kit, ran down to Grindelwald, swung our legs over our bikes and headed for home.

That was another fateful date in the history of the Eiger. Our giving up was only a minor incident. The same day Hias Rebitsch and Wiggerl Vörg appeared on the scene, but we did not meet. However, something else was happening unbeknown to us which we only learnt about when we got home. A pair of climbers from Salzburg had attacked and were caught in the storm. They succeeded in traversing off and reaching the Mittellegi ridge, but at this point Gollackner died of exhaustion and Primas had to be rescued in a state of collapse.

Rebitsch and Vörg brought down the body of Gollackner. Right from the outset, their party stood under an unlucky star. No sooner had they recovered from the effort of the rescue than they made an attempt on the face, but had not climbed 300 metres before they found one of the victims of the year before. It was Hinterstoisser. Naturally they gave up their attempt and carried down the body.

Thus they lost several fine days. The weather became unreliable, but they made another reconnaissance as far as the Hinterstoisser traverse, across which they fixed a rope taken up specially for the purpose. Satisfied with this achievement, they turned back. Their careful preparations and wary approach to the mountain show that this time there were experienced men at work who were up to the task they had taken on.

Three weeks now elapsed before they ferried ample loads in two stages up to a niche beyond the Hinterstoisser traverse, where they spent the night. Next day began the serious work.

Even they had underestimated the scale of the face. Instead of the five pitches they had allowed for, the second icefield gave them 20; and instead of one hour it took them five. In the process of hacking steps in the glassy ice Vörg broke his axe and from then on had to use his ice-hammer instead, which is always a poor substitute.

The wall of rock dividing the second icefield from the third was everywhere plated with ice. In vain they looked for a way around, but finally Rebitsch got to work and cut a way up, drenched in the spray of a waterfall. On the way he found an old piton with an abseil sling left by their predecessors.

In the course of the struggle they had quite forgotten the weather, and now got an unpleasant shock as they noticed that dirty grey clouds were beginning to form around the face. Were they too condemned to retreat? They had not yet reached the upper crags.

It was another 100 metres over steep, rock-interrupted ice before they reached the point where Sedlmayer and Mehringer had last been seen. Here they expected to find the latter's corpse, but the only trace was two pitons hammered into the wall. From here on it was up to themselves to find the way. After an attempt to continue straight up they realized that it would take too long, so they roped down and traversed left-wards towards a conspicuous ramp. Here they found such a stream of water that they hurriedly retreated.

They settled down for the night on the ledge below the two pitons and waited with chattering teeth for dawn to come. The hope of better weather proved illusory, but they waited on for a while. Then a gap in the mist revealed a bank of black cloud rolling in from the west. There was no point in hesitating any longer; the retreat began at once.

All through the day they abseiled downwards on the hard-frozen rope in their soaking clothes, continually menaced by stonefall and avalanches. It was 5 p.m. when they reached their first bivouac site at the end of the Hinterstoisser traverse. There was still plenty of daylight and they could easily have crossed the traverse and descended somewhat farther. For them it was not a trap in which they were caught, as the fixed rope guaranteed an easy return to the rocks below the Rote Fluh. But perhaps the weather might improve after all?

They spent the night thinking and talking about the tragedy that had been played out the previous year a few metres below where they lay. If only the others had left a rope across the traverse too. . . .

Next morning the weather was more miserable than ever. Now there was no more question; the only course was to get off the mountain as soon as possible. The rain was torrential, and the abseils ran down a line of temporary waterfalls. The two climbers had to slit their breeches at the bottom so as to let out all the water that poured in at the necks of their anoraks. It took them the whole day to reach the foot of the face.

Joy at winning their way back to life outweighed the disappointment of failure. When all was said and done, they were the first to spend over 100 hours on the Eigerwand and live to tell the tale; moreover, they had demonstrated that with the necessary prudence and foresight the face could be climbed.

CHAPTER IX

Interlude

ALL THIS I only learnt much later. Back at home, I felt far from downcast or defeated. If Hias had succeeded I would have been genuinely pleased for his sake. Simply, the dream of the Eigerwand would have been over. But what then? It had already become a nightmare. I had enough other experiences to keep me abundantly happy.

One morning in Bayrischzell I found a telegram from my friend Hans Steger in Bolzano. For many years he had been the best and also the best-known rock climber in the Südtirol, and had now become a qualified guide. The telegram said that Leni Riefenstahl wanted to climb with him, but he had an engagement with the King of Belgium. "You take her. Rendezvous Wolkenstein today." Everyone knew about Leni Riefenstahl from Arnold Fanck's mountain and ski films, and she had produced and starred in a fine mountain film of her own, *Das blaue Licht.** It was also well known that she belonged to Hitler's most intimate circle. Party leaders often had film stars among their friends and followers, but in her case the rumour was that she was one of Hitler's closest friends, if not more. That she was a star did not trouble me in the slightest, but the connection with Hitler gave me food for thought. Up until then I had had no contacts with governmental or party big-shots. No matter. Naturally it did not occur to me to turn down such an offer. I travelled to Wolkenstein and asked at the hotel for Miss Riefenstahl. Immediately I was treated with exquisite politeness. It is quite remarkable the bowing and scraping and dashing to and fro occasioned by names and money.

My future client had gone out for the day with a climber I knew well, Xaver Krayse from Kaufbeuren who, however, was not a professional guide. After a few hours she appeared looking radiant and more beautiful than I had imagined her to be in reality. Her feminine charms and untroubled naturalness

* *The Blue Light.*

soon dissolved my inner reservations. Whatever her relations with Hitler might be she was obviously a fabulous woman, and her years spent in the company of Arnold Fanck's casts of outstanding climbers and skiers seemed to have taught her not to play the star or the capricious diva among mountaineers. What she was worth as a climber herself I would soon find out.

When we discussed the routes we might do I suggested the west ridge of the first Sella Tower as a training climb, knowing full well that there was a pitch of Grade 5 on it. If she had trouble there, she could find another guide and I would go home. I was arrogant in those days and interested in nothing but the difficult stuff.

To my vast surprise, and I may say to my pleasure also, she had no difficulty on the crux pitch. Indeed, she positively danced up it. Knowing little about women, I would never have believed it of such a delicate-looking creature. When she explained that before going into films she had been a ballet dancer I began to understand why her movements were so graceful and sure. Thereupon we undertook a series of harder and harder climbs, including the Schleierkante, which we knocked off in two and a half hours as a party of three. This success made me presumptuous, and for our next climb I suggested the Guglia di Brenta, not just the ordinary route but the Preuss route.

As we walked up from Madonna di Campiglio to the Brentei hut we got to talking about her film *Das blaue Licht* which she had shot in this district. Hitler had been so impressed by it that he had commissioned her to make the films of the National Socialist Party Meeting and the Olympic Games.

Before I had set out from home my brother had drawn my attention to these matters and had drummed into my head that I should on no account let on that I knew next to nothing about her and had never seen one of her films. That was bad advice. At every bend in the path she kept asking if I could remember the scene she had shot there, until like a fool I confessed that I had never even heard of the film. That offended her and she went into a sulk. Just wait till tomorrow, I thought to myself, and I'll cut you down to size so that you forget your own film. In fact she was to be cut down much smaller than I intended, and that was my fault again, because after the experience on the Schleierkante I had simply overestimated her ability.

I fixed our time of departure at 10 a.m. sharp. We wandered gently up to the Tosa hut, had an agreeable midday rest, and reached the foot of the route by two o'clock in the afternoon. I was reckoning on three hours up and one down, so that there was plenty of time even though we were a party of three. However, this was adding up the bill without the tip. I was feeling my oats, and right at the beginning decided there was no point in following the ledges across the Bergerwand when a convenient corner led straight up towards the Preusswand. Unfortunately, this corner turned out to be much harder than it looked. Half-way up Leni suggested: "It would be a bit easier out there on the left." I was of the opposite opinion, but experience gave in to inexperience, a thing that should never happen in the mountains. The somewhat easier rock led around to a good stance on the east face, but there everything came to an end. So back to the corner. I took some tension on the rope, then climbed free to the top of the corner and gave the word to follow. That was easy enough to say. Leni peered around the edge, took one look at the smooth wall and overhangs in the corner, and refused to move another step. In this she was fully within her rights. I called down that I would abseil back so that we could return to the hut. At this she grew angry and insisted on continuing up, but not at this particular place. In reality we had no choice; there was not enough time to go any farther. At this point, however, she made the mistake of informing me that she had engaged me as her guide and that I must do as she said. In a sense she was right, but not in these circumstances. There was nothing for it but to go down so that she could find another guide who would do as she told him.

I kept the belay rope over my shoulder while I hammered in a ring piton for the abseil. Suddenly, without any warning, there came a violent tug and Leni pendulumed across into the corner. I therefore hauled in the rope with all my strength and before long she was standing in front of me, her eyes red with weeping. Xaver followed, grinning with embarrassment. Only now were we at the foot of the Preuss route proper. Normally people allow four hours for this, and it was 5 p.m. already.

"The sensible thing would be to turn back."

"No, I want to go on."

All right by me. Up we go then. I turned and started climbing without further delay. Even today the route cannot be described as easy, and it kept us busy until 8 p.m., by which time it was dusk. Whether a bivouac was inevitable or not did not bother me in the slightest, but out of the west a black wall of cloud was bearing down on us flickering with blue lightning. It was essential to get off the summit with all possible speed. I found a niche between two blocks on the north face.

"Right, this is where we bivouac. Now it remains to be seen how we survive the storm."

"But you don't expect me to spend the entire night here?" sobbed Leni. "I mustn't catch cold, I'm not well. . . ."

The rest of her words were drowned in a terrifying crash of thunder. Hail poured over us, while the lightning flashed and glimmered incessantly in the black cloud.

"This is unpleasant. Let's get down farther."

Going on implied abseiling, hammering in pegs by the harsh glare of the lightning. Xaver had to descend unbelayed on the two 40-metre ropes in the pitch darkness. Leni could only be belayed on a thin cord for the first 25 metres. The shower of hail had turned into a cloudburst. We abseiled on all night, arriving exactly where we had left the sacks at the bottom of the climb. It was either pure chance or sixth sense, as most of the time I had no idea where we were.

It was far too dark to follow the route back to the Tosa hut, but in the gully running down to the coomb below a faint light shimmered off the ice. Nothing much could happen to us now, and by cutting our way step by step down the gully we at least kept moving. The weather had relented a little, but cloud came up from the valley, enveloping us in a Stygian gloom compounded of fog and darkness. Luckily we had just got off the ice. Although we had no torches, we could at least move forward in a sitting position. For me there was nothing new in that. Leni and Xaver did not care for it, but wanted even less to bivouac. We missed the little track leading through the coomb and found ourselves in a wilderness of blocks the size of tables or even houses. After I had tumbled over one of these I found my readiness for self-sacrifice exhausted, so I stretched out and announced that I was going to sleep until it got light. In a moment I was snoring. Xaver had to spend the rest of the night comforting and rubbing Leni to keep her warm. As soon as day broke they wakened me; despite the wetness and cold I felt fresh and fully revived. By climbing back up again we soon found the track, up which the hut warden and his wife in a state of great concern were already coming to look for us.

After we had had three days of rest at the hut, Leni Riefenstahl's friends gave a banquet for us at the Hotel Greif in Bolzano. There were heated discussions over the table concerning modern mountaineering techniques. The subject of the Eiger was brought up. One of the older men looked deep into my eyes and said: "Heckmair is the man who will climb the Eigerwand." I was taken aback, having believed that nobody knew anything of my intentions. However, his confidence did me good, as in view of my failure and defeat on the Grandes Jorasses I was not at all sure of myself.

It was now September, and Leni had to attend the Party Meeting at Nuremberg as Hitler's guest of honour. As she wanted to convert me, she insisted on my coming too. Afterwards I was to accompany her to Berlin, where everything I needed would be placed at my disposal at the national stadium so that I could keep in training. For an offer like that it was even worth attending a Party Meeting; what harm could it do anyway if one regarded the whole thing with disapproval?

At Nuremberg we were lodged at the Gauleiter's house. Everything was costly and hyper-refined except the Gauleiter himself. So that was the face of National Socialism! Hitler himself was staying at the Deutscher Hof Hotel. Naturally, the whole place was hermetically sealed off, but Leni had a special pass that opened all doors. We went to the hotel for afternoon tea. Leni took up a position where the Führer could not help but see us when he came in. It worked perfectly. He went straight towards her with outstretched arms and complimented her on her appearance. We were invited to sit at his table in a neighbouring room. Thus I found myself sitting beside Leni in immediate proximity to Hitler and could study his face at leisure. I make no claim at all to being a profound connoisseur of men, but I could find absolutely nothing so extraordinary about him.

Leni told Hitler about her experiences in the mountains

but he seemed neither impressed nor enthusiastic. Instead, his brow drew down and he growled: "How can you risk your life so lightly when I have entrusted you with so great a mission?" She answered that for this very reason she had employed a guide to see to it that her life was in no danger. Now, for the first time, he looked straight at me and I came into the conversation. Far from being stupid, the questions he put to me were very much to the point, although it was clear that he had not the faintest idea about mountaineering. What interested him was the "why" of it all—what one would feel and experience on a severe climb as opposed to a simple walk in the mountains. Without any intention of embarrassing me he bored his way relentlessly into every aspect of the subject. In all this my own person interested him not a straw. It was the phenomenon that absorbed him, and apparently he had never before discussed it with a mountaineer.

Thus the meal went by. Outside darkness had fallen and a torchlight parade began to march past. The Führer's adjutant—I do not know if it was Bormann—came up behind him and murmured that it was time to go out on to the balcony. As we got to our feet Hitler asked me another question which called for a lengthy answer; nobody dared to interrupt us, and so it was that I accompanied him out on to the balcony, still talking, there to find myself in my grey suit amid all the uniformed Party dignitaries. Below us the crowd clamoured its unceasing cry of "Heil". The torchlight procession came to a halt. Hitler saluted it with stiffly outstretched arm, something rigid in his gaze as though staring into the distance. For the first time in my life I raised my hand in the Hitler salute. My situation as an anonymous, unpolitical and unbelieving climber standing beside the fanatically acclaimed leader struck me as so grotesque that I felt like laughing out loud. The march past lasted two hours, and throughout this time I stood at his elbow. As the umpteenth thousand marcher paraded past us yelling I thought of the loneliness of the mountains and of the hordes of humanity below. Naturally I came to no conclusion; I simply found the whole thing remarkable, disturbing, somehow inexplicable.

The following day I stood beside Leni Riefenstahl on the tribune of honour watching the parades and the march past of Party members, wondering how people could be herded around like that and why they let it happen. One could not help admiring the organization, yet I felt a kind of shudder in my soul. I understood that something was in motion that was going to sweep everything away with it, but where to I could not tell. In Berlin I needed a period for reflection in order to digest the experience. Leni was set on dragging me off to the mass gatherings on the occasion of Mussolini's visit, but I had had enough of it all and preferred to go running in the woods. Each time I ran farther until I was doing 40 or 50 kilometres every second or third day. Deliberately I suited my training to my projects for the following year. This time I intended to get the Eigerwand climbed.

All this preserved me from the temptations of city life and from getting involved in politics. I was unwilling to give way to this suggestive urge which could not be rationally explained. That world was not mine: it was too alien to me and I too matter-of-fact for it. Above all, I had my own goal.

Not until winter had set in did I get back to Bayrischzell. A couple of weeks later I took a job as a ski teacher in the "Strength through Joy" organization. To introduce these simple, mostly working-class people to the beauties of the wintry mountains was far more satisfying than instructing the would-be socialites of the St Moritz travel agencies.

CHAPTER X

The North Face of the Eiger

WITHOUT DELAY I began to tie up the loose ends for the summer. My first act was to write to Hias Rebitsch in Innsbruck and say that we should stop stupidly competing with each other and join forces instead. He replied by return that he was all in favour of the idea, but that he had been invited by the well-known expedition leader Paul Bauer to go to Nanga Parbat, an 8000 metre mountain in the Karakorum. In his place he recommended his companion of the previous year, Wiggerl Vörg, with whom you could happily try anything. Wiggerl Vörg: wasn't that the nice fellow I had once overtaken in a cross-country skiing race and who had protested on my behalf when I had been placed behind him? I had no idea that he had become a climber into the bargain. If Hias recommended him, he must be good. I therefore wrote off at once.

Again the answer came by return. He had been invited to join an expedition to the Hindu Kush, but it was not at all sure whether anything would come of it, and he would be glad to team up with me. So it came about, and we agreed by post to meet in the Kaiser on a particular date to begin our training.

For a whole week I sat at the Gaudeamus hut waiting for sight or sound of Vörg. Perhaps he was already on his way. What should I do? First of all a few climbs, even though solo.

I wandered up the south ridge of the Karlspitz, steep slopes with a lot of flowers and here and there an overhang between, taking pleasure in it all. As I strolled back down to the hut in the evening light I saw two climbers looking towards me expectantly. Both were on the short side, one thin, the other plump. Yet there was something in the bearing of the fatter one by which I could divine the tiger climber. That would be Wiggerl Vörg. And so it proved to be. The introductions were short and hearty; his thinner companion was his brother. After a few moments it was as though we had been together for years, but in the intervals we looked long and penetratingly into one another's eyes and each thought his own thoughts. We had both heard too much about each other to be in any doubt, yet somehow it was strange to be face to face with a person with whom one was bound in a pact for life or death. The same evening a couple of friends from Munich arrived to stay for a few days. Nevertheless, our plans remained a strict secret. Only the hut warden Mother Maria, so called by everyone because she really was a mother to all mountain climbers, knew or rather guessed what we had in mind, and fed us like fighting cocks.

We remained at the Gaudeamus hut for two weeks, doing all manner of climbs. Quite against our will it worked out that although Wiggerl and I were sometimes on the same face at the same time we were never on the same rope until, on the last day, we did the hardest climb of the holiday, the east face of the Karlspitz. Never had I had a climbing partner so much the opposite from myself yet with whom I could climb in such perfect harmony. He was outstandingly kindly and good-natured, which I cannot claim for myself. This was a factor destined to play a major role in the ascent of the Eigerwand; without it events might have taken a completely different turn.

We decided on 10 July 1938 as our date of departure for Switzerland. The last week beforehand was spent in Munich assembling our kit, which had been worked out down to the last detail. By contrast to all earlier attempts, including our own, it was chosen in the light of the concept that the north face of the Eiger was an ice climb rather than a rock climb. Nowadays this discovery seems ridiculously obvious, but up to then all our predecessors had come to grief on account of primitive and unsuitable equipment. Not only pitons, crampons and rope needed to be of appropriate design, but also our clothing and bivouac outfits, so that we could stand up to bad weather and several bivouacs without coming to harm. All this process of selection postulated not only experience but also the eradication of deeply rooted traditions and attitudes.

The question of packing arose. In order to avoid being recognized as Eiger candidates we put everything into suitcases. Only the ice-axes caused headaches; try as we might we could not get them in. In the end we had to carry them under our arms, thus rendering all our camouflage pointless.

According to plan, we left on 10 July. We had deliberately chosen this date because I knew from the previous year that in June and early July melting on the face causes such water-falls and consequent stonefall and avalanches that an ascent during that season is not to be thought of. We wanted to keep the nerve-racking period of siege as short as possible. For this reason we had purposely started training late. Our opinion received melancholy confirmation when two Italians, Bartolo Sandri and Mario Menti, attempted the face during the critical period in June and lost their lives.

It was not easy to keep to our chosen date. Even while we were up at the Gaudeamus hut we had received the news that four Viennese climbers were camping below the face, among them Fritz Kasparek and Heini Harrer, whom we knew by reputation. However, we managed to remain calm and stick to our plans. If by doing so we lost the first ascent, it would simply mean that fate had decided otherwise. I held to this notion with a stubbornness that in retrospect surprised even myself.

Upon reaching Switzerland we stocked up with special food for the face and also certain medicaments that were easier to obtain there than at home. Among these was a roll of Thermogene. This product had been earnestly recommended to me by a solicitous lady. It consisted of a kind of pink cotton-wool which persons suffering from rheumatism could place over the afflicted part, whereupon the skin burnt like fire. What burns cannot freeze, I reasoned to myself, and in view of the well-meant advice bought a jumbo-sized pack.

The weather was rainy, so we lazed away a couple more days in Zürich, enjoying the pleasures of the big city. Not until 12 July did we reach Grindelwald. The visibility was good, and a single glance was enough to sum up the condition of the face: it was still damnably white. This in fact was very comforting, as it meant that our rivals could not have snatched the prize from us. We now had the advantage, in that (a) we were fresh from training, (b) we probably knew the face better, and (c) we must be better equipped. The combination of these factors gave us a feeling of great security, which naturally soon drove us up to the foot of the climb.

From our earlier attempts we already knew a place where we could camp safe from the eyes of inquisitive tourists and still more inquisitive journalists. In no time Wiggerl had the tent pitched, while I went to gather wood. At first I disregarded the smaller sticks that lay around in abundance and instead dragged over thick branches and trunks which I then attacked violently with the ice-axe, with the result that after about five minutes the shaft broke. I pulled a face and Wiggerl grinned meaningfully. There could be no question of attacking the wall next morning; first we should have to go back down to Grindelwald for another ice-axe. However, the delay was not without a favourable side. We would be acclimatizing to the altitude and could make a few minor additions to our supplies. The weather was also not yet quite what we would have wished.

Next day turned out decidedly rainy again. We passed the time in a peculiar way, improving the camp site in spite of the weather. In order to keep our clothes dry we took them all off and ran around naked as Indians. It was not long before we began to feel the cold, so in order to warm ourselves we set to work like wild men. First we dug a ditch around the tent to keep the surface drainage away from it. Presently the ditch grew so deep that we needed a bridge. Wiggerl dragged over some enormous slabs of rock which I then made a professional job of laying. Next the trampled area in front of the tent began to trouble our aesthetic sensibilities, so we paved this too and in between the slabs I planted grass and Alpine flowers —what was the use of being a gardener otherwise?—so that we finally had a beautiful terrace.

On Sunday 17 July the weather began to improve, but the Eiger was still cloaked in thick cloud; in any case, it is a more hopeful sign when the conditions do not improve too suddenly. On Monday we went down to Grindelwald, having thought of a few more provisions to take on the face. In front of the tourist office stood a man from Vienna intently studying the weather forecast. He told us that it had been in the news that we had arrived in Grindelwald, and Kasparek and Harrer were going to attack the mountain that very day.

Now there was no holding us. We went straight back up to our camp and made our plans: first a good night's sleep and a good meal, then pack our sacks and set out by midday.

The plan was carried out to the letter. We got up at ten o'clock and I started cooking right away while Wiggerl carefully laid out all the gear we should want for the climb: 30 ice-pitons, 20 rock-pitons, 15 karabiners, two ice-axes (one long and one short), an ice-hammer, a piton hammer, crampons, two 30 metre ropes, two thin 30 metre cords, a petrol cooker, a litre of petrol, a packet of Metafuel for priming, plaster, kletterschuhe, two pair of socks each, a change of underclothing, two pullovers, spare shirt, two anoraks, over-trousers, sou'westers with chin straps, face masks, two pair of mittens, not forgetting the bivouac sack and the roll of Thermogene, which weighed nothing but was unbelievably bulky. On top of all this Wiggerl slung his Contax camera, at which I protested. In the first place I thought it weighed too much, and in the second I did not want to waste time taking photographs. Wiggerl, however, was of the opinion that any photographs we might take could afterwards be an important record. I gave in on the condition that the camera should be the first thing to be jettisoned if the going got tough and we had to lighten our loads. Knowing that I was in deadly earnest, Wiggerl agreed. Not until much later did I realize that he was in the right.

Food was another whole problem area in itself, and one that gave us many headaches. Again and again we argued the question through, bringing all our experience to bear on the matter, and at last we thought we had found a solution. The basis was hot drinks—chocolate, tea, coffee, Ovomaltine, sweetened and unsweetened condensed milk—together with three kilos of lump sugar, glucose (especially Dextro-Energen), biscuits, bread, bacon and sardines in olive oil. Wiggerl was against these last but I insisted on them, very much to my own subsequent regret. On top of all this we took a cured shin of pork which we later had to leave behind on the mountain on account of its weight and indigestibility, a deed which haunts even yet.

As we sorted everything out we kept glancing up at the north wall. Meanwhile the morning had gone by. We forced ourselves to gulp down all we could, and by half-past twelve we stood ready to go.

A shiver passed through my limbs as I lifted my rucksack: it weighed at least 20 kilos, and Wiggerl's was just as heavy.

It seemed impossible to climb with them, yet there was nothing we could leave behind. Somehow I could not bear the thought of parting from the shin of pork. Slowly we plodded up the steep ground below the snow slope at the foot of the face. Already we had to stop a couple of times to get our breath. My morale was close to zero; I could not see how we were going to manage the climb with our overloaded rucksacks. Wiggerl comforted me: "After the first bivouac they'll be a lot lighter because we'll put on all the spare clothes for the night and leave them on after that. Anyway, you get used to the weight." Cold comfort indeed.

Right from the beginning the snow slope was steep and hardened by the avalanches that had poured across it. We were glad to have this excuse to strap on our crampons, which already lightened the load.

As we climbed Wiggerl told me about a chimney with a jammed block in it at the end of the first snowband. It seemed that this offered a good way on to the face. Instead of a chimney with a fallen block, however, we found a steep groove of snow. Clearly, there was significantly more snow than the previous year at the same time. That was a good thing, as with our crampons we could gain height quickly. Slanting across to the right we reached the first buttress after 300 metres From here on we were on rock which tended to form ledges and terraces.

At this point we found a splintered ice-axe handle, then a torn rucksack a few metres higher, and above that some other odds and ends. We did not search any farther, as we knew that there were two bodies still on the face. Only one of the Italians had been brought down, and Karl Mehringer had also not been found. We had no wish to disturb the peace of the dead in case they disturbed ours. However, we resolved to return and search after we had climbed the face. Unfortunately, we did not keep this resolution.

Meanwhile we had reached the split pillar. The climbing was more difficult and we began to feel the hindrance of the sacks. We therefore tried hauling them after us over one of the overhangs. It proved a complicated manoeuvre and wasted a lot of time.

Above the pillar we came upon a cave, and what should we find there but two full rucksacks with a ticket on them saying: "Please leave where found. Belong Kasparek and Harrer." Well, well! So they had already been up and cached their kit. The certainty that they had gone down again had a sort of liberating effect on us.

"All right then, we'll just carry on for a few pitches and the others can see if they can catch up!"

The next few ropeslengths were not pleasant at all. Water was falling from the second icefield, and there was nowhere suitable for a bivouac. We therefore decided to retreat to the cave and spend the night there. There were drips in the cave too, but Wiggerl declared: "They'll soon stop when it gets properly cold."

It got cold soon enough, but the dripping failed to stop. I lay right at the back where it was worst, with a stone in the small of my back just to help matters. Wiggerl lay unroped at the edge, so that I did not dare make the smallest movement for fear of pushing him over. Our first night on the face thus turned out to be neither exciting nor romantic. The perpetual dripping on my face and down my neck soon became positively unpleasant. At about four o'clock in the morning we crawled out and made coffee. Our enthusiasm had waned considerably, and the weather, or rather the outlook for later, was not very encouraging. The horizon was angry red, with black, fish-shaped clouds outlined against it.

"Take a look at the altimeter."

"It's gone up 60 metres!"

This meant that the pressure had dropped about three points. Our morale dropped correspondingly. Wiggerl chose his words carefully:

"Of course, I don't want to go down . . ."

I agreed at once that the idea was not at all to my taste either. However, if we wanted to play it safe we must have settled weather. An old proverb says "Fish-clouds in the sky bring rain by and by". Quoting these pregnant words to one another, we decided to leave the sacks in the cave and descend.

The sacks were packed away and we were just about to start when suddenly a form hove into view on a snow slope to the left of the pillar, closely followed by another. Not particularly pleased with this development, I called down: "Hei-yo!" and received the same reply. It was Kasparek and

Harrer. As we had never met, we introduced ourselves some-what formally and with a shade of embarrassment.

"Sleep well?"

"Not too well," we admitted, and then asked in our turn: "Are you going on in spite of the weather?"

"Yes, we're going on. It's got to be done sometime. We've been camping around in tents and barns for five weeks now, and we're down to a franc and a half. We think the weather's going to hold out, so we're going for it."

"Our altimeter's rising and the weather doesn't look too hopeful," I warned them. But Kasparek repeated obstinately: "We're going on."

Wiggerl looked at me:

"What do you think?"

At this moment yet another party appeared on the scene. They were two Viennese, Freissl and Brankovsky. I asked: "Are you together?"

"No, it's each party for itself."

The six of us stood there and laughed a little forcedly at the coincidence. In fact it was not really so extraordinary, since obviously all the parties that had been lurking around were bound to meet on the first fine day. I would not have been surprised if several more parties had appeared, since we knew that there were some Italian climbers in the vicinity who represented serious competition. The name of Cassin had even been mentioned, and of all possible rivals he was the one I feared most. The arrival of the second party was, however, already enough to confirm our decision to retreat. No matter how good they are, six men cannot help getting in each other's way. On a face such as this, the objective dangers would be heightened to a point where an accident would be inevitable. That was my opinion at the time. Nowadays, when the conditions are good, parties climb one behind another. Have the conditions or the climbers improved?

However that might be, we had resolved to turn back and remained true to our decision; things would just have to take their own course. Nevertheless, we assured the others that if anything went wrong they could count on our help.

Secretly we believed in our own weather forecast and reckoned that the others would soon be back too. As we descended, however, the weather got finer and finer and our faces longer and longer. By 10 a.m. we were sitting among grass below the face, knowing that far above us "the competition" were at work. Wiggerl, normally so placid, was utterly discouraged and in despair. When I spoke to him he was too lost in his thoughts to hear. However, I was fortified by the thought that we had acted rightly throughout.

Since we were already down, we decided to continue to Alpiglen at once so as to follow the progress of the other parties through the fixed telescope. Before long we were standing among a crowd of inquisitive tourists who had nothing very intelligent to say. A woman announced importantly:

"I saw them on the way up yesterday afternoon."

This in fact referred to us, who stood in their midst, but nobody had noticed us climbing down. A man who had elected himself spokesman explained to his eager listeners:

"Those are doomed men. Do you see that tree growing in the icefield? That's where they are now. Today they'll get to that ledge, tomorrow they'll reach that one, and then it'll be all up with them because they'll be out of food and they won't be able to climb down."

Seldom had I been forced to listen to so much earnestly intended drivel. I began to wonder whether it was we who were sane or they. Meanwhile, we had pressed forward to the telescope, where we found to our astonishment that the first party was making extraordinarily slow progress. The second party was not visible at all. This perplexed us, but after a few more hours of observation we came to the conclusion that for some reason or other they must have turned back. The idea affected us like an electric shock. If that was the case, we could go back up; four on the face was not too many.

Swiftly we telephoned to Grindelwald for a weather report. The meteorological chart showed a flat anticyclone over the Baltic, a flat depression over the British Isles. It seemed as though everything was flat except the face. If we weren't scared of that, surely there was no need to be scared of the flat depression. Now we felt no more doubt. We were going up again.

I could have turned somersaults of joy. We ate a good lunch at the Gasthaus at Alpiglen, where the kindly landlady knew us and kept our secret. The accompanying tankard of beer soon restored our mental equilibrium. Another look through the telescope showed Kasparek working his way up from the first to the second icefield, hacking away furiously with his axe. Probably he lacked twelve-point crampons and was having to cut his way step by step up the almost vertical ice-groove, a tedious and time-consuming task. It suited us all right, as it meant that they would not build up too great a lead.

Wiggerl was for going straight back up to the bivouac without more ado, but I still had horrible memories of the night before and also considered that an immediate attack would be premature. It was finally agreed to stay down on condition that we set off at midnight. To this I agreed sanctimoniously and undertook the responsibility for waking up at the right time, thinking to myself: "You can stuff your midnight. Two o'clock is early enough." Once before I had started up for a big climb at midnight and remembered how we had sat freezing and shivering at its foot until daylight came. I wanted to avoid a repetition on the present occasion.

During the afternoon we got into our sleeping bags and lay down under a shady tree by our camp site. Seldom had I felt so well in myself, without a trace of nervousness. We were in a mood of supreme confidence. At six o'clock we had an ample meal. There was pineapple for dessert. Originally we had intended this for victory celebrations, but we philosophized: "Success is not so certain after all. The pineapple will taste just as good now, while we are alive, and if something happened to us somebody else would eat it." An hour later we lay down again in the tent and fell asleep straight away; it was astonishing that we could sleep so deeply and peacefully. In the middle of the night I woke up. It was exactly two o'clock.

Enough of inactivity. Out!

The night was cool and clear. As we looked up at the pale loom of the face a light suddenly flamed up from the rocks below the second icefield and immediately went out. We learnt later that the other party had lit their spirit cooker at this moment.

Three-quarters of an hour later we left the camp, finding our way with the help of a candle lantern. It was a good thing that we knew the way so well, as the darkness was intense. We did not go astray by so much as a metre and reached the snow slopes in the dawn twilight. By the time we set foot on the rocks it was day, so we stuffed the candle lantern into a cleft with the intention of returning for it after the climb which, however, we never did. At 4.30 a.m. we were already at our bivouac site of the previous night. Here we recovered our kit, roped up, shared out the pitons and karabiners, and pulled on our kletterschuhe.

"No more fooling about. Let's go."

The crack leading up to the Hinterstoisser traverse was covered in ice and I found it so difficult to lead that I had to take off the sack. This pitch has now become popularly known as "the difficult crack", and more than one party has met its match there. The ability to cope with extreme technical difficulty is only one of the preconditions for a successful ascent of the face. We were fully aware of this, whence our intensive training and long period of mental conditioning that now stood us in good stead.

The sack-haulage once again proved extraordinarily time-wasting and exhausting. I started to take in but the sack immediately got caught up. I heaved fit to thin the rope with the strain, but still it would not budge. Finally Wiggerl had to climb up and butt it free with his head, so that at last I could haul away. We resolved to avoid sack-haulage as much as possible, and as we had now reached easier ground we began to climb at top speed.

The Hinterstoisser traverse, over which a waterfall usually tumbles and which had been the undoing of the 1936 party, was quite dry but plastered in ice. The fixed rope with which Rebitsch and Vörg had kept open their line of retreat was still there. That was good, as it saved us time. Damaged as it was by avalanche and stonefall it was risky to use, but by protecting myself with our own rope the worst I had to fear in the event of the old one breaking was a big swing.

In 1957 a German and an Italian party met at dawn at the beginning of this traverse. For reasons that nobody can explain it took them the whole day. Their ascent ended in particularly tragic circumstances. In my judgement it was doomed to failure from the start; the north face of the Eiger is not the place to learn how to do rope traverses.

At 8 a.m., climbing on our twelve-point crampons, we reached the first icefield. As we stepped on to the slope we found ourselves in the fall-line of a hail of ice-chips and stones dislodged by the others, who were cutting steps above us. The steps which they had cut the previous day were no more use; melt-water had flowed over them in the afternoon and frozen during the night, so that no trace remained even of the biggest. This did not worry us, however, as with twelve-point crampons no steps are needed, except that a stance must be cut out and protected with an ice-piton at the end of each run-out, since climbing at high speed on the front points only is very hard on the calf muscles. It was the first time that I had used twelve-pointers, which in 1938 were still absolutely new-fangled. Nowadays everyone has them, even for stumping around on flat glaciers, although their only advantage is in climbing steep ice-slopes.

I was surprised at the way the two front points bit in and the security they gave even on ultra-steep ice. After no more than a few minutes the first icefield lay below us. The route to the second icefield lies either up the notorious "ice hose" or else up a black 40-metre wall of rock. We opted for the rock. Off came our crampons, the sacks were tied to the rope, and in the end the wall turned out to be not so bad as it had looked. Nevertheless, there were a couple of overhangs, and hauling the sacks occasioned more drudgery.

The second icefield consisted of blank water-ice. Very carefully but steadily Wiggerl balanced upwards, while I panted behind with the big rucksack. We had allocated the weight so that the leader could climb with a lighter sack, the second managing as best he could with the heavier.

At eleven o'clock we reached Kasparek and Harrer's line of steps at the upper end of the second icefield. Now there was no more trouble. We could have trotted along with our hands in our pockets.

"Look, Wiggerl, we're catching them already!"

The icefields had not looked particularly big from below, but in reality they are huge; the second is a good 20 ropes-lengths across. The pair in front of us had performed a titanic labour, cutting their way step by step. Indeed, "steps" was no longer the word—they were real bath-tubs. Now we could stroll along them together. Quite soon we were within shouting range and yodelled gaily to one another. At half-past eleven we caught up with them.

Now I saw why they had moved so slowly and needed

such big steps. They had made the same mistake as all the parties that had been lost on the face, and that we ourselves had made on our first attempts: they were equipped for rock rather than ice. In fact they did not have so much as an axe, and Harrer did not even have crampons. Kasparek had had to cut all the steps with an ice-hammer, working the whole time in a bent-over position. I pointed out to them that at this rate they stood small chance of getting through, and advised immediate retreat. However, mountain climbers are obstinate characters, and Kasparek was particularly so. He simply replied:

"We'll do it all right, even if we take a bit longer over it."

It was a tricky situation. We were faced with the grave decision whether to overtake and press on, leaving them to their fate. I was close to doing this, but not Vörg, who was far better-natured. It was he who found the redeeming word:

"Then let's form one party and rope up together."

I did not want to start an argument and therefore agreed, rather against my will. However, I must own that during the ascent our association turned to comradeship and after it to lifelong friendship. That was by no means an inevitable development, mountaineers being only human and endowed with their share of human frailties. Among us there were no petty jealousies about who was the best climber. On the north face each one had his job and did it, and could rely on the others to do theirs.

Joining together also brought some undeniable advantages. With the weight distributed among four, I could lead with only a very light sack. The bivouacs were not so lonely, and above all the other two knew the way down the other side of the mountain. But for this it would have gone badly for us.

Before long we were standing under the rock buttress below the third icefield. The way up was supposed to be a difficult chimney, but there was so much ice that it was invisible. It was an example of how changeable conditions are on the face. Well, we were equipped accordingly.

By the time all four of us were sitting beside the third icefield it was 2 p.m. Wiggerl pointed at the rock:

"Look, there are the pitons placed by poor Sedlmayer and Mehringer."

Silently our thoughts turned to the two friends. We hacked

The east face of the Sass Maor

Bivouac on the Eiger, 1938. Settling down

Bivouac on the Eiger, 1938. Preparations

out big stances and heated some Ovomaltine, which did us all good. As we wanted to eat as much as possible to lighten the sacks we chewed away at some bacon, but nobody really cared for it. Our stomachs simply refused to absorb solid food. The shin of pork began to annoy me, but I was reluctant to abandon it in case my appetite returned in force.

About this time the hitherto cloudless sky began to haze over, but we did not worry unduly. The route, by which I mean the route that we had worked out in advance, was so firmly fixed in our minds that there was no peering around and wondering where to go next. The weak points of the wall and where to attack them were worked out in advance. We were all in agreement about them.

So the four of us crossed the rib of snow on the third ice-field on to untrodden ground. To get across to the so-called "ramp" we first had to climb down a short stretch of steep ice where the differences in the lengths of our ice-axes really became significant. The longer axe came into its own on the downhill cutting.

The ramp is a gully running diagonally up the face. One side of it proved relatively easy to climb—almost too easy, it seemed to me. I became quite anxious lest it should continue thus to the top. Before long, however, I was to be fully reassured on this point.

For about 150 metres the route went comparatively easily up snow-covered, icy slabs which then culminated in a ring of cliff. The only way out of this was a vertical chimney which higher up ended in a rib. One side of the chimney was yellow, overhanging and loose, in a word unclimbable. The other wall was smoother but more suitable, except that a waterfall came tumbling over it so merrily that anybody attempting to climb it would be soaked through in a minute. None of us wanted to bivouac in wet clothes.

It was seven o'clock when the four of us stood together in the hollow below the ring of cliff. We decided to celebrate. The hollow did not seem a good place, as its floor was covered with avalanche debris which had built up into a steep, icy surface over which the water sprayed and flowed. We therefore climbed back down into the ramp and set about preparing for our bivouac. Suddenly the clouds parted and we found ourselves gazing down into depths so tremendous that although

D

we were accustomed to such sights we shuddered slightly. For the first time we understood how exposed our position was, and with a couple of powerful blows hammered another anchor-piton into the rock.

We pulled on every stitch of clothing we had with us. With loving care I took out my Thermogene and packed it around my knees and toes, informing the others that it would keep me fine and warm. Next we got into our long underwear, over which came climbing breeches and overtrousers, two lots of pullovers and anoraks, and anything else available. Wiggerl, the voluptuary, even had a pair of fur bootees. I had to wear my climbing boots, as my kletterschuhe were still wet through from the Hinterstoisser traverse. Ropes, rucksacks, etc., were laid on the ice as an underlayer to sit on, and the sleeping bags spread out ready. Had I been a fakir I could also have sat on my crampons with the points upwards, which might have added further warmth.

Coffee was what we most craved, and Wiggerl busied himself producing mighty quantities. We were thirsty but not hungry. I still could not get rid of any of the damned shin of pork. One must eat something, however, so I opened a tin of sardines. Nobody else wanted any, so I ate the lot. This was to cause me trouble during the night.

In the meantime it had grown dark. The lights of Grindelwald glittered up at us and we felt fine on our airy perch. Before long we got into our sleeping bags and everyone settled down to get as much sleep as he could. By the light of my torch I took a last glance at the altimeter. It showed 3400 metres, which was extremely satisfactory for the first day. As I was trying to put the altimeter away, something slid down the slab and vanished silently into the depths.

"Damn it again, what was that?"

Naturally it had to be the altimeter, which was nowhere to be found. Cautiously I inquired how much such a gadget might cost.

"Oh, around about 150 marks," replied Wiggerl drily.

I could not get to sleep for anger. In addition, it gradually got so cold that we began to shiver. Only the parts covered in Thermogene remained marvellously warm. I thought with gratitude of the fair lady who had given me this good advice; it was as though the padded places were being caressed.

The time would not go by. When I thought it must surely be almost dawn it turned out to be only eleven o'clock. It is a form of natural compensation: as the hours fly past like minutes when we are climbing by day, the minutes have to turn back into hours at night when we are bivouacking.

Just as I began to get bored I was seized with a violent stomach-ache. In order not to worry the others I said nothing about it. The fevers and chills and dizziness were so powerful that I began to fear that there was something seriously wrong with me. Presently Wiggerl noticed, and everyone sprang into action. Heini Harrer was of the opinion that hot tea would be the best thing, and immediately got his cooker going. A few minutes later I found myself sipping peppermint tea, a drink I had never been able to stand, yet never had a brew tasted better or done me so much good. The sardines promptly settled down in my stomach and we all nodded off again for a while.

Cooking started again at 4 a.m., but not until seven o'clock were we ready to go. As we packed up the altimeter came to light. One should avoid getting angry; it seldom helps and is often pointless.

Our first moves were a bit stiff, but the sight of the wall that I now had to climb made me feel warm. The waterfall over the smooth left-hand wall was no longer there, but in its place was an icy crust. As the chimney was free of ice higher up, I started up it without crampons, prudently placing a couple of pitons, one of which was really firm. In order to avoid the ice I used holds on the loose, overhanging side, and managed to surmount the overhang, even if not very elegantly. Just half a metre more and I could get in another peg. My right hand reached a hold above me, but it broke off even before I could put much strain on it and a lump the size of a coffee pot landed on my head. I found myself hanging from the good piton under the overhang.

That was the first fall. Well, these things happen, I thought to myself. Strapping on my crampons I tackled the left-hand wall. I had never done anything like it before. It was ice climbing in the purest sense, but it went.

Well above the level where the hold had broken off I returned to the chimney, and after a few more metres found myself standing in an ice-filled groove where I cut a stance and belayed the others. While doing this I glanced up to see where we could go next, but the possibilities did not seem very clear. The only remotely feasible line appeared to be an ice-choked corner capped with an ice overhang.

It was the task of the last man to take out all the pitons, not so as to complicate the task of subsequent parties but in order to economize our stock in view of the unknown above, where we might need all we could muster. As leader on this difficult ground I no longer wore any sack at all. The others were thus all the more heavily laden and arrived so out of breath that they needed a few minutes to recover.

Every metre gained in the direction of the ice overhang made me more uncertain how to get over it. Finally the difficulties came to a head at the end of the corner, right under the roof. In front of me a curtain of wonderful icicles hung from its edge, but at this moment I was little disposed to the appreciation of the beauties of nature. In fact I was in despair to know what to do to get any further. The first thing was to place a safe piton under the roof. Now I could take tension and knock down the icicles with the axe, naturally after warning the others to take cover, as these icicles weighed a good 50 kilos and went whizzing down most impressively.

Leaning as far out as I could against the rope-tension, I was finally able to reach the stump of one of the icicles. In those days we did not have the now usual étriers, or we would have used them. As I swung my weight on to the icicle it snapped off and I shot down as far as the last piton, which luckily held. It was clearly impossible to get up here, but there was no alternative. Were we to be defeated by this ridiculous overhang? This was the Eiger, and we had to expect some difficulties.

I prospected to the left and then to the right, but it was no good. By this time I was really in a temper and resolved to go for it all out. Above the ice-piton that had just held so well, an icicle as thick as my arm had grown down until it had joined on to the ice again, thus forming a handle-like structure through which I threaded a sling. Once again I took tension on the rope and leant out. With a supreme effort I managed to hammer in my biggest ice-piton just at the edge of the overhang. When it was only half in I could tell by the ringing noise that it was sound. That was enough——quick, a kara-biner——"Take in tight!" I got the upper part of my body over the edge. Now the battle was as good as won. With my left hand I swung the pick of the hammer into the ice, with my right the ice-axe. A quick pull-up, and I got my cramponned feet up on to the slope.

"Slack!"

I took a few hasty steps. Five metres higher I could finally cut a good stance and plant two ice-pitons for protection. Then it was the turn of my companions to climb up with their heavy rucksacks—we had long ago given up sack-haulage. It had been the hardest part of the climb so far. I was satisfied, but not inclined to wish for any further heightening of the satisfaction.

The slope to which we had won our way was blank and steep. The ice was so hard that I needed to cut some steps even for the crampon-wearers. We were getting close to its upper end when suddenly a fearful uproar broke out. Thinking it was a stonefall we all instantly ducked, only to find that it came from an aircraft flying close to the face. Seen from below, the slope on which we stood looks tiny, but it was almost ten ropeslengths long and took over two hours to climb. Next we followed a band to the rocky step that bars access to the long gangway leading across to the "white spider". The spider is the ice field in the upper third of the face from which icy gullies and ledges reach out on all sides into the surrounding rocks.

The previous year, as we had carefully studied every possible way up the face through the telescope, this step had looked distinctly doubtful to us, and the others had independently come to the same opinion. Now that we stood in front of it, it did not look bad at all. Though vertical and about 50 metres high it was finely articulated and therefore probably well-equipped with holds, so that I did not think of taking off my sack and crampons but simply tied the ice-axe to the sack.

However, starting up the step was not at all so easy as it looked. The holds were small and the rock overhanging. Placing the front points of my crampons on tiny holds I forced my way upwards. It was a completely new technique to us; none of us had ever climbed on such iced-up rock before. What would we have done without our twelve-pointers? Nevertheless, it was hard on the arms, which were going numb with the effort. I was not too far from falling off when suddenly the aeroplane came blasting by again shamelessly close. A thunderstorm approaching out of the west was shaking it about, and I had visions of it crashing into the cliffs at any moment and the whole lot raining about my ears. I was genuinely relieved when it disappeared into the clouds.

Three o'clock in the afternoon: where had the hours gone to? We felt not a trace of hunger or tiredness. On the contrary, as we heard the first rolls of thunder our wills hardened with the resolve to fight a way through. There could be no more thought of retreat. In the interests of speed we divided up into pairs again. I wanted at all costs to reach the spider and get a view of the way forward before the arrival of the cloud that always goes with a storm. To get on to the spider we had to cross a few metres of bare ice. I found I was out of ice-pitons.

"Wiggerl!" I called. "Bring the ice-pegs."

"Ja mei, Heini's got them!"

As last man it was Heini Harrer's task to take out all the pitons, and as we had used them all he now had the lot. It seemed best to wait for the others to catch up, but as we were standing there several stones went whistling past. It only needed one of them to hit one of us, and that would be the end. Suddenly we found our stance very inhospitable.

"Come on, never mind the pitons. We'll belay with the spikes of the ice-axes." And as this technique seemed to me of doubtful effectiveness, I added: "Only we mustn't fall off!"

In fact the ice had softened up and steps were not absolutely essential. Nevertheless, 150 metres had to be climbed in this way. After each run-out we cut a stance, which was to prove the salvation of the others.

Thus we did not take long to reach the foot of the summital rock-bastion. Initially there was nowhere to stand, but it was possible to hack a couple of stances out of the ice. I also found a crack in the rock that would accept my very last ice-piton, which was a particularly thin one. It is extremely rare to be able to place an ice-piton in rock, but if it can be done it constitutes an especially safe anchor. With heavy blows I drove it deep into the crack, little guessing how vitally important it was to prove to us. A glance up at the face comfortingly revealed a whole system of cracks and grooves, one of which must surely provide a way forward. Now the storm could come, although to half stand, half hang where we were was not the most agreeable of prospects. Thirty metres below, a pulpit of rock cropped out of the ice, offering a level, table-like top.

"What do you say, Wiggerl? It would be pretty good to sit down there."

"I'm all for it, only the rope won't reach."

"It doesn't matter. Go on, I'll belay you."

As soon as the rope had run out, I unclipped from the piton and climbed carefully down without any security. We settled down on the rock as though it were a throne and looked around critically at the weather.

"Doesn't look too good."

During this time our friends were just traversing on to the spider. The light was gradually growing more and more dismal, and before long it began to sleet. Lightning and thunder followed, but we had endured enough storms in the mountains not to be dismayed. Only the increasingly frequent whistling and hooting of invisible stonefalls in the mist got on our nerves.

Following our tracks, the two Austrians had now reached the middle of the spider. The sleet had changed to hail, and we had pulled the tent-sack over our heads for shelter. In order to see how the others were getting on we raised it. Suddenly Wiggerl gestured towards the ice groove directly above us:

"There's an avalanche coming!"

Out of the gully came hissing a stream of ice grains that broke over our heads and poured on into the depths. I jumped up and stabbed the pick of my axe into the ice so as to resist the pressure. Wiggerl was unable to emulate me because there was no room to do so, and sat exposed on the edge of the rock. We had no anchor whatever. I held on to the pick with one hand and with the other grabbed Wiggerl by the scruff of the neck, convinced that our comrades must have been swept away by the mainstream of the avalanche that had broken over them and that we were about to follow them at any moment. In the meantime I just tried to hang on as long as possible. In my imagination I could already see us tumbling over the crags.

However, things had not quite reached this point yet. I was astonished myself at how long I was able to withstand the tremendous force. The bare hand that was holding on to the axe had turned white with the cold, and I took the risk of letting go for a moment to draw on a mitten. The sleet and hail particles had built up a wall as high as my hips, over which the avalanche split into two and rushed past on either side. Luckily the steepness of the ice slope had caused the enormous mass of powder to slide by quickly. Slowly the air cleared and the pressure eased. We could hardly believe that we had come through, but so it seemed. What had happened to the others? The cloud thinned out, and . . .

"Wiggerl! They're still there!"

It seemed impossible, almost a miracle. We were overcome with joy. Only when you again see friends you had believed dead do you realize how deep the feeling of comradeship can be.

"I'm hurt!" called Kasparek. "Throw me a rope."

First we had to get back up to our piton, and that turned out to be not so easy. The stream of hailstones was still pouring down. When we reached the rock wall above the spider we found ourselves separated from the peg by a runnel down which the hailstones were rushing like a torrent. I was for risking a jump, but Wiggerl would not hear of it. It was a good ten minutes before we could get across to our piton. It and the karabiner had grown ice-spicules several centimetres long. The phenomenon was curious, but we had no time for scientific reflection. However, it did occur to us to wonder how we would have fared if we had remained standing there.

The belay was clipped in, the ropes tied together and the end thrown down to our friends. In order to reach it where it lay on the ice some 60 metres below us Kasparek had to climb up about another ten metres. Finally he was tied on. The knowledge that we were all linked together again was like an assurance of salvation, and from that moment we remained roped in one party all the way to the summit and down to Scheidegg.

The others soon reached our stance.

"Where are you hurt?"

"Ugh, my hand looks awful."

All the skin had been torn off the back of Kasparek's hand, and at the time it looked much worse than it really was. In order to be sure I gave it a hard squeeze, reasoning that if a bone was broken he would feel it, whereas if the injury was superficial he would only start cursing. To my relief it was the latter that occurred. Quickly I got out the first aid kit and bound up the gaping wound with sticking plaster. By this time it was 6 p.m.

"Shall we bivouac here?"

Following the storm the weather had improved, but nevertheless did not look promising. We had just had a taste of what the snow slides could be like when concentrated in a funnel. If the weather should really turn nasty it would be fatal to try to climb the ice gully up which the rest of the route lay. After a short council of war we therefore decided to continue despite the Alpine rule of thumb that one should settle down to bivouac two hours before dark. Our reasoning was that it was still relatively warm and the ice soft, so that this was the most favourable time to try it.

The gully began with an overhang which I tackled on the left. However, I had been in too much of a hurry, and after three metres had to jump down again. In the process I got my crampons tangled up and only avoided a fall thanks to our belay. Over on the right, where at first the rock had looked too formidable to try, it turned out distinctly easier. The ice proved to be in good condition, and I was able to stab in the blade of the ice-axe with one hand and a stout ice-piton with the other, then pull up on them and walk my twelve-pointers up quickly. Nevertheless, it was very hard and risky work. But what alternative did I have?

If I spent time looking for more security it would have cost us all the remaining daylight, and the following morning we could scarcely have escaped the terrible avalanches in the gully. It was always a principle of mine to accept subjective risks in order to avoid objective ones, and the four of us held to it on this occasion. The higher we got the narrower and steeper the gullies grew. In between they built up into overhangs, which we took as they came. Harrer groaned under the weight of his increasingly heavy rucksack. In order to climb more safely at the front we had been passing back some of the contents of our rucksacks to the others on every possible occasion. Heini and Fritz had relieved us of everything they could in a spirit of evident comradeship, and to this was added the weight of the pitons which accumulated as they took them out. The last man began to look like a porter. The two of them accepted the monstrous effort without once complaining. It was this teamwork which enabled us to win through. Fritz never said a word about his hand although he must have been in great pain; the plaster binding up the wound was saturated in blood.

We now needed to find a spot in this system of grooves and chimneys where we could be moderately safe from avalanches and stonefall. After climbing an ice bulge I came upon a ledge protected by an overhang. It was outward-sloping and exposed, like everything on the Eigerwand, but at least it was sheltered.

I drove a ring spike into a little crack right up to the ring. To get any other piton into the rock was a work of art, as the rock on this final wall was much looser than elsewhere. With a great deal of patience we nevertheless ended by hammering in a sufficient quantity to tie our gear and ourselves to. The previous evening had taught us that everything which was not attached slipped from our hands to be lost for good.

Unfortunately, we could not sit together. Three metres away there was a second place where it was possible to belay and cut away some of the shelving ice, and Fritz and Heini worked away to install their bivouac there. Between us we stretched a rope along which we could pull a billycan clipped on with a karabiner.

As on the previous evening, the good-natured Wiggerl did all the cooking. Kasparek's spirit stove had long since joined my shin of pork on the road into the depths. We still had no inclination for solid food. All we wanted was to drink, preferably coffee, and of that we had ample supplies. We still had enough food to last us a week, but it remained untouched. I was not anxious to repeat my experience of the night before. None of us was particularly exigent in the matter of space, but this ledge really was annoyingly narrow. I just could not find a comfortable position. There was no question of lying down. We had already spent the night before sitting up, but this time it could not even be called sitting. With my crampons stamped into the ice (which meant that I had to keep them on) I slumped from a sling around my chest, suspended from the piton.

If only Wiggerl would at least sit still! But he just went on

peacefully boiling one can of coffee after another, and in our
hearts we could find nothing to say against that. He would
take a swig, pass the can on straight away, and immediately
set another on the petrol cooker, the humming of which gave
us a feeling of well-being. Quite apart from that, we felt
perfectly calm. We knew what we should have to face next
day, and that the weather would be bad. Only Fritz grumbled:
"When I get down again I'm going to light a dry cigarette
with a dry match!"

We two had purposely taken neither alcohol nor tobacco
with us. Kasparek, however, who could not do without his
smoke, now found his cigarettes and matches unusable,
whence the complaint. It was only to be expected, as although
we were not absolutely soaked to the skin we were nevertheless
quite damp.

For me this latter circumstance had a particular significance,
as the Thermogene had got wet. This had happened during
the course of the day, and the wadding, which was only supposed to be applied to rheumatic spots for a couple of hours
at most, was now burning my knees and toes horribly. No
longer did I feel pampered as at first, but really tortured.
"Better to let it burn," we decided. "At least it will prevent
any freezing." Unfortunately, we were very much mistaken.

At last Wiggerl stopped cooking and began to prepare for
the night. With indescribable calm he proceeded to change
his clothes and draw on his bivouac slippers, whereas we had
just settled down as we were. Darkness had long since fallen;
it was already after eleven o'clock. Even Fritz had kept on his
crampons. I would gladly have taken mine off, but as already
mentioned I needed them to stop myself sliding. Wiggerl's
antics took him a good hour, and then at last we could pull
the bivouac sack over our heads. His broad back was turned
towards me and I could lean against it comfortably. He was so
soft and warm that I forgave all the disturbance he had caused.
As peace returned my eyelids closed and I fell fast asleep.

A violent cold shower woke me up again and set our teeth
chattering. I was astonished to see that it was light already.
In fact it was 5 a.m., and I had slept through the whole night.
The others told me that several avalanches had swept over
our heads without my noticing.

"Go back to sleep," said Wiggerl settling back into the

position that I found so comfortable. I noticed for the first time that it must be extremely uncomfortable for him.

"Have you been able to sleep?"

"Naturally not. But when I noticed how well you were sleeping I kept still, because you are the one who is going to need it most. Go back to sleep, Anderl. In any case it's snowing at present and we can't do anything for the time being."

However, now that I knew my rest was causing him agony I could not settle down again. On top of that, I was too cold and also worried about the weather. The snow was falling dry. We could hear the storm but not feel it, as we were in the wind-shadow of the west ridge. But from the ridge and the summit came the sound of its roaring. Every so often, as the weight of snow piled up on the summital ice slopes, it would break away in avalanches. We were able to observe their route and timing exactly. It was lucky for us that we had climbed this far the previous evening, as below us everything falling from the summital slopes was gathered as into a funnel. Only a small side-stream fell past us, and on our ledge we received no more than the whirling snow dust.

Wiggerl carefully resumed his task as cook and produced hot chocolate made with tinned milk. We knew that this would be our last meal until we got back to the valley, yet we did not throw away the ample provisions we still had. One never knows.

Our every move was being observed from the valley, and a Munich journalist who had reached Scheidegg at exactly the right time telephoned the following dispatch to his paper, the *Münchner Neuesten Nachrichten*, that evening. It was entitled "Between hope and fear".

At 12.30 p.m. on Saturday the weather turned bad over the Eiger. A slate-grey wall of cloud, dark and threatening, rolled towards the Lauterbrunnen valley. After a severe five-hour struggle the four climbers had surmounted the slanting gully, which perhaps contains the hardest pitches on the face, and traversed the snowband above the yellow cliff on the right of the gully. At one o'clock they stood in a row at the left edge of the snowfield. Heckmair, the mountain guide with the hardest training and perhaps the greatest experience on ice, was in the lead. For the next half-hour the climbers were hidden in cloud, but at 2.30 it cleared again. They had crossed the snowband and the leader was just reaching the overhang before the so-called "spider". Without stopping, Heckmair—who remained in the lead all day—traversed on to the spider. We watched him wielding his ice-axe powerfully and swiftly forcing a way to the middle of the slope. Immediately, he ran out the whole ropeslength to reach a snowband running up to the top left-hand end of the spider. Vörg followed up as second man. Heckmair went on again at once up the steep snowband or, more accurately, gully, until he reached a brown rock where he stopped and belayed Vörg, who came up equally fast. They then sat down on the rock to wait for the others. Their performance, their powerful axe work, their careful belaying and astonishing speed clearly showed us, as we watched them excitedly through the telescope, that they were in great form and still full of energy.

Meanwhile Kasparek and Harrer had been resting at the end of the lower snowband. From 3 to 3.30 p.m. the face was again veiled in cloud, and as it cleared the watchers crowded around the telescopes. The leader of the second party was just traversing on to the spider as Heckmair reached the rock in the upper snow gully.

The second party moved definitely slower than the first, but just as carefully and safely. Heckmair and Vörg were now at 3600 metres. At ten past four the face clouded over again, leaving us alone with our hopes and fears once more. The four climbers still had 350 metres to go before the summit.

The weather began to look very threatening again. Throughout the day it had been impossible to decide from one hour to the next whether it was finally going to get better or worse. Now the air over the Lauterbrunnen valley was dirty grey and the Jungfrau and Mönch were lost in cloud. The glacier ice falls glimmered pale blue in the failing light. Between the rain clouds was a patch of blue, and over the Grosse Scheidegg the sky was still clear, but the weather was rolling up inexorably. The party must still be in the funnel of the spider.

At 4.25 p.m. it began to drizzle, and five minutes later there was a cloudburst. It must have broken over the face like an ocean comber. Suddenly a cry of horror was torn from the throats of the watchers: "The face!" The whole breadth of the north face was one appalling waterfall. The water cascaded over the rocks in ten, twelve, fifteen broad, white, foaming bands. A beautiful rainbow was arched above Alpiglen, but who had eyes for it or the marvellous play of its colours? Up there the pair on the snow slope were fully exposed to the plunging torrent. Would they be able to hold on?

At last the cloud cleared and it became possible to see through the telescope. There was the snow field and there, yes, there they were. Calmly and deliberately, they were already in movement again. They had come through the deluge! Having been able to take shelter below the rocks at the side of the gully, Heckmair and Vörg probably had an easier time of it. But already the face was covered over again; the last we saw was that one of the upper party had climbed down some way, presumably to throw a rope to the others and safeguard them.

At 6.15 we were able to see that they were all together again and heading for the upper end of the snow gully. Heckmair was standing straddled, belaying the others. Then he turned and continued, cutting steps. At 7 o'clock all four were at the top of the snow gully. An hour later they were still climbing, having either found no bivouac site or, more probably, preferred to keep going as long as daylight should hold out, in order to get as near the summit as possible. They were now at 3700 metres, far above the spider, and had thus achieved an outstanding performance in the last fourteen hours. The weather was looking more hopeful for the time being: patches of blue showed between the dirty-looking clouds, which were not getting caught up in the crags, so that the climbers had some visibility.

At 8.30 it began to rain again, but in the intervals we could see the party still under way. After half an hour they seemed to be preparing a bivouac site. For Kasparek and Harrer this will be the third night on the face, for Heckmair and Vörg the second. In wet clothes and on probably exiguous stances it will be a testing experience, although all four are iron-hard men.   .

Our last observation was at 10 o'clock. The sky was

starry. In the middle of the face floated a light-coloured cloud, and below it shone the strange light of the Jungfrau railway Eigerwand station. Otherwise all was dark. For the four men up on the face the problem now was to hold out through the hours of darkness. They had enough food for five or six days. Probably they did not sleep much but passed the night crouched over their cooker making hot food and tea. There could be no more question of retreat; they must get up at all costs. They were at 3750 metres, which left some 200 metres to the summit.

On Sunday morning we awoke to rain. The windows were blind with cloud. The weather has broken, and there is nothing to be seen of the face. Up there it must be snowing. Kasparek and Harrer have now been on the face for 65 hours, Vörg and Heckmair for 43. At 5 o'clock it was raining, at 6 o'clock it was raining, at 7 o'clock it was raining; at 11 o'clock there was still nothing but uninterrupted, pouring rain.

Up on the face, however, we had no inkling of the anxiety that we were arousing. All we knew was that we could reckon on no outside help.

The decision to leave our sheltered spot and climb up into the storm was difficult but did not take long. Like Merkl and Welzenbach on the north face of the Charmoz we might have waited for better weather, but somehow I did not have the nerve, since even after the weather had cleared up conditions on the face would not be much better at first. We were unanimous to push on.

After packing our rucksacks, we roped up in the same order as before and set out to face what in the circumstances were to be the hardest hours we spent on the face. It was still snowing and snowing, as it had the whole night. The avalanches came down at regular intervals, and each time we had one hour in between to climb farther. The sight of the route that we must follow was appalling. The rocks were coated with ice, on which the treacherous new snow was building up. I used to have the naïve idea that where snow settled there must be a hold underneath, but what I did not know was that in clouds the humidity can be supercooled to −39°C. Mixed with snow, this humidity in suspension was being swept against the wall, forming a layer of clear ice to which the snow was sticking even below the overhangs. Very romantic to look at, but just about the worst that could be encountered on a climb of this order.

Wiggerl was unable to stop taking photographs even in these circumstances, just as he had during the bivouac. Knowing that I had been against the whole business of photography from the outset, he grinned at me apologetically. He was in fact right to obtain this record in spite of my disapproval.

I fought my way up to a small jut of rock. When I looked back down at my companions I could not suppress a smile; they were leaning against the wall like a bunch of icicles, as an avalanche had just shot past and left us well and truly frosted.

There were two possibilities: a groove down which, according to our observations, a branch of the mainstream of the avalanche flowed, or an open wall that was indeed safer but also much harder. At first I opted for the latter, but as the first few metres already called for several pitons it seemed to be absorbing too much time and energy. I therefore went for the groove.

To get into the groove it was necessary to descend, so I hammered in a piton at once and abseiled. The top of a small pillar just at the edge of the groove offered a stance, but the problem was to reach it. I had a good hold for my right hand, but the left could find not the smallest purchase on the ice-glazed wall. Finally I tried to lurch across but slipped and found myself on a small ice patch two metres lower down, where my crampons immediately brought me to a stop.

Wiggerl, who had held me on the rope, grinned down at me shamelessly from his stance out to one side. I immediately tried again and promptly fell off once more, only this time I did not stop but pendulumed into the groove. With the help of the others Wiggerl once again held firm, but he had stopped grinning. I had taken a considerable blow on the behind, but was accustomed to pain in this quarter from my earliest schooldays. Nevertheless, I had now been cut down to size and traversed modestly around the pillar, which turned out to be fairly easy from the other side. I hacked the ice off the top of the pillar so as to get a good stance and inserted a belay piton. No sooner had I done this than an avalanche came sweeping down over the face like a thick veil of mist. In our position it was as though we were standing behind a giant waterfall, otherwise we could hardly have resisted the pressure. In addition, we got a certain amount of cover from the over-hangs, and were protected by the ice-piton. The real danger was that we might inhale the whirling ice dust and suffocate, so we drew our scarves up around our noses.

After the last trickles had finally ceased I climbed into the groove, very much aware that the mainstream of the next avalanche would pass down it. Before that happened, I must be above its well-nigh vertical top section. It was no place to hang around. The ice was much harder than it had been the evening before, and it was correspondingly more strenuous to front-point upwards without cutting steps. Well, we could not choose our conditions. The degree to which ice climbs change in difficulty is so great that they cannot be graded.

With the ice-hammer I chipped nicks to use as handholds. After I had run out about half the length of the rope the angle eased off somewhat and I could cut a stance. Already I could see that the groove ran out somewhere into the upper slopes, so I yodelled joyously down to the others. Before long Wiggerl was beside me, while the second pair had moved up to the top of the rock pillar. At this moment the expected avalanche began to fall, and this time we could observe it exactly. First a white trail appeared far over at the right-hand side of the face. It took three or four minutes before it spread like a curtain across the whole width of the face to a point above the gully in which we stood. It was obvious that we were directly in its path, even though it would only be a subsidiary flow. There was just time to hammer a second piton into the rock, then it was upon us.

With our rucksacks over our heads and our scarves wound round our faces we waited for the shock. The pressure did not tear us from our steps, but forced our crampons deeper into the ice. The important thing was to make sure that the snow did not build up between our bodies and the slope, as this might have pushed us over backwards. There were no stones; we were already too high for that. The snow was very fine, so that it did not have too much weight, in addition to which the main mass of it shot past over our heads. Already we were in high spirits again and rejoicing at this new view of the drama of nature which neither of us had experienced before.

"We stood up to that one all right," we told each other.

We shook ourselves like a pair of wet poodles, and while Wiggerl brought up the others I climbed on. Suddenly from the west ridge we heard a long-drawn shout, which was repeated after a pause. It could only be meant for us, but I realized at once that an answer would only lead to misunderstanding. The distance was much too great for communication, and unintelligible cries could too easily be interpreted as appeals for help. I therefore passed down the word:

"Keep quiet, don't answer!"

Later we learnt that the guide Schlunegger, who had distinguished himself on the rescues in 1935 and 1936, had taken the trouble in spite of the weather to climb the west face to the summit in order to find out whether there was anything to be seen or heard of us, and if necessary to get a rescue party under way. That we should remain so active and cheerful in such circumstances seemed unimaginable, so he returned to the valley with the report that in these conditions no living creature could possibly survive on the face. At this time we were in the best of spirits, being certain of reaching the top before long.

The gully, which had become less steep, suddenly reared up once more.

"Wiggerl!" I shouted. "Watch out, it's getting difficult again."

The steadily falling snow did not in itself bother us, but the flakes were now much bigger and we could feel that the air was growing warmer. The next avalanche would probably be longer coming, but all the heavier when it fell.

Now indeed it was snowing wet and heavy. It had been a long time since the last avalanche. I had better climb the overhang quickly. The layer of ice was no longer thick enough to hold pitons, which after the second blow either fell out or bent against the rock. At the overhang I had to place my feet one directly above the other since the old ice had shrunk to a narrow strip and the new lay too blank and thin over the rock. The point of the ice-piton which I was using as a dagger now hardly penetrated, and the axe-pick fared no better. Suddenly both skidded at the same time. Had I been in a bridging position I might have been able to keep my balance, but with my feet in line there was no holding it.

"Wiggerl! Look out!"

And away I went. Wiggerl took in as much slack rope as possible as I shot straight down towards him. It was more of a fast slide than a fall, as I had still been below the overhang when I slipped. At the moment of falling I turned face outwards in order to avoid going over backwards. After all, we all like to see where we are flying to.

Wiggerl dropped the rope and tried to grab me with his hands. In the process one of my crampon spikes drove into the ball of his thumb, flipping me upside down. As I shot by head-first I grabbed at the rope. This gave me a jerk so that I completed my somersault, to my own astonishment landing upright some distance below the stance with my crampon points bedded in the ice. The momentum with which I had thudded into Wiggerl had knocked him off, and now I was able to hold him too. Quickly we scrambled back up to the stance. The peg had been torn out, so I put in another one at once. The whole affair had taken only a few seconds; it was an instinctive reaction that saved us. Our friends below were blissfully unaware that anything had happened. Had it been otherwise the rope that bound us together would have plucked them off after us in a great bound over the face.

Meanwhile Wiggerl had tugged the mitten off his wounded hand. The spike had gone right through, and blood was spurting out on both sides. It was dark, so not arterial. By way of further diagnosis I suddenly squeezed it as I had Fritz's lower down. He grimaced with pain, but as he did not keel over I took it that no bones were broken. Only he had gone so pale, perhaps from shock, that if he had any colour left at all it was green.

"Are you going to faint?"

"I'm not too sure."

I anchored him again and placed myself so that he could not fall whatever happened.

"Pull yourself together, everything depends on it."

I glanced up at the face. Thank God the avalanche was holding off. Whipping off the rucksack, I bound up the hand with plaster. In the first-aid tin I came across a phial of heart-stimulant drops, given to me just in case, by an anxious lady doctor in Grindelwald with the remark: "If Toni Kurz had had drops like these, he might have survived the crisis." We were only to use them if the situation was really serious. I thought to myself that the moment had come. There were perhaps ten drops in the phial, but I did not take the time to count them. I shook half of them into Wiggerl's mouth and drank the other half myself because I was thirsty. A couple of glucose tablets on top of that, and we were fighting fit again. There was still nothing to be seen of the avalanche.

"Wiggerl, I'm going to try the overhang again right away."

"OK, but please just don't fall off on me again," he answered in a weak voice.

I concentrated every ounce of nervous energy on getting this delicate and dangerous pitch behind me as quickly as I could, even to the point of doing without any intermediate security. Although I ran out the whole rope—almost 30 metres—I still could not find any stance. At that point, however, I was at least able to get in a small rock-piton. It went in really well, and no sooner had I clipped into it than the feared and long-awaited avalanche arrived. A kindly fate had held it back just long enough, but now it broke over us powerfully. I was out of the worst of it, as the groove led out to the side. Fritz and Heini, who were the farthest down, received the full weight of it, and Wiggerl too could not complain of neglect. All I could do was to take in the rope as tightly as possible so as to back up their own belays. I also watched the force of the avalanche and when particularly heavy waves came down yelled:

"Now! Hold, ho-o-o-old. It's coming thick!"

In fact these were mere cries of despair. Afterwards nobody mentioned having heard a thing, but at the time I had the feeling that I was being of enormous help. Suddenly everything went dark and my head was smashed against the wall by a mass of falling snow, leaving me with a lump on the forehead. It only lasted a few moments, then I was free again, but the others were still getting a drubbing. The avalanche seemed to be going on forever; it was the consequence of the long time it had taken to build up.

"It's getting light . . . no, look out! Look *out*!"

Another heavy wave came down, some of which also reached me. Once again I bellowed:

"It's nearly over, hold on, hold on!"

After what seemed an eternity it began to ease off somewhat, but we still had to wait a while before the last trickles were over and Wiggerl could come up to me. The others followed, and then I could go on again. Ouch, my ankle! I had turned it in my fall, and now felt it for the first time. However, it could not be broken or I would have known it at once, and nothing else mattered even if it hurt.

The gully now flattened out, but the possibilities for belaying became still fewer. The end of the gully was in sight when we again heard the voice from the west ridge. "Don't answer" was again passed down the line. We were too familiar with the procedure. First comes a lone observer, peering around. If he hears anything, the whole rescue apparatus is set in motion. On this giant mountain it would have been hours before he had got down and the rescue party up, and in the meantime we could get out of it by ourselves. True, we were all a bit the worse for wear, but we still had plenty of fight left in us. Yet we were cheered by the thought that somebody cared enough to go to the trouble, and it gave us a renewed incentive.

Soon after this we reached the end of the gully. We had overcome the rocks, but were far from having reached the summit. Before us rose a steep ice slope where we had to use our last remaining pitons in order to avoid being swept away by avalanches. The snow continued to fall more and more thickly. Avalanches thundered down the face one after another without a pause, but we were now beyond their reach.

Now for the first time we were exposed to the full fury of the storm. Long before the rope had run out it was impossible to make oneself understood. Our windproofs iced up to such an extent that we could only move in jerks. I felt like a knight in armour, in addition to which the saturated Thermogene burnt horribly. Every so often, in order to relieve the irritation to which I was helplessly subjected, I had to jump up and down. Wiggerl, who had got rid of his Thermogene long before, remarked that I must be suffering from altitude madness. Resigned to my fate, I stamped on through the storm towards the summit. The thongs of our crampons also began to contract, cutting into our feet and sending them numb. However, we were finished with the face and would get through now whatever happened. It was up to ourselves. The dangers and difficulties had been overcome, and even the storm could no longer kill us.

In spite of this the conditions could not be described as pleasant, and we nearly fell through the cornice. The last part of the ridge is horizontal, but in the thick fog it looked to me as though it slanted steeply upwards. We had climbed the final ice slopes, swept bare by the wind, in a series of zigzags. Now I made another, and with the next step I was out over the cornice. One metre behind me, Wiggerl was in the same situation. Suddenly he yelled:

"Stop! Get back! There are rocks below!"

We were looking down the south side of the mountain. It would have been bad luck to have got up the north face alive only to fall down the south face because we had not noticed the summit.

Somehow we had imagined the experience of standing on the summit having solved the last and greatest problem in the Alps as much more solemn. The storm allowed no respite to think of anything else. We shook hands, scratched the ice away from our eyebrows so that we could at least see, and immediately carried on down the west face, into the wind. It was now a great advantage that Fritz and Heini knew the way. Only a few days before, they had climbed the Mittelegigrat and down the western flank of the mountain.

Now we could see how much new snow had fallen in the course of this one day. Owing to the lesser angle of the west face it had settled to a depth of half a metre in places where it was neither drifting nor being blown away. It was not pleasant new snow such as one gets in winter, but a heavy, porridgy mass lying on icy slabs. Quite often the whole lot would slip with us on it, but almost always stopped at once.

Now that the excitement of immediate danger was gone, a leaden weariness invaded our bones. Probably I was in the worst state, as I had all the pains in the world to keep up with the others. I just thought to myself: "I've done my bit, now they can do theirs and get us down." As last man on the face, Heini Harrer had made a gigantic physical effort carrying loads, but had used up less of his nervous energy than the rest of us. Now he took over the lead. As for myself, I mostly waited until the others disappeared into the mist and the rope was taut, then sat down and shot past them on the seat of my pants so that the three of them had their work cut out to hold me. It was not an ideal example, but then what is exemplary on the Eiger?

On one of my little slides I burst the elastic on my overtrousers so that they kept on coming down, taking my climbing breeches and underpants with them. I did not care about that, but the direct contact with the snow was so unpleasant that I carried on a running battle with my nether garments which consumed the rest of my nervous energy.

All that mattered was losing height. With every metre the storm lost something of its force and the snow fell less thickly. But we were not to get away without one more test of my sorely tried nerves. In the impenetrable fog, Heini had led us too far to the left. Luckily Fritz and Heini soon noticed the mistake, or we should not have avoided a further bivouac. In our then state it would have been fearful, and none of us would have escaped unharmed. In 1957 a German party that had just climbed the north face lost their lives on this very descent.

Nevertheless, at that moment, we almost bivouacked again. A momentary clearing in the cloud showed that we should have to toil our way back up for 200 metres in order to cross a cleft that separated us from the west ridge. To me in particular it seemed worse than the hardest part of the north face. I felt a total disinclination to go back and was all for trying to descend over the overhang. My friends simply dragged me uphill in spite of my protests. I was the only one to kick up a fuss; the others said not a word.

A thousand metres of descent lay behind us already, and at 3000 metres the storm was no longer so violent as it had been at the top. Our ice-armour began to thaw, with the consequence that we were soaked through to the last stitch. Now that we had crossed the cleft we were certain of reaching the valley the same day and began to wonder if we could get a room at the Kleine Scheidegg Hotel without money, and whether they would let us have some dry clothes. Harrer asked me:

"Anderl, have you any money so we can get a room?"

Naturally I had no money, that being about the last thing you require on the Eigerwand, so we decided just to make the best of it and go on down to the tents as we were. We had completely forgotten that we had been watched and that people had been anxious for our safety. Thus when we got down out of the cloud an hour or so later it came as a surprise to see a seething mass of dots in front of the hotel some hundreds of metres below. That it had to do with us did not cross our minds.

For the time being we were still on rock and clambered carefully on down amid grunts and groans. Presently a Swiss lad came storming towards us. Goggling at us as though we had just landed from the moon, he asked with embarrassment:

"Have you just come off the north face?"

"Yes, but what's going on down there?"

"That's the Mountain Rescue. They've come up to look for you."

Quite suddenly we realized that it was to do with us, and slowly, very slowly, joy began to burgeon inside us at being given back to life. Down below, the crowd became more and more turbulent, then started swarming up the hillside like ants. Soon the swiftest were within 50 metres. For a moment we hesitated, then, all weariness forgotten, bounded towards our friends. They fell around our necks with whoops of joy and whirled us around in war dances. We joined in with a will, and nobody thought any more about all the aches and pains that had been so torturing us a few minutes before.

Freissl and Brankovsky, the two Viennese climbers we had met on the face the first day, were there too. Once our success seemed assured they had not withdrawn from the scene in a sulk but had taken over the job of communications with our friends who kept telephoning from Munich. Now they were the first to welcome us. Freissl held out a flask of brandy and said boisterously:

"Drink some of that. It'll do you good."

With our friends had come reporters from all over the world, and there was a continual blaze of flashbulbs around us. Among the journalists, whom we climbers generally look on with a good deal of suspicion, were two who became our friends, Guido Tonella from Geneva and Ulrich Link from Munich, author of the account quoted above. These two and the late Kurt Maix from Vienna have throughout their careers related the doings of mountaineers with accuracy and honesty, certainly no easy task in view of our sensitivity to attempts to manufacture sensations at our expense. However, those—regrettably few—that understand climbers and climbing and gain our confidence not only become friends but finally become members of the circle.

An American reporter asked us to set up a bivouac on the spot for his benefit. That was asking too much, and escorted by our friends we literally fought our way through the excited crowd.

Now others took over and did our thinking for us. Warm rooms were ready waiting, and our friends brought dry clothing. We badly needed hot baths. Wiggerl was already standing in the tub as I came into the bathroom. He stared at me with the wide, soulful eyes of a dying calf. "Poor fellow's a bit touched. Why doesn't he sit down?" I thought to myself, and without more ado climbed into the tub. A moment later I shot out again as though I had landed on a spring. Quite apart from first-degree frostbite, my feet were still fiery red from the irritation of the Thermogene. They stung as though simultaneously pricked with a thousand needles. However, a climber always finds a way out of any situation. We let our feet hang over the edge and lowered ourselves into the hot water up to the neck.

For three days we had eaten next to nothing. Now our hunger was so gigantic as scarcely to be satisfied. One schnitzel after another disappeared before the gaze of our astounded public. A uniformed official from the embassy in Bern turned our dinner at the festively-decorated table into a kind of victory feast over which he made a speech full of unpleasant nationalistic phrases despite the fact that we were in Switzerland. The victory of the Schmid brothers on the north face of the Matterhorn had indeed been made the occasion of a celebration in Zermatt, but that had been within a restricted circle and therefore bearable. The pile of congratulations and invitations that now poured in from all over the place was enough to submerge us. All through the night they continued to arrive, including one from the Reichskanzlei in the name of Hitler, stating that he wished to see us. From this there could be no escape. Admittedly it might have been construed as a great honour, but I would much rather have carried out my plan of travelling over to Chamonix to attempt the Walker spur on the Grandes Jorasses.

Things even went so far as a little reception by the guides of Grindelwald. It had not been easy for them to have to watch us pick off "their" face. Consoling words were found on both sides.

A week later Riccardo Cassin climbed the Walker spur. By this time we were already "received in audience by the Führer". It was the third time I had stood face to face with him. Naturally, he had not the faintest memory of having held a long conversation with me on the motivation of mountain climbing, and I did not let on for a moment. He showed us the most gracious side of his nature and surprised us with his searching and knowledgeable questions.

"Now you need to recuperate," he announced.

The "Reichssportführer" was standing by and took over at once. He had us put on board the *Columbus*, which was setting out on a Scandinavian cruise. We were just loaded aboard and our opinion was not asked at all.

CHAPTER XI

The Consequences

AFTER THE EIGERWAND we were no longer masters of our own fate. We were quite simply taken over. Not very tactfully with regard to neutral Switzerland, fully uniformed staff officials from the Sonthofen Ordensburg appeared and swept us off "home to the Reich as national heroes". Many years later it is easy to see what we should have done, but at the time we were more or less stunned by the reaction to our success and submitted to the will of others.

At Sonthofen a great reception was given for us, and in the Ordensburg we were immediately enrolled on the staff as "Bergsportführer" at a salary of 300 marks. It was the first time in my life that I had received a salary, and it represented a step up in the social scale that I found very pleasant. Less acceptable was an address by Dr Robert Ley, head of the Reichsorganization, in which he harangued us as Party members and expressed his pride in our performance. We were not Party members. My sole relation to the Party was that I had been in Hitler's company for a couple of hours and had spoken with him. We were lined up, clothed, and generally brought into line. The fact that for ten years I had had no fixed address, had not reported anywhere and had spent most of my time wandering around abroad was not mentioned, although for someone else such behaviour might have entailed trouble and perhaps worse.

At this point I should say a few words about the political consequences of the first ascent of the Eigerwand, since I am still questioned about them up to the present day. In many books the four of us are branded as fanatical Nazis who climbed the Eiger as a kind of "National-Socialist Greater German Record". As late as the spring of 1971 the editors of the English magazine *Mountain* came to interview me in Oberstdorf and cross-examined me about the matter lengthily and in the greatest detail.

These editors suggested that climbers from fascist countries were primarily interested in the Eigerwand for reasons of nationalistic ambition. I replied that, put thus, the suggestion was pure nonsense, and pointed out that I and many other such climbers of that period had taken little or no interest in politics. It was the fuss in the papers after the ascent celebrating us as "heroes" that gave the impression that the Nazis were behind it. The Italian government and press caused exactly the same misunderstandings over Riccardo Cassin's ascent of the Walker spur, yet I am sure that, like ourselves, Cassin and his companions were only interested in success in mountaineering terms.

To questions regarding our reception and decoration by Hitler I answered that just like anybody else we felt honoured at being picked out of our obscure existence and presented to the most powerful man in Germany, and at being decorated by him. It could have happened to a dancing bear. As young men with no interest in politics we had no way of seeing where Nazi policies were going to lead. Not until the outbreak of war did the real political situation become clear. Nevertheless, I replied, I could not blame people in other countries for thinking as they did. The Nazis did indeed build us up into such stars that people believed that we had been backed and financially subsidized by the Party. However, that is simply not true.

I told the English journalists that I was glad that since those days the mountain-climbing world had freed itself from this type of pressure and had quickly grown into a genuinely international sport. We then discussed the nationalistic motivation that still sometimes exists behind big expeditions, perhaps Japanese ones in particular. When one of the Englishmen objected that only recently a German politician had complained of the lack of German success on the highest mountains in the world, I replied: "Dann ist er ein blöder Hund", which he translated as "Oh, he was just a silly fool".*

I attached a condition to our being enrolled on the Ordensburg staff by the Nazis, namely that we should be able to organize an expedition to the Himalayas. This fitted in perfectly with the projects of our then leaders, who were out to further German prestige abroad by every possible means. There was nothing modest about our claims. Not wanting to

* *Translator's note:* the German is stronger.

have to beg for every penny, we asked for a round sum of 100 000 marks, which was granted at once. Thereupon I signed on as an Ordensburg guide. The only activity we were called upon to perform was as agreeable as anything we could have thought up for ourselves: "Get to know the Allgäuer Alps." We did one climb after another at our own pleasure. In between, we made highly amateurish preparations for our expedition to Nanga Parbat. Our first concern was food supplies, and when we had bought 17 000 marks' worth we turned to the matter of equipment. At this point a stopper was put on our activities. What had happened? Permission for the expedition to start depended directly on the Führer's personal consent, pending which all preparations must be shelved.

"How can we obtain this consent?"

"The best thing would be to go and see the Führer in person."

The opportunity arose at Christmastime. I was detailed off to take a picture to Hitler as a present from the Ordensburg. First of all I had to call on Ley, who had a house at München-Grünwald. He arranged for me to go to the Christmas feast of the Party veterans in the Löwenbräu cellar, where Hitler was to be present. I therefore drove off in my Opel Olympia in the direction of the cellar, only to find that I could get nowhere near it. The Stiglmaierplatz was barricaded off and packed with people. How was I to get through? I backed up to the gateway, kept my hand on the horn and drove flat out at the wall of humanity. As though by magic a way through opened before me down which I recklessly hurled the car. Even the screen of SS men shot apart, and I drove up to the portal in an elegant curve. Immediately I was surrounded with SS and even saw several drawn pistols.

"See to the car, the Führer is expecting me!"

With that I sprang out, the picture under my arm, and made off up the steps with the whole SS pack at my heels, by no means sure whether it was all true or whether they were dealing with a madman. Again a lane opened up before me through the room as I strode towards the Führer, who sat there blinking at me in astonishment. Suddenly recognition dawned on his features and he invited me to take the place next to him; whereupon the SS officer who had been occupying it instantly vanished. Hitler had actually recognized me. When I mentioned to him that he had once pumped me on the subject of mountaineering he also remembered the conversation. Now for the first time he began to see how the pieces fitted together. This seemed to me the strategic moment to press my claim, after passing him the picture, which he did not so much as glance at. He frowned and said:

"I need you and your comrades for quite a different task."

What on earth could he mean? What other task could we perform as mountain climbers? I hinted at the importance of a success in the Himalayas for German prestige, but he had entirely stopped listening to me and concentrated on his speech to his veterans.

It was a real Bavarian meal consisting of unlimited quantities of roast pork with potato dumplings and beer. Hitler ate spaghetti with tomato sauce and drank only mineral water. A couple of passages from his speech still remain in my memory. The first went as follows:

"When there is a row in the home, the crockery starts to fly; when there is a row between peoples, what flies is high explosive. Czechoslovakia sticks like a spear into the side of Germany, and must be broken off."

The second was:

"From among us German people no one can opt out. As soon as we are out of baby napkins our place is in the Jungvolk movement, then in the Hitler Youth, and later in the SS or SA, or if there is no use for us there then in the armed forces."

The implication of these words could not be mistaken. Deeply cast down and at one stroke cured of many illusions I slunk out of the hall before the proceedings were over. It was clear to me that war was not merely possible but probable. If that happened, it would be the end of freedom in the mountains. There could now be no question of fulfilling our plans. It was a profound disappointment, and the certainty of impending disaster oppressed me. I felt like emigrating.

After this wreck of our projects, hope flared up again when the Himalayan Foundation took up the idea and even requested us to bring our plans to completion. At the last moment, however, everything fell apart again through the obstructiveness of someone behind the scenes. Not more than one of us was to be allowed to go on the expedition. The only one who was quite free and independent was Heini Harrer, so I rang up and harangued him to the effect that he should go with the official party in order to gain influence with the Foundation for the following year. Thus Heini went off to Nanga Parbat, the war broke out, and he was interned in India. The rest of us were called up and clothed in field grey. Vörg was killed on the eastern front on the first day of the Russian campaign. Nobody attached the slightest value to my mountaineering experience, and I landed up in the infantry, also on the eastern front. This happened as follows.

In March 1940 I was enrolled in a Jäger or mountain regiment at Sonthofen and sent to France the following month, by which time the campaign was over. One day I was informed that I had been posted u.k., in other words "unabkömmlich" or reserved for essential duties. All Ordensburg staff members were needed for a special task on the eastern front, although I was not told what, and were therefore assembled for political indoctrination at Falkensee in Pomerania. We skived out of an introductory address by Reichsleiter Ley, and were caught playing cards in a tent by a lout of an SS man who made an almighty row about it and sent in a special report. In the course of all this a lengthy questionnaire had to be filled in, obviously for purposes of finding out where we stood politically. "How long have you been a Party member?" "What Party distinctions have you received?" and so on. My questionnaire remained practically blank, as I could only answer each time with a dash. Thereupon I and a couple of others were posted available for active service again on grounds of political unreliability, and there followed unpleasant months on the central sector of the eastern front.

However, at Fulpmes near Innsbruck there was an army school of mountaineering, and I knew that Rudolf Peters, my rival for the Grandes Jorasses, was serving there as an officer. I therefore wrote to him that I too would rather be up in the mountains than in the morass of the eastern front. He replied by return of post that he had requested the High Command to have me posted as an instructor. I was overjoyed, but heard nothing more for half a year. During this time I might have been killed not just once but umpteen times if my sharpened perceptions had not enabled me to dive under cover at the last moment. At long last, however, I found myself on my way home, and reported for duty at Fulpmes, where I found all my old climbing friends, among them Hias Rebitsch, Hansei Lucke and August Vörg, Wiggerl's brother. Rudl Peters, who had the rank of captain, was our chief.

From that time on the war was won as far as I was concerned. Although an order came around stating that no able-bodied man was to serve more than nine months on the home front, none of our regularly changing Commanding Officers let us go. Our Alpine experience was simply too valuable. Thanks to our efforts there were no accidents during mountain training, whereas elsewhere there were continual fatalities. Cheap as human life might be at the front, obituary reports were the more frowned on at home. Our Commandants thus preferred to hold on to us, and we had less than nothing against that. Thus we lived through those terrible years until one day the dream of empire and final victory was all over. I had no desire whatever to be taken prisoner, and therefore walked over the mountains to Oberstdorf where I had set up house.

My first action was to dig up a small garden and start growing vegetables. Before long we had a boarder who wanted to be guided in the mountains; this client led to others, and presently I had enough to do and to live off. When the German Alpenverein was refounded it fell to me to take in hand the training of mountain guides. I attached great importance to making it clear to future guides that they should not only impart technique to their clients but also point out the beauties of the mountains. The basic principle was to keep all expeditions well within the client's capabilities in order to foster his or her desire for more. It was taken for granted that a modern guide must be a mountaineer through and through and know all about every aspect of the subject taught him during the course of a three-year training.

In the summer of 1947 the newspapers carried the news that the Eigerwand had been repeated. The names of the two climbers were Lionel Terray and Louis Lachenal from Chamonix. Despite the fact that we had been widely accused of unhealthy nationalistic competition, it was a genuine pleasure to me to learn that French mountaineers had made the second ascent. On impulse I sent them a telegram of congratulation, and was interested to see how they would react. Their message

At Kleine Scheidegg after the first ascent of the Eiger. From left to right: Harrer (with hood up), Kasparek, Heckmair, Vörg (with rope)

The north face of the Grandes Jorasses. The Walker spur descends towards
the camera from the left-hand summit

of thanks was equally spontaneous, and included an invitation to Chamonix.

At one stroke, this remarkable second ascent of the north face made it once again a major objective of mountain climbers from all over the world. Just as during the 1930s, it made the headlines more often than any other mountain in the Alps. We who had made the first ascent in 1938 had never thought for a moment that we were the only ones capable of the feat. That same year the Italian climber Riccardo Cassin, who made the first ascent of the Walker spur immediately afterwards, was lying in wait. If we had not done it he would certainly have tried—and succeeded.

At the time we had the most advanced technique, equipment and clothing; but development never ceases, and nowadays all that has long been out of date. Later climbers of the face have had quite different postulates. The wall has not become any easier or the dangers any less, but they have had equipment made of plastic, more highly developed rock- and ice-pitons, and so on. After many successes and further tragedies and victims, in 1961 this evolution finally made possible a winter ascent of the face, which nobody would so much as have dared to think of in 1938. The successful climbers were Toni Hiebeler, Toni Kinshofer, Anderl Mannhardt and Walter Almberger. The ascent was planned down to the last detail in every respect, ranging from types of piton to the choice of companions. The struggle lasted seven days, and by their victory they proved that the impossible no longer really existed.

It was not long before the inheritors of the tradition appeared on the scene. In 30 days of extreme climbing they drove a "direct" route up the face, also in winter. The moving spirit behind this venture was Peter Hag, and his companions were the Stuttgart climbers Karl Golikow, Siegfried Hupfauer, Jörg Lehne, Rolf Rosenzopf, Günter Schnait, Günther Strobel and Roland Votteler. Teamwork as perfect as theirs could only be achieved through total mutual confidence. During the climb they found themselves in rivalry with a party led by the American John Harlin, one of the best climbers of his day. His companions were the American Layton Kor and the Scot Dougal Haston. On the twenty-seventh day Harlin fell to his death when a fixed rope broke. The two groups finally

E

joined forces and reached the summit after being on the face for a month.

Opinions concerning this performance were very various. I was sceptical myself, and tended to the view that an enterprise of this order could also be carried out with paid assistants who would fix the ropes and could be regularly replaced. When everything was ready the so-called climbers could come along, clamber up the ropes and celebrate their victory. Time and money would count for nothing. In international climbing circles a real furore grew up over the meaning or lack of meaning of such an undertaking, and a meeting to discuss the matter was convened at Lecco by Riccardo Cassin. Unfortunately, only one of the people who had been concerned with the ascent was present, the English climber Don Whillans. As nobody was keen to discuss the Eigerwand ascent in the absence of the "accused", only the subject of regulations for mountaineering was heatedly discussed and unanimously rejected.

At another discussion in Trento the majority of the party were present. I had to revise my former prejudices entirely. The climbers of the Eigerwand direct revealed themselves as genuine mountaineers. My questions were more than just testing, they bored right through to the nerve. Gradually I was forced around to the view that this manner of mountaineering also represented progress.

Perhaps it is by such means that certain still apparently impossible Himalayan peaks will be climbed. Evidence in support of this theory was provided in 1969 by Japanese climbers—five men and a woman—who drove a superdirect route up the Rote Fluh, surely the most "impossible" of all the Eigerwand's "impossible" features,* with an outlay on equipment that in our day would have been simply unthinkable; yet the Japanese deliberately carried out this month-long ascent as training for forthcoming adventures in the Himalayas. We must now wait and see what the next developments will be. Nobody has yet succeeded in foretelling the future, so why should it be any different in mountaineering?

With the Japanese superdirect route the Eigerwand was finally degraded to a training crag. Nothing is spared our

* *Translator's note:* It has since been climbed in winter by a Swiss party.

north face: it is described as a "wall of death", although that is
the fault of the climbers rather than the climb. On any mountain expedition an oversight or deliberate neglect regarding
clothing and equipment can lead to complications and in
some circumstances even to death. On a climb such as the
north face of the Eiger any infringement of the unwritten
laws of mountaineering or any failure to grasp them can
only lead to catastrophe.

In addition to the many victims and the hardly describable
tragedies that were played out on the face, there have been
grotesque occurrences and even Alpine swindles that had to
be settled in a court of law. On one occasion pictures of a
further ascent of the Eigerwand appeared before the editors
of a newspaper, among whom, however, were people who
knew something about the subject and called them into
question. They were placed before me without comment. My
opinion was that they were taken on the Eiger, but certainly
not on the north face. Toni Hiebeler followed the matter up
and had the photographers brought to court. Kurt Diemburger
and I were nominated as expert witnesses. The two persons
concerned insisted that they had climbed the face in fog, but
it was obvious that the pictures could not have been taken at
the places claimed, and in any case it is unusual for climbers
to peddle their pictures around. The modesty of these two was
a sham for the benefit of the court. To initiates it was clear
that their ignorance of mountaineering matters was such that
they could not possibly have climbed the face. Finally Diemburger, who had made the thirteenth ascent, discerned a
memorial plaque to the Italian climbers Sandri and Menti
on one of the negatives. It had been claimed that the picture
had been taken on an ice overhang on the ramp, but the
plaque is let into the rock at the foot of the face. In the whole
history of mountaineering, which extends back over 150 years,
there have been very few dubious ascents indeed, as it is part
of the unwritten code of honour that climbers should stick
rigorously to the truth regarding their deeds. On the Eiger,
however, nothing is impossible. . . .

In 1958, on the occasion of the twentieth anniversary of
the first ascent of the Eigerwand, I was particularly honoured
to receive a specially struck gold medal at the reunion of
mountaineers which is always associated with the Trento

International Mountain Film Festival. Riccardo Cassin also received one for his first ascent of the Walker spur of the Grandes Jorasses, and those who had repeated the two routes were given silver medals. There was a great deal of applause and the atmosphere, if highly official, was outstandingly friendly.

Naturally I was happy, yet in my inmost being I am against honours of this sort, since mountaineering is not the kind of sport in which outstanding performances are rewarded with prizes. Sportsmanship is indeed needed in the highest measure, but the performance represented by a great first ascent cannot be precisely gauged and evaluated. In the last resort all that counts is the subjective joy, the memories and the friendship that often arises from combat and victory. Whether one is subsequently glorified or despised on account of the pointless game is a matter of complete indifference. I am sure that other mountaineers feel the same way.

The real pleasure on this anniversary was that it provided an opportunity for everybody to meet everybody else, so that it really developed into a celebration free of all envy and pretension. Each of us knew what the others had achieved and endured, and could evaluate it from personal experience. When human beings meet in these circumstances there are no more distinctions according to nationality or political creed; all that matters is the individual and his worth. The fine thing about a meeting is that climbers from all over the world metaphorically rope up together. For me this rope began to be formed just after the war with that exchange of telegrams with Lionel Terray and Louis Lachenal and their invitation to Chamonix.

CHAPTER XII

The Walker Spur

IT WAS NOT possible to follow up the invitation to Chamonix right away. In 1947 there was still no question of getting a visa to visit France. Three years went by before I was able to return to the Mont Blanc range at last. However, we remained in touch by post. They asked how things were going and what I was doing; I replied that as far as food went nobody was bursting out of his clothes. This was mainly intended as an indirect apology, but they took it literally and sent me a parcel of goodies almost every week. Where was the hereditary enmity between France and Germany that had been drummed into us for so many years? Real climbers feel neither jealousy nor nationalistic hatred. Mountains do not divide us but unite us in the same ideal. I could feel that already in the friendship that was growing up through this correspondence.

In 1950 it was the French who made the first major postwar Himalayan expedition, and who became the first to climb an 8000-metre peak. The mountain was Annapurna, and together with Maurice Herzog and Gaston Rébuffat, Lachenal and Terray were the outstanding members of the party. Their names became world famous, but far from growing conceited they repeated their invitation.

At this time I got to know a young climber called Hermann Köllensperger whom I liked particularly for his open nature. His name had become well known on account of a number of extreme climbs in the Wettersteingebirge. One day as I was going up for a traverse of the Schüsselkarspitze I saw a solo climber descending the slabs from the Leutascher Dreitorspitze. He was much too far to the right, so I shouted up some directions which he gratefully accepted, and before long we stood face to face. It was Hermann Köllensperger. We exchanged a few friendly words and each went on his way. A few weeks later he came over to Oberstdorf and we agreed to take up the invitation to Chamonix the following summer.

If all went well, we would try to fulfil my old dream of climbing the north face of the Grandes Jorasses.

The days of bicycling were finally over, and we sat in the train to Geneva like any other tourist. Leafing through an illustrated magazine, I came upon a full-page advertisement extolling the fragrance of the spicy Swiss Toscanelli cheroots. I enjoy this kind of smoke, and as a stall was already open on Geneva station when the train rolled in at 4 a.m. I treated myself to a packet. They were strange-looking Stumpen, just like gnarled roots. Not having eaten, I felt rather shy of trying one out straight away. A small café already stood open for the first-shift workmen, and one sturdy character was downing black coffee with a shot of grappa in it. Although I was less sturdy I felt strong enough for that and ordered one too. It tasted loathsome, and that on an empty stomach, but as I would have to pay for it anyway I drank it. After that I lit up my Toscanelli and we strolled back to the station. Just as I reached the steps I went all pale and had to sit down before I fell. Though I blamed it for the way I felt, the Toscanelli still tasted good, and to the horror of my friends and family I have remained faithful to the brand to this day.

In Chamonix we wandered pleasantly through the well-remembered streets, feeling happy that everything was as it had been and that I had survived the war to see it again. It is true that there hardly exists another mountain resort to compare with it for ugliness, yet somehow it emanates a special charm compounded out of so much Alpine history. There is nowhere else quite like it.

There was a man sitting outside a café opposite the guides' office. It must be Terray. I went and stood in front of his table without saying a word. We had never met: would he also recognize me at first sight? Surprised, he glanced up, and yes, he knew me straight away. We embraced like old friends, and despite the language problem had no difficulty in communicating as we could read each other's eyes. The first errand was to visit Terray's friend Louis Lachenal, who greeted us no less heartily. In reply to their query as to what we had in mind we gestured towards the Walker spur. Immediately their faces clouded.

"Il y a beaucoup de neige et de glace," said Lionel.

We indeed knew that there had been a hard winter, and that the rock was not yet clear.

May as well have a look, we thought, and went up to the Leschaux hut.

The little hut had changed, having been enlarged before the war. It was deserted, and everything was spotless and tidy. From the presence of a number of typically feminine articles we deduced that the hut warden was now a woman. In one corner a bed was properly made up with sheets. With great difficulty resisting the temptation to climb in, we rolled ourselves in the usual blankets in the other corner. After all, we wanted to set out at one o'clock.

We woke up punctually, but the night was not to our liking. The sky was mainly overcast and it was far too warm. With an undeniable "certain relief" we pulled the covers over us with the intention of sleeping until noon. We had done right; when hunger finally drove us from our warm nest with bones aching from lying around it was streaming with rain outside.

A rather weary-looking party of two ladies and two gentlemen were heading towards the hut. As we were already cooking we put some tea water for the newcomers on our petrol stove, just like in the old days. They accepted our thoughtfulness with gratitude and duly invited us to join their evening meal. When they inquired about our goal and we simply pointed meaningfully at the north face, which had just cleared for a moment, their expressions became thoughtful but their hospitality warmer than ever. They even conjured up an alarm clock, which woke us again at 1 a.m. out of a deep slumber.

It was Thursday, 2 August 1951. By contrast with the night before it was cold. We resolved at all events to go up as far as the foot of the rock, which is at 3010 metres. Having carefully packed our rucksacks with the strict necessary minimum of gear the previous evening, it was not long before we stepped out into the dark on the Leschaux glacier and plodded up towards the start of the climb. The bergschrunds were soon crossed, and our twelve-pointers bit reassuringly into the hard, steep snow-ice. Everything seemed to promise rapid progress, and I lulled myself with hopes of reaching the top in a day and a half, perhaps even a day. Seldom have I been so far out in my reckoning.

When we reached the Rébuffat crack we stared. It was a pitch that would not have been out of place on the north face of the Cima Grande. Only a few sparse pitons showed where our predecessors had passed. Higher up we found abseil slings, tokens of earlier retreats during which pegs had been hammered in at impossible places.

After the crack came a fine stance, but already we had to buckle our crampons on again; the traverse across the ice slopes was too long for us to consider cutting steps across without them. Every so often we had to take them off to climb a piece of awkward rock, then repeat the whole business. It all cost a lot of time, but in the prevailing conditions there was no other way of overcoming this steep zone. It fitted in perfectly with Terray's predictions about the state of the face. At last we reached the end of the traverse and the foot of the 75 metre corner. The guidebook called it Grades 4 to 5, which we thought rather an underestimate.

We had been looking forward with some anticipation to the traverse and pendulum rappel that lead across to the right-hand side of the buttress. The supposedly easy traverse turned out to be completely iced up. In the meantime we had come to an agreement that I would keep on my crampons and lead the icy bits, while Hermann would take over on the stretches of bare rock. The continual changeovers from one to the other kept us busy, and we failed to notice how the hours were flying by. In due course the sun sank behind the Aiguilles. We looked despairingly for a bivouac site where we could at least pass the night half sitting, half standing. There was not a minute to spare; by the time we had hammered in the pitons it was pitch dark.

Although we had spent most of the day battling among ice and snow, it happened that on the spot where we had bivouacked there was not a spot of snow anywhere. Our throats were completely parched. Apart from Ovomaltine and Nescafé our rations consisted of bread and sausage, but without fluid we were unable to force down so much as a crumb. Being familiar with this state of affairs from the Eigerwand, I had purposely brought a flask of cognac and some egg powder which I now mixed with plenty of sugar in a shaker. Despite my well-meant entreaties, however, Hermann, who was an absolute teetotaller, refused to touch a drop of this agreeably burning and warming energy-food. For my part I felt a pleasant warmth diffuse through my stomach and was glad that I had often

In the Karakorum,
1954

Crossing the Hunza river

trained on alcohol. At least I was able to get through the night
not too disagreeably.

Before leaving the Leschaux hut I naturally had not wasted
time pouring the brandy out of the bottle into a small flask. As
we were travelling light I had just stuck the bottle into my
rucksack with the thought that if it became a nuisance I could
simply hurl it away. This turned out to be unnecessary; on the
contrary it became so valuable, at least to me, that I remain
convinced to this day that it saved our lives. Consumed
medicinally a swig at a time, the bottle lasted out the whole
four days. My companion, who refused to swallow so much as a
mouthful, subsequently suffered from frostbite of the hands and
feet, whereas thanks to my good blood circulation I escaped
entirely. For me it was a proof that, taken in moderate doses
over a period of time, even considerable quantities of alcohol
do no harm.

Towards morning it began to snow and hail, which under
our bivouac sack sounded as though somebody was pouring
peas over us. Suddenly an avalanche shot past, covering
our bivouac site with hailstones. By shovelling them into our
mixing bowl until they melted, we were at last able to obtain
some much-desired fluid for our morning coffee.

Our second day on the face began with an extremely severe
pitch at the top of the black slabs. In fine weather the subsequent climbing up the slabs of the grey tower would have been
pure pleasure, but in the circumstances, with stiff, cramped
fingers, we could only work our way upwards with extreme
caution. Once we had got out on to the ridge of the tower the
difficulty seemed at last to ease, but it proved to be an illusion.
The weather began to get worse. On this less steep ground the
snow was able to settle, so that one could only guess at the
whereabouts of the small holds. A broom would have been
the ideal instrument for clearing the rock, but unfortunately
we did not have one with us.

In the course of climbing a smooth slab I discovered a
splendid undercut hold at the bottom of a flake of rock. No
sooner had I seized it than the whole great flake broke off and
went hurtling down. After a bound of ten metres it landed slap
on my new nylon rope, cutting clean through the outer sheath.
As I had just paid 15 000 old francs for the rope in Chamonix
before setting out on the climb, the flake hurt me as much as if

it had fallen on my own foot. Fortunately, the nylon strands inside the sheath remained undamaged, and subsequent events showed that the rope was not seriously weakened.

After reaching a small hump on the ridge we were hard put to it on account of the snow to know whether to climb on the snow or the rock. Both were so unpleasant that after placing a firm peg ten metres above the hump I decided to go back down to it and sit out the increasingly bad weather.

It was just noon. We hoped that after a few hours we should be able to go on and bivouac higher up. Snow, rain and hail continued to pour down on us. Thanks to the peg ten metres above we were secure on our ledge, and above all absolutely safe from avalanches. As the storm did not abate we spent the second night at this spot, where we could at least stretch out somewhat under our bivouac sack. This was very necessary, as we were racked by cramp alternately in the legs, stomach and back.

We got our Esbit cooker going, but under the tent-sack the stink was unbearable, while outside the storm extinguished it at once. The only solution was to bring the shaker into action again. It worked automatically: we only needed to hold it in our hands and our shivering did the rest. This gave us a nice little pastime throughout the night. A shakerful of snow mixed with glucose or a bonbon would be reduced to a lump of ice by the shivering action. Then came a moment of deadlock when more violent movement was required; this also helped to warm us up. The lump would fall apart into an ice-broth and finally, if we were patient enough, the broth would turn into water which we could vary with Nescafé or Ovomaltine. So it went on all night. The sausage, bread and butter in our rucksacks remained untouched.

As morning approached the weather showed no sign of improving. Retreat was out of the question; we were already too high. No one else could help us out of our fix. Fear was no help either. There was nothing for it but to climb on.

Wearing crampons on my feet I first climbed up to the piton, then traversed across to an icy cleft which in turn led to a projecting spike of rock. The ice was exceedingly steep and so hard on account of the cold that when I tried to cut steps whole scoops of it broke away. It therefore seemed better to do without steps and to work my way up as best I could. The closer I got to the spike the steeper it got. Below the spike there was a hollow space between the rock and the cortex of ice, so that I could use the edge of the latter as a handhold. Just as I got within reach of the spike a snow slide came sweeping down from above and broke over me. This put too much pressure on the ice rim, which broke off. One metre below I had been able to plant a good ice-piton, but it was torn out by the shock. Like lightning I spun around facing outwards in order not to trip over my crampons and turn upside down, then shot down the whole pitch and the length of the rope beyond. Hermann reacted with great presence of mind, and as the rope went slack from the fall swiftly started to let himself down from the anchor piton to the hump on the ridge below. Before he reached it, however, the rope came taut again, dragging him several metres upwards. I fetched up hanging just above an overhang; the anchor peg had held. If it had been torn out Hermann's only remaining chance would have been to jump down the other side of our bivouac ledge. Thank God it had not come to that. The fall was intercepted. The astonishing thing about it was that the sack I had been wearing on my back was now on my front, and that I was holding one mitten in the other hand. I had let nothing drop, but had received a heavy blow on the back that I could still feel a fortnight later. Hermann yelled:

"Are you all right?"

"Nothing missing."

I hauled myself back up the rope to my companion. Where the strength came from I still do not know.

Nevertheless, a shock has its effect, and suddenly I felt a natural urge coming over me with positively unnatural force. With an understanding grin, my friend held me on the rope while my bottled-up fear found an explosive outlet. After this morale was restored, but I had no inclination for further icy adventures and gladly let my rubber-soled companion take the lead up the rock. The cloud grew ever more impenetrable and the storm more violent. In the conditions, pitches graded 5 in the guidebook seemed harder than normal 6. At the stances it was only possible to belay hanging on a loop of rope from the piton.

Just to make everything perfect I found that I had lost my hammer, which must have been torn from its sling during the fall without my noticing. We still had a hammer-axe which

Hermann was using as he worked his way up the pitch. Suddenly I heard an oath, a ringing sound and a whirring in the air. The head had broken off the axe and vanished into the depths. All we had left was the second rock-hammer, which would now have to be lowered on the rope after every pitch so that the pitons could be taken out. This meant that we could only clip one rope through the karabiners, which amid difficulties of this order seriously reduced our safety margin.

The last 20 metres of the pitch were less steep. They were thus all the more thickly plastered in ice, and this was the cue to bring my crampons into action again. In any case it was high time, as Hermann had reached the end of his strength.

According to the guidebook description an easy groove now led to the traverse to the red tower. On this occasion it certainly did not look easy. The rock was coated in black ice with an overlayer of loose powder snow covering the few rugosities that could be used as holds. Like the earlier grooves, this one began with an overhang that I had to climb free. For lack of the hammer-axe I found myself standing despairingly in the icy groove, hesitating before every move at the thought of the fall I had already taken. The idea of retreating to bivouac below the overhangs passed through my mind, yet clearly the pitch would look no easier after another day. In despairing rage I lashed out against the bare ice with the hammer—and behold, a great plate of ice broke away, revealing a marvellous hold on which I could stand and blow my nose at last.

For another 20 metres I had to tiptoe my way up the hard, glassy surface like a tightrope walker, then at last I reached a large block that served as a belay and enabled me to bring up my companion. Twenty metres higher again under an overhang and out to one side was a big flake of rock which looked like a suitably sheltered place for a bivouac. Hermann wanted to climb on and escape from the face at all costs, but it was already 7 p.m. and we had another 200 metres to go. The cold and the blizzard had increased in fury so that we could see nothing but whirling flakes all around. Moreover our garments were utterly soaked inside and out. The net effect was that our flesh crept at the thought of a bivouac, but higher up the ridge or on the summit the conditions would certainly have been worse still. In spite of my companion's repugnance, therefore, I resolved to bivouac behind the flake.

The damp, stiff-frozen rope served us as insulation from the ice and snow. So grateful does one become in such circumstances for even a little comfort that things seemed better as soon as we had pulled the tent-sack over our heads. We could neither lie nor sit properly, but just huddled together. In order to keep out the piercing cold we drew up our feet and rolled the edge of the sack under us, but this meant that we had to bow our heads, a most uncomfortable position. The moment either of us tried to stretch out even a little the storm would find a gap through which to come blasting in, inflating the sack like a balloon and spraying us with powder snow.

There exist theories about what one should do on a bivouac, for example putting on dry clothing. And indeed, I still had a pair of dry stockings and a spare pullover in the rucksack, but it was quite impossible to change. In the tent-sack we were safe from freezing to death, but not from just freezing. The colder it got outside the more the condensation formed on the inner surface of the tent, trickling continually and disagreeably down our bodies. The shaker was brought into action again, but in the circumstances our enthusiasm for this kind of exercise was very much diminished. I told myself not to grow apathetic, that I must fight back against the hostile forces around us, and continued shaking. In addition, I deliberately bothered my companion by shifting around so that he could not get to sleep, since I feared that if supercooling were added to exhaustion he would never wake up again.

Everything has an ending, and even this night finally went by. The snow still splattered over us without interruption. Resignedly I emerged from the sack and was astonished to see the peaks opposite flooded in sunlight that was reflected in the snow which was falling over us. In all seriousness I thought: "I'm having hallucinations. That kind of thing doesn't happen." The snow crystals cascaded past like myriads of glittering diamonds. The sky had cleared, but the gale persisted and was sweeping the new snow up the south side of the mountain so that it showered over the north face on which we stood. The air was wretchedly cold, causing our saturated clothing and boots to freeze solid. Well, complaining would serve no useful purpose, so up!

Hermann reacted to my call to action, but had stopped speaking. I began to climb with extreme care, knowing that

I could no longer rely on him to hold me if I fell off again. Presently I emerged into sunlight on the upper part of the ridge, but we obtained no warmth from it. The gale continued to lash the powder snow into our faces, building up an icy crust on them. Our mittens had hardened into solid balls, so that in difficult places I had to take them off in order to climb with bare fingers. In no time they were numb, white and hard as wood. I knew what that meant, and sought feverishly to restore the circulation by rubbing and moving them. The pain was terrible and yet comforting. After six hours of struggle I stood under the metre-thick cornice of new snow at the top of the ridge desperately looking for some means of safeguarding myself while dealing with this last obstacle. Once again I struck out at the bare ice in helpless anger with the blunted hammer until a whole flake broke away, revealing a magnificent ring piton, the same one that Cassin had symbolically hammered into the last metre of rock in 1938. To me it came as a real life-saver. With a yell of triumph I clipped into it and swung up over the cornice on to the summit.

Despite the clear sky, the gale that greeted me was so strong that I was unable to stand up. Communication with my companion was impossible; only by the tugging and pulling on the rope did he realize that he should come. At last his head popped up over the cornice into the sunlight. It was ten o'clock in the morning. We embraced, then let ourselves slither a few metres down the gentle summit slopes so as not to be blown back over the north face. In spite of the sunshine it was far too cold and stormy to rest, so we started down right away in the hope of reaching a warmer level. What looked to us like a harmless ice gully descended on the southern side of the gap between the twin summits, named the Pointe Walker and the Pointe Whymper. Slipping on his rubber soles, Hermann went first, while I kept on my crampons and belayed him over an icy bulge.

"Don't slide!" I called. "Face outwards and stamp in your heels!"

At this point I made the mistake of starting down behind the taut rope. Suddenly Hermann slipped again and tore me from my footing. With a powerful bound into some deep new snow I tried to restrain him, but in vain. We shot over a couple of ice steps and plunged into the depths accompanied by an

avalanche of snow. Even as we flew through the air I felt furious
that this should happen after winning our hard battle. The
important thing now was not to let my crampons catch and set
me spinning, but I was unable to stop the rear points punching
through my breeches into the knee beneath. The gully was so
steep that although I was aware of blows I actually felt nothing
in particular, cushioned as they were by the snow. Three
hundred metres lower down we shot out on to a hanging glacier.
It ended in space, and a few metres before the edge we came to
a halt. I jumped up at once and looked around. The only
thought in my head was: "Well, at least we don't have to climb
down that bit."

Ten metres away to one side Hermann lay motionless in the
snow. However, he was only resting and was not at all pleased
at having to get up again. The hole in my knee was bleeding
copiously. Luckily it was only a flesh wound that was soon
bound up. Hobbling rather than walking, we sought the way
on down, which offered no further difficulties. We were extremely fortunate that the sky was clear. It was difficult enough
to find a route down the glacier as it was; in weather such as we
had had on the north face we would never have made it.
Even so we managed to miss the hut and had landed ourselves
in new difficulties when suddenly a form appeared. It was the
warden of the Grandes Jorasses hut. He stared at us as though
we had fallen from the skies and showed us the way over the
last few slabs of rock, where we had the joy of seeing the first
flowers and green grass for some days.

Not until we reached the hut did the warden grasp where we
had come from. Immediately he was full of eagerness to help,
fitting us out with dry clothes and dressing our wounds. In
the process it emerged that Hermann had second and third
degree frostbite in his fingers and toes as far up as the second
joint. Apart from my minor cuts and bruises there was nothing
the matter with me, although, unlike my companion, I had
kept swigging away at the brandy bottle until I had chucked
it away empty shortly before reaching the summit. Profoundly
disturbed about Hermann's frostbite, I was in favour of carrying on down to the valley without delay, but had to allow him
a night's rest. I knew that every hour gained in getting him to
a doctor might save him from amputations. To get back over
to Chamonix became an obsession, so we went straight up

from Entrèves to the Torino hut on the Col du Géant. First, however, another nice episode occurred.

Just as on the Eiger, in the heat of battle we had completely forgotten that others would be worrying about us. It is reassuring to know that people care, but it can lead to the unfortunate consequence of a major rescue party being organized, as in this case. I first became aware of this when I heard a gesticulating bunch of people discussing an accident on the Grandes Jorasses, upon which I made the mistake of telling the good folk that we were the climbers who were being searched for. My object was to see that the right quarters were informed of our safe return to the valley. This, however, was not understood; they simply saw from our appearance that we must be the climbers mentioned in the press. In a moment we were surrounded with a crowd of chattering, gabbling tourists. Cameras were produced, bambini thrust into our arms and perched on our shoulders, photos were taken of us from in front and behind. Nobody could or would understand our desire to telephone the guides' office in Chamonix, and not speaking Italian we were unable to do it ourselves. The first to grasp what needed to be done were some guides at the Torino hut, who put the call through at once.

With the feeling of having done our duty we then set off down the Vallée Blanche in spite of the cloud. I knew what it meant to find the way through the icefall to the Requin hut in fog, and got quite excited when Hermann wanted to call for a bowl of hot soup at the hut, which failed to materialize for a long time. At 7 p.m. we reached the Leschaux hut. After five days the north face of the Grandes Jorasses stood in front of us again, looking extremely forbidding and in its upper portion completely plastered with ice. The sight did not make us feel puffed up with our success, but rather small and insignificant. Thankful for our luck, we gazed up at the mountain that had given us such a profound experience. That may sound like a platitude; but it is precisely in climbing mountains that a man learns his limitations and becomes humble.

CHAPTER XIII

Journey through Lapland

ALTHOUGH THE NORTH faces of the Eiger and the Grandes Jorasses were climaxes in my climbing career, they were very far from being conclusions. Practically all keen mountaineers long to see the more distant ranges of the world, and I was no exception. As a very young climber I had had a faint hope of going on the 1932 Nanga Parbat expedition, for which I helped to pack the crates and transport them to the station. The crates went along, but not me.

My second run-up was stopped short by the war. After the climb on the Walker spur the time seemed ripe to try for the third time. The Alpenverein proved very interested in the idea of new initiatives for an expedition, but its coffers were empty and I lacked the experience to recruit funds from any other quarter. I was therefore excited to receive an invitation from some Scandinavian mountaineers to visit them and climb in their mountains.

For the first time since the war I climbed aboard an aeroplane. At Stockholm I was met at the airport by Henk Bjerberg, who drove me to his house. In one of the rooms he had set out everything he thought essential for a traverse of Lapland, mainly food. The mere sight of it made me sit down and stare, after which I asked shyly whether he had hired any porters to transport all these masses of material. He answered that this lay beyond his financial means. This was an argument for which I always had a great deal of understanding, so I began to thin things out, especially the food. Even if we reached no supply point for two weeks, it would still be enough to take food for only ten days. Better to take in our belts for the last four days than to eat the last salami sausage after our arrival. The good Henk could not see this at all, but he was to be convinced by experience.

Even our reduced load proved enough to carry during our march from Kiruna to Abisko, where we elected not to follow the usual route along the King's Trail, but to pass through some rarely travelled valleys in order to cross some out-of-the-way summits. For the last three days, however, we were back on the King's Trail and met plenty of tourists almost crushed under their packs who were only too thankful to unload some of their food on to us. We rounded off our programme with some tours in the neighbourhood of Narvik. Among these we climbed the singularly beautiful Stetind, which rises out of the Steffjord like a pillar. At Narvik I received a telegram from Dr Karl Herrligkoffer asking me to join an expedition to Nanga Parbat in 1953.

Dr Herrligkoffer is a step-brother of Willi Merkl who died on Nanga Parbat before the war, and he had organized this expedition in his memory. It seemed that the ambition of my life was to be fulfilled at last. I threw myself into the organization of the expedition with enthusiasm, but differences of opinion arose over the choice of members. As we were unable to agree I withdrew from the party. In the event this was not too tragic an event, as my old friend Hias Rebitsch had invited me to join another Himalayan expedition which he had got up with the full support of the Alpenverein.

Thanks to Hermann Buhl's incredible solo ascent, Herrligkoffer's expedition was crowned with success, even though there was some distasteful friction afterwards. Mountaineers are no more than human. I was glad not to have been involved.

CHAPTER XIV

In the Land of the Hunzas

THAT SAME YEAR Mount Everest was climbed, a feat which
ushered in the period of conquest of the Himalayan giants. We,
however, had no intention of climbing so high. In order to
obtain funds we were obliged to take along a large group of
scientists whose goal was the still imperfectly known Hunza
valley. At the entry to the valley stands Rakaposhi, an icy
giant which in those days still awaited its first ascent. We chose
this mountain as our objective and were promptly rebuffed.

There were twelve of us on the journey out in April 1954—
seven climbers, four scientists and a cameraman. My view was
that if we really had to have one then he should be the best we
could get. In the event we obtained Eugen Schuhmacher, who
brought back the wonderful film *Im Schatten des Karakorum**
which enabled us to recoup the major outlays.

We were also lucky with regard to the scientists. Not only
did they gather valuable geographical, geological and botanical
data and collections, but they backed up our mountaineering
activities whenever possible. During the journey I became
very friendly with one of them in particular, Karl Heckler, a
geodetic surveyor from Stuttgart, who sadly was drowned in
the Hunza river.

And so I finally reached the Himalayas at the age of forty-
eight. They were certainly impressive, but I must admit that,
knowing it all in a sense from pictures and travellers' tales,
my expectations were too great. The impression made on me as
a boy by the Lalidererwand in the Karwendel was stronger and
more overpowering.

Before you can attempt to climb one of the highest mountains
in the world you must reconnoitre it. You cannot just set off
with a whole expedition, including the outlay on hundreds of
porters, without knowing the slightest thing about the terrain
and the conditions. Two of us, Martin Schliessler and I, were
therefore detached to reconnoitre Rakaposhi.

* *In the Shadow of the Karakorum.*

We left Gilgit with five porters. The Karakorum range, which is only brushed by the end of the monsoon after it has broken over the Himalayas, is as dry as a desert. Up to a height of 3000 metres the mountains, and even the valleys unless artificially irrigated, are totally arid, so that the effect is all the more beautiful when one reaches this altitude. First whin and furze begin to sprout from cracks in the rock, then come tamarisks and even juniper, which in these parts grows to a height of 20 or 30 metres, and finally stretches of green with clumps of wild rhubarb, gooseberry and numerous other plants which in Bavaria one only finds in gardens. The most typical plant of the Karakorum is the dog-rose, which grows everywhere, even on the glacier moraines.

In the few spots where it is possible for people to settle they farm on built-up terraces. In such surroundings it is strange to see nut and apricot trees with trunks a metre in diameter. Apricots in particular are the gold of the Hunzas. The fruit is dried and oil is crushed out of the stones, so that supplementary food is available all year round. The very first time we stopped to rest we were offered dried apricots, on which I promptly broke a tooth.

It is said of the Hunzas that they are the healthiest folk on earth, but it proved no more than a saying. We saw men with goitres bigger than their heads and children with all kinds of infectious diseases. In view of the thousands of flies that swarmed around us up to an altitude of 4000 metres it seemed no wonder. Swatting and slapping was pointless. Only I had a defensive weapon in the form of my Swiss Toscanelli Stumpen, of which I had brought along ample supplies. They drove away not only the flies, but my companions as well.

After two days' march we reached a cirque at a height of about 4000 metres out of which the snow- and ice-clad flanks rose for another 3000–4000 metres. Dimensions are deceptive and not easy to grasp. Not until we place ourselves in relation to them and begin to reckon how long an ascent would take do we become fully aware of the scale.

Right in the background, still some kilometres farther on, a steep ice gully rose up to a gap in a ridge. True, it was well garnished with hanging glaciers, but it seemed to offer a possible way up. We were just surveying it through binoculars when suddenly some overhanging séracs high up broke off and

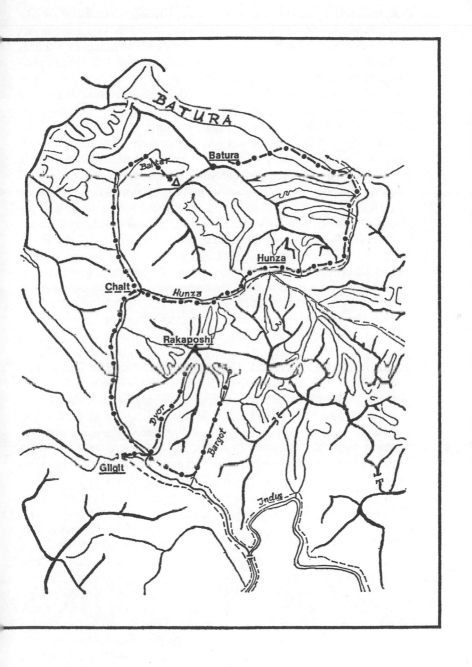

came down in an avalanche. Ice dust whirled up into the air like an atomic cloud. The strangest thing about it was that apart from the initial boom the whole event took place in silence. The ice dust had absorbed the sound entirely. We were spellbound by this drama of nature, but the desire to climb the ice gully had left us. To climb the face, equally well furnished with hanging glaciers, seemed just as impossible. We therefore returned to Gilgit with our negative report.

Hias reproached us for not having immediately reconnoitred the next parallel valley in order to see if it contained any better hope. There was no need for him to tell us twice; we set off again next day with the same group of porters. This valley proved to be much longer and higher, and was relatively densely populated. From its broad, U-shaped, rolled-out formation we deduced that there must be a mighty glacier at the end of it. We passed through several large villages. The most impressive thing, however, was a bewildering scent that pervaded the whole valley. It was given off by a blossoming tree that grew everywhere.

We had not been mistaken; at the head of the valley a glacier came down from far above. But what a sight! It was a regular rubbish-heap. Glaciers in the Karakorum are mostly what are called fluvial or gorge glaciers formed by the debris of ice avalanches that bring down with them all the rubble off the mountainsides. In addition, the glacier tongue was so ruptured and rent that with the ass we had hired at the last village we could only make progress between the edge and the lateral moraine. The ass meekly carried the greater part of our food and equipment, but jibbed at the prospect of climbing a rock step as high as a room. There was no way around it, however, so while one porter mercilessly whipped the beast from behind, another dragged and tugged at each leg until I could not bear to look on any longer at such ill-treatment. The donkey seemed quite unconcerned and peacefully bit off a thistle which it continued to chew with pleasure throughout the whole operation.

We toiled along this glacier for at least 15 kilometres. Evening was not far off when we discovered a little track leading up on to the lateral moraine. From this vantage point we could see that the glacier described a huge curve, on the inside of which there was an "alluvial island" or patch of ground formed behind the ice. It looked like a garden of Eden with its wonderful short grass dotted here and there with conifers. No landscape artist could have done a better job. We were instantly unanimous that if a way up Rakaposhi were found from this side, this would be our base camp.

Unfortunately, it was not to be. As we advanced the following day we once more encountered ice avalanches that spread out across the whole width of the glacier. A man may choose to run a risk for himself, but not for an expedition and especially not for the porters that are called upon to carry up supplies. It had already happened once that an entire German expedition (to Nanga Parbat) had been wiped out by a single avalanche, with the exception of one man who was up in the top camp. There was therefore nothing for us but to turn back hoping to find a safer route on the northern side of the mountain.

In the event Rakaposhi was indeed to be climbed from the north-west, not by us but by a British party ten years later. Thus successive expeditions are able to profit from the experience of their predecessors until one day the problem is solved and the goal attained.

Disappointed, we returned with our message that once again there was nothing to be done. Hias came half-way to meet us with the entire expedition. They had been unable to stand the idleness in Gilgit any longer. There were long faces as we made our report. At this moment a note arrived from our scientists, who were carrying out their tasks in the neighbourhood of Batura. "If Rakaposhi is proving too difficult," ran the message, "come over here. There are masses of unclimbed summits just as high, one or other of which is sure to prove climbable."

It was exactly the encouragement we needed at that moment. We changed our plans and together with 100 porters and a score of high-altitude porters marched up the Hunza valley, initially towards Chalt.

This time we went for a mountain which had no name; we did not even know its height. We liked the shape of it, there seemed to be a feasible route, so we wasted no time in getting down to work. Once again Martin Schliessler and I formed the scouting party and reconnoitred the mountain towards a col from which an apparently climbable ridge led to the summit.

At this point I did something stupid that almost cost me my life. Having got back to base from the reconnaissance late in the afternoon, I returned alone up the Baltar glacier to Camp I. Normally this took three to four hours, but in my eagerness to report that we were to push on to the col next day I ran up in two. In fact the news was not really so important and I could perfectly well have sent a porter, but we were going to need them next day and I did not want one of them to drop out from fatigue. It did not occur to me to take it easy myself. As I reached Camp I new supplies had just arrived, so that perforce I lent a hand with the heavy job of unpacking the loads until late at night. When this was finished I returned to base, which I reached at 3 a.m. just as the others were getting ready. I joined them without stopping to rest, and on the upper part of the climb even took over the task of breaking the trail.

After some 24 hours of unremitting effort I had begun to feel a certain fatigue, but the cornice fringing the col tempted me on to cut a way through. At last I stood in the sharp-cut gap, soaked to the skin from inside and out. Now I had had enough. I left the job of making camp to my companions and contented myself with belaying them. This was the biggest mistake of all. In addition to the icy wind a snowstorm blew up. There could be no question of changing my clothes. Two hours went by before the snow cave was big enough for me to crawl in, and by then it was too late.

Everything I had on was frozen stiff, and so was I. Finally I could lie back in my sleeping bag, but I did not feel too good. The rarefied air did its work. Presently I began to shiver violently. The others now noticed that something was wrong. They put extra covers over me, gave me plenty of hot tea, and generally did what they could. By the time morning came I was unable to lift a finger. In books I had read of cases that had begun like this and ended fatally. Knowing that I could never recover if I remained at this altitude, I begged my companions to take me down. We had descended no more than a couple of ropeslengths when I began to feel so well that I would gladly have climbed back up to the ridge. However, I had also heard about euphoria, a sensation of extraordinary well-being which sets in before the last mortal stage of illness. It might not be that, but one could not be sure. I therefore said to the others:

Foothills of the Ruwenzori, 1960

In the Hoggar
mountains of the
Sahara, 1960

"Look, you can see how much better I am. You go back up and continue the climb. I'll go right on down with one porter to help me."

They looked at me anxiously, but I looked and sounded so cheerful that they finally gave in to my urging.

On the way down I hurried so much that the porter could hardly keep up. We passed Hias coming up with his column 100 metres away to one side. He called out, but I did not reply as I was unable to explain and the terrain did not lend itself to traversing across.

Down, down: I could think of nothing else. I noticed that black spots were beginning to appear before my eyes again. At last we reached the level Baltar glacier along which the route now lay. I wanted to reach the doctor at Camp I, but was incapable of taking another step. I lay down on a slab of rock and wished to die.

The porter, however, was having none of this. Gesturing with upraised arms he begged:

"Sahib, sahib, go farther."

I wished him to hell. Why could he not just leave me alone? It was so pleasant just to switch off completely. Thereupon he simply drew me up on to his broad back and tried to carry me. He was still soaked in sweat from our headlong descent and did not smell very pleasant. This had the effect of bringing me back to my senses. Forcibly I freed myself from his back and stumbled along in his tracks, continuously trying to send him away so that I could lie down. Perhaps he understood what this would have implied, as he left me no peace.

Our strange behaviour on the glacier had been observed by our friends at Camp I. Immediately they hastened to meet us. I was aware of people standing around me, then I fainted. When I came to I was lying in the tent with the worried face of the expedition doctor above me, then I lost consciousness again. The next time I had a glimmering of consciousness I was shivering so violently that the whole tent was shaking. Two men were kneeling on me to hold me down. I felt very well and thought it great fun.

Later the doctor was to tell me that I had had extreme fever and that he had diagnosed acute pneumonia. Injections and tablets improved my condition but gave me a violent head-ache. I would never have believed that a head could hurt so much. There was something wrong with my eyes too; I could no longer see out of the right one. Through the other, however, I could distinguish enough to see that it was raining and that the whole expedition was assembled at the camp. I reckoned that they had gathered to bury me. Well, things had not got that far yet; they would just have to wait another couple of days. And in fact it never did get that far. I recovered surprisingly fast, and quite soon I could stand up and walk.

Now I was granted fool's licence and could do or not do whatever I pleased, but only under the eagle eye of the doctor, who did not trust me out of his sight.

Those were halcyon days. I could laze around, take photographs, eat to my heart's content, do what I would. Everyone was nice to me. I was treated like a raw egg until finally it all began to seem too silly and I insisted on resuming the push towards the summit that had been broken off on account of my illness and the onset of the monsoon.

Everything was prepared the evening before we were due to start back up the mountain. The loads had been shared out and packed. Down in camp it began to grow dark, while the summits 4000 metres above were still bathed in sunlight. Rapt and reverent we gazed upwards. Suddenly a wall of séracs broke off to one side of our peak and went roaring down across the whole width of the glacier up which our next morning's route lay. Hias and I just glanced at each other.

"We going up there?"

"Nah!"

Our desire to climb up that glacier had completely evaporated. Once again it was the scientists who helped us out of the mess. Next day we were fiddling around without any sense of purpose when a messenger arrived with a slip of paper on which were written the words: "There is a safe route up the highest peak in the whole range from the Batura glacier." And here were we tussling with a mere outlier!

Now we had a good reason for leaving our troubles behind, quitting the Baltar glacier and going over to the Batura valley, which lay on the other side of the main crest of the range. Nevertheless, this implied a march of a week or ten days, the enrolment of over 100 porters and all the work of organizing them. Such decisions are not taken lightly.

It was a real release to get going. I walked with a group

containing my close friends Hias, Martl and the doctor. The latter was somewhat mistrustful of my swift recovery. A ten-hour march is part of the normal order of the day in the Himalayas. I held out, but in the evening by the campfire I noticed that all was far from being well. Luckily we were in an inhabited area, and next day somebody found a horse for me to ride.

I am no very eager rider, but as I was having more and more difficulty walking there was no alternative. Going along the Hunza valley I found myself alone on my nag on the "raffig", a kind of artificial path built up with nothing but dry stones across the cliff-face, far above the foaming river. The body of the expedition was ahead, the camera team a day's march behind, and the porter who was supposed to be escorting me had loitered in his home village as we passed through. I hung on to the horse's neck and hoped it would not do anything silly like stumbling over the edge.

In a village called Aliabad—although any connection between it and baths* seemed very remote—I noticed a barrack-like building. During the 1920s, I knew, the British had built a military sick-bay somewhere in the Hunza valley. Perhaps this was it. I pressed the old nag's head around until it was pointing in the right direction. The clever beast seized the point and ambled over. A handsome, intelligent-looking Pakistani emerged from the door. I asked: "Doc?" He nodded. I slid off the horse and knew nothing more for a couple of days.

When I came round I was lying in a clean bed. It was twilight, but whether in the morning or the evening I had no idea. Beside the bed were the Pakistani and our expedition doctor. It is strange how slowly one's thoughts return after a long period of unconsciousness. At first I did not understand anything at all, then I recognized the expedition doctor, and slowly it dawned on me that I was on an expedition and what was wrong. The presence of doctors comforted me so much that with a deep sigh I fell into a wholesome sleep. After two weeks I was able to get up again, but one of my eyes still smarted and watered. The iris was torn. In the doctors' opinion, that had no connection with the pneumonia, but I did not believe them.

* *Translator's note:* in German "Bad" = "bath".

At this time I received the following letter from Hias, which simultaneously gladdened and saddened me:

28 July, Camp II, 4800 metres.
Dear Andreas,
    We have now got stuck into the Batura glacier and have already dug ourselves an ice cave. However, we shall soon have to move out, as a crevasse that was quite a modest size at first keeps on widening day after day and will soon divide Martl's work of art in half.
    To take things in order, after three reconnaissance probes from base camp we made our way up via a difficult ice route. At this point the Skipper found a better way around through some flowery pastures. But like an idiot I have forgotten to explain first about the nut we are trying to crack. It is the unnamed highest peak (almost 7800 metres) in the Hunza-Batura massif—the one we saw from the other side when we were on the Baltar glacier. From here it looks easy; Jochen Schneider says it is a ski slope. The lower part of this ski slope appears to be a wild 2000 metre-high icefall barring the way to the snow bays above. By dint of pitching three camps we overcame this rather dangerous icefall with a good deal of difficulty, and yesterday Dolf and I reached the plateau, from which the way to the summit looks straightforward. Tomorrow we are going to carry supplies up to Camp III at 5400 metres and then push on farther. If nothing goes wrong, the summit should be reached in about 14 days. From one of the cols we ought to be able to climb three easy 7000ers.
    In a way I am afraid of depressing you with my report, but on the other hand I want to keep you regularly informed. If we can reach this summit, taken together with the work of the scientists, it will make a great success of the expedition and we shall be able to celebrate a triumphal campaign in Pakistan. Skipper has already become a great mountaineer and is very helpful, and Wixling is also leading columns of porters on his own. However, I am missing you greatly and have to try all kinds of expedients to make up in some degree for your absence.
    How are you getting on? If you are neither better nor worse it would probably be best for you to go down to

Minka with Eugen. Otherwise better to stay at Aliabad and wait for us at Baltit on the way back. It won't be long now before the journey homeward together, and we shall certainly find fine things to see on the way.

I shall be needing my Leica now that you are no longer available as an extra photographer. Please send it by return together with the lenses (I no longer remember what I lent you).

We shall be back in Baltit in three to four weeks. In the meantime keep your fingers crossed for us and stay well. Everybody sends greetings. Goodbye for now.

Yours,

Hias.

For a lifetime I had looked forward to visiting this distant range, and now, through my own fault, it had got the better of me.

My companions did not in fact attain the highest summit, but at least reached a subsidiary one, so that the expedition had some modest mountaineering success. How lucky they had been was shown a year later when a British party with a German member, Hirschbichler from Bad Reichenhall, lost their lives in an avalanche in the icefall.

The scientists were already on their way back, and I looked forward with longing to a visit from them. Instead, there came the news of Karl Heckler's accident. The entries in my diary read as follows:

Aliabad, 26 July. Today I feel deeply depressed again. Pillewitzer and Heckler were due for a visit. I waited the whole day in vain. Not that it is of much importance, but I feel so excluded from everything that has been happening that a visit from my comrades would have cheered me up.

27 July, noon. The doctor has just broken the news to me as gently as possible that Karl Heckler fell into the Hunza river yesterday on the way from Gulmit to Baltit, and that his body has disappeared. I cannot seem to grasp this news, but understand why nobody was able to spare a thought for me. . . .

I now insisted on quitting the sick-bay and took up an invitation from the Mir of Hunza to recuperate at his castle in Baltit, where I ran into the other scientists. Soon I was feeling so well that I would have liked to hurry back and join the climbing party, but I was informed that they too were now on the march out.

It was another disappointment. That is how expeditions are: one has far too many rosy visions. Expeditions are not pleasure trips. They bring hard work, renunciation, adversity and disappointment, one after another. As recompense one has the great experience and, with good luck, success. If your luck is bad, they can cost you your life. All this should be taken into account, but when adventure beckons it rarely is. Prestige and fame often do not enter into the picture, or soon vanish. Yet the memory remains. With this harvest of experience I journeyed home.

CHAPTER XV

Youth Hostel Work

AT HOME IN Oberstdorf a very nice, kindly, old gentleman was waiting to see me. He turned out to be the famous Professor Ernst Enzensperger, who with his brother Josef had been one of the outstanding Alpine pioneers around the turn of the century. He was an idealist of the purest kind. Together with Richard Schirrmann he had been a founder of the German Youth Hostel Association.

It was a great joy to meet this deserving man, whom I had looked up to all my life. It proved to be no courtesy visit. He was following a carefully weighed course of action which was to give my life a new and significant orientation.

Enzensperger told me how the Association had hostels scattered all over the country, including the Alpine regions. There were already two in Oberstdorf. Except in schools, one never found so many youngsters gathered together as in Youth Hostels, which therefore offered an opportunity to do something in the educational line. He asked if I would be willing to take on the job of guiding hostellers in the mountains. In fact I could not imagine myself in this role at all, but as it is difficult to disappoint somebody as nice as Enzensperger I agreed. The more I thought about it, the more it seemed that I could indeed make a contribution, particularly as the assignment included the training of teachers, educationists and youth organizers in mountaineering matters, and I had already been running the training courses for German mountain guides for many years.

Working with young people of all ages is something very vital for me. It does not worry me at all to go for little outings and walks. The age groups range from as young as six up to twenty-one, with a majority between fourteen and sixteen. Most of them have never seen mountains before. Sometimes we even get problem children and deaf-mutes.

I had a particularly interesting case one winter. On winter courses I lay emphasis on touring and using skis as a means to an end. A group of long-haired youths arrived from Hamburg who had hardly seen snow, let alone skis and mountains. The course organizer asked me to cope with this bunch in person. I was highly sceptical, but after we had fitted them out with skis I decided to test the boys by taking them for a tour lasting several hours over flat terrain. I was all set to deal with mutiny and found myself speechless with surprise when one of them slapped me on the shoulder and announced that he had never dreamt of anything so beautiful. After that everything was easy. They practised all the exercises from side-slipping to stem-turns with fiery enthusiasm, and after a week I could take them on proper ski tours. Such experiences are profoundly satisfying, and I am grateful to old Professor Enzensperger and the Youth Hostel Association for giving me the possibility of working with young people and leading them into contact with nature. In this respect it sometimes stands me in good stead to refer to my experiences, after which they believe what I tell them and follow me without question.

CHAPTER XVI

A Meeting on the Heilbronner Trail

IN THE COURSE of my new duties I did not forget my mountaineering dreams, and my wanderlust was far from being satisfied. Among my private clients was Otto-Ernst Flick,* whom I had met in the course of a walk along the Heilbronner trail in the mountains of Allgäu. He had asked me if I would be willing to guide him too. Before committing myself I wanted to know what he had in mind. The answer came straight back: "the Matterhorn." With the exception of the first time, storm and cold had always been my lot on the Matterhorn and I had had my work cut out to get my clients off the mountain safe and sound. OE suggested engaging a second guide. To this I agreed, since there is nothing to compare with the knowledge of a local man. Yet even that did not satisfy me.

"If necessary, I can get you up and down blindfold," I said.

"Then you will thank me, perhaps pay double the fee, and I shall never see you again. I would rather you climbed the mountain easily even in awkward conditions, and thus acquired an appetite for more."

Nonplussed at my direct manner of speech, he looked at me. "What are you driving at?"

My suggestions were carefully noted down in his diary. Over the next two years we carried out all these tours, during the course of which he proved himself very strong and possessed of great powers of endurance. Ten-hour walks did not put him out at all, even in pouring rain. There was to be no question of technical difficulties; the man was not a climber, only a very powerful mountain walker. Before putting the Matterhorn project into action, therefore, I deliberately took him on a few trips such as the Kopftörlgrat in the Kaisergebirge which are difficult for a non-climber and were beyond his standard on rock. My aim was to prepare him for the impending difficulties

* *Translator's note:* One of the richest and most powerful industrialists in Germany. The Heilbronner trail is one of the classical Alpine high-level routes.

F

of the Matterhorn. He took it all in his stride. The experiment had been worthwhile, and we had grown closer to each other as human beings in the process.

Provided a guide takes the trouble to offer his clients something more than merely getting them safely up and down and collecting his fee, he establishes a close human contact with them which may become friendship and even comradeship. I thought to myself that in the circles frequented by my industrialist it must be very rare to find anyone willing to undergo all the fatigue and hardships of mountaineering. Yet in this case it was true, and somehow the fact helped me to develop a special patience.

We soon came to an agreement that he would call me by my first name and I him by the initials OE. This was adhered to throughout the adventures we subsequently shared. Right from the beginning I made it plain that we mountain climbers are not flunkeys and in the interests of safety sometimes even have to be blunt and hard. In practice it never came to a scene, as I always took care to keep our undertakings within his powers—which, moreover, were very considerable—in order to preserve his will to effort and his love of the mountains.

A further quality of OE's was not only to remain calm in the worst situations, which no doubt partly stemmed from his confidence in me, but also never to lose his ironical sense of humour. He was always able to find a joke about himself and his surroundings, a characteristic which stood us in good stead both in the Alps and on our later journeys to Lapland, Africa, and North and South America. Naturally such a stinkingly wealthy man has quite a different outlook on life from ours, but in the mountains, where money and social distinctions have no part to play, he showed his real character. Unless guide and client can get on together, it is no good. The latter has to suffer hunger, thirst, cold, heat and fatigue like his leader, and must not sulk or lose heart—naturally, he has a right to blaspheme. If in spite of all this he loses neither his temper nor his enthusiasm, then that is something exceptional on the part of anybody coming from such an environment. OE united all these qualities. He had always been a brilliant, passionate rider, but mountaineering, that special form of freedom which is attained through much hardship, and the immediacy of nature, meant still more to him.

But I digress. After some ascents around the Jungfraujoch in order to acclimatize to altitude we fairly polished off the Matterhorn. OE was radiant and announced that he would now like to go to the Himalayas.

I was frankly shocked. At great heights every mask falls away and there is no longer any formal politeness. Who knew whether we would be able to stand each other's company for long in such circumstances? I therefore suggested:

"How would it be if we made a journey through Lapland lasting several weeks as a trial run?"

My idea was to see how we got on together for a prolonged period in primitive conditions.

"Done!" he said. "You can go ahead and make the preparations."

We carried out our plan in 1957, but before that I had another narrow escape.

In September 1956 I was sought out by Wiggerl Gramminger, my old friend from the Munich mountain-rescue team, who wanted to know if I would accompany him to Zermatt where a pair of German climbers were missing on the west face of the Matterhorn. Two of their friends who had just returned from an attempt on the Eigerwand wanted to look for them, but the parents of the missing youths wanted two experienced mountaineers to go along. I agreed willingly, and next day the four of us were on our way to Zermatt with rescue equipment and stretchers.

Basing ourselves on the Schönbühl hut, we began by searching the avalanche cones at the foot of the face. Owing to the danger of stonefall this had to be done early in the morning while the face still lay in shadow and everything was frozen hard. We found nothing, but at the side of the face an ice gully led upwards to the Zmutt ridge. Perhaps we would see something from up there.

We roped up at the bergschrund. I let one of the youngsters lead off, but only gave him ten metres of rope to play with. This was enough for crossing the crevasse, so I tied on at this point. However, he was unable to surmount its upper lip and had to climb down. Meanwhile his friend had tied on to the other end of the 40 metre rope, and, having found a better place to attack, got up at once. The party was now under way. Gramminger tied on between me and the one who had failed. Once up into the gully, we all climbed together. In principle one should not do this, but when everybody trusts one another it is common practice. After all, they had just come from the Eiger, so they ought to be pretty good. The pace was too hot for Wiggerl, and as we had to search on all sides in any case he untied and pushed off on his own. We carried on, but had not climbed 20 metres before Wiggerl suddenly yelled out. I looked at him; he pointed upwards, and I saw a body shooting down towards me. The leader had fallen off. I had neither a stance nor a belay. The best I could do was to plunge in my ice-axe and pass the rope over it with a clove-hitch. However, it was no good: the axe was catapulted out and away I went. The third man received such a tug that he shot over my head. I was pulled one way and then the other. So it went on for 200 metres, then I shot head-first over the bergschrund and lost consciousness as I landed on the other side.

A sharp pain in one shoulder brought me back out of the darkness. I recognized the north face of the Dent d'Hérens, but what had happened to me and what was I doing here? Slowly I began to remember that we were on a search party, then everything went black again. In the far distance I heard a voice that I recognized saying:

"Here comes Wiggerl. It'll be all right now, he'll help us."

After we had shot past him, Wiggerl took three-quarters of an hour to climb down the 200 metres that we had descended so swiftly. With the calm of a seasoned campaigner he took stock of the situation. The bird of ill omen who had caused the accident was hanging in the bergschrund, so he was hauled out straight away. Apart from abrasions there was nothing wrong with him. The other one had landed on his back and was wailing horribly, but only had grazes and bruises. I was lying crumpled up and unconscious, with one arm sticking out in an unnatural position.

Wiggerl immediately put the shoulder back into joint; he knew the trick of this better than anybody. This brought me back to my senses. It was as though the pain had been blown away. All together they helped me to my feet. There seemed to be something else wrong, as although I could stand I was unable to hold up my head. Also the pain in both sides was so bad

In the Cordillera Blanca, 1963

The members of the Cordillera Blanca expedition

Anderl Heckmair at the Youth Hostel in Oberstdorf

Three sixty-year-olds: Heckmair, Fischer and Gramminger

that it was difficult to breathe. Any attempt to carry me hurt still worse, although I am not given to complaining. We seemed to get along best if I held on to Wiggerl's sack and leant my head on his shoulder. Step after step, we eventually reached the Schönbühl hut after seven hours. Next day I was carried down on a stretcher. At the clinic in Zermatt they found that the seventh cervical vertebra was fractured, my shoulder dislocated and all the ribs in my back broken.

Enveloped in plaster, I was able to travel home in the Volkswagen. Once again I was X-rayed from head to foot, and a fractured pelvic vertebra was found. Since I was completely unable to move anyway, I was spared a plaster jacket. In mid-December they let me out of the hospital fully cured, and by Christmas I was giving ski lessons again.

In the hospital I was visited not only by my own family, but also by representatives of the government and by friends who had travelled a long way to see me. I was deeply touched. Instead of flowers, those who knew me well brought a bottle of high-proof fluid that, "taken in medicinal quantities . . ." I had learnt this lesson long before, and no doubt it contributed to my rapid recovery. One visit gave me particular pleasure and had far-reaching effects. This was from Helmut Münch, at that time Warden of the Kurzschule* at Baad, who for professional reasons was taking the courses and examinations to become a mountain guide. We got on well together and soon became friends. I welcomed the advent of university graduates into the guiding profession, which in those days was still a rarity although it has now become a matter of course.

Helmut asked me if I would like to make a journey with him to Mount Athos, and instead of flowers or schnaps brought a whole bundle of literature on the area. I had plenty of time for study. In May 1957 we drove to Salonika via Yugoslavia, where at times my old Volkswagen could only advance in first gear. In the glove compartment we had a personal letter from the Queen of Greece which opened all doors.

The community of monks in the monasteries of Athos is the oldest republic in the world. Since the year A.D. 1000 nobody but monks has lived there, and women are forbidden even to set foot on the peninsula. This is carried so far that even female animals are excluded, so that there are no cows or

* *Translator's note:* similar to an Outward Bound school.

chickens. Only cats shamelessly yowl their love songs, as they are needed to keep down the mice, which are also not an exclusively male community.

We wandered along from monastery to monastery through a kind of subtropical park landscape, accompanied by the twittering of birds that we hardly ever saw among the thickets of furze, laurel and other plants unusual to us. At each monastery we were welcomed with ouzo—an aniseed-flavoured spirit— Greek coffee and sweet confectionery. A room would be got ready for us, and when our royal letter was read we were sometimes promptly moved again to the chamber of honour. As special guests we were also shown the treasures of the world-famous libraries, among them a fifth-century Byzantine Bible in which wonderful miniatures were painted on parchment. I regretted not knowing more about the subject and only being able to stand and admire. Helmut, who had had a completely different education, was lost in enthusiasm.

On one occasion our letter had not the slightest effect. In the most south-easterly monastery, which we entered through the back door, a gloomy-visaged monk advanced towards us. We handed him our letter, but he showed no interest at all; probably he could not read. Addressing us in insulting tones and in a language of which we understood not a single word, he conducted us through the building to another door which led back into the open air. The door slammed to behind us and we heard the bolt being drawn on the inside. Well, not to worry.

As we anyway wanted to climb Mount Athos, we bivouacked under a tree on a spur of the mountain. It was the most beautiful night of the whole trip; we felt positively grateful to the unfriendly monk. The sun sank glowing into the western sea just as the full moon rose like a golden ball out of the east. Around us was total silence, and we drifted off into reverie. When we reached the summit next day it was in cloud. Scorning the disused mule-track, we clambered up a rock ridge on the eastern flank. On the top stands a small oratory containing valuable ikons, though at that season still half full of snow— Athos rises 2100 metres out of the sea. We were greatly admired for this "feat". From a mountaineering point of view it is, of course, no feat at all. The most beautiful part of it was the night out which we owed to the monk.

At the next monastery, which was on the western side of

the mountain, the monks were once again extremely friendly. It was a school of painting, and we were proudly shown the masterpieces which they painted in the old style and even sold. We also made a short excursion to see the hermits dwelling among the cliffs just above the sea. Here our climbing abilities really came in handy, as we were able to clamber down cracks and grooves. Suddenly we found ourselves standing before a meditating anchorite. He did not utter a word but made friendly gestures and prepared the usual coffee for us. These hermits are partly supplied from the sea, drawing up their provisions in nets as their predecessors have done for more than a thousand years.

Hermits were indeed the first men of religion to settle on Athos. Subsequently monasteries were founded, the first of which was Lavra, still the most important. Two cypresses dating from the time of its foundation stand in the cloister garden; they are over 1000 years old. Most of the monasteries are now inhabited by only a few monks. At the Russian Pantelcimon, for example, which was built for 3500, there were only 60 in 1957. We were told that the republic had survived many such crises in its millennial history, and the monks look to the future full of trust in God.

After Athos we visited the monasteries of the Meteora, which by contrast are now no more than museum-pieces. They were built in the Middle Ages perched high on enormous outcrops of conglomerate to which the monks could retreat in time of danger. In those days there were 23 of them, but now no more than five remain. Determined to see an abandoned monastery, we circled an outcrop which we suspected of holding a ruin, but without finding any possibility of getting up. The monks must have drilled and bolted their way up, then taken out the equipment and hauled up their supplies by rope. Our latest climbing technique is not so modern after all! We had no ironmongery with us and had to give up.

Finally we wanted to climb Olympus, but the Gods were ill-disposed to us and opened the floodgates of the heavens so wide that we were literally washed away home.

That spring I was able to make the planned journey to Lapland with OE. We flew to Stockholm, then took the train to

Kiruna, from where we climbed Kebnekaise, the highest mountain in Sweden. We also made some nice tours from Abisko. Then there happened what must happen when people are together for a long time.

A march was planned to Unallakaz and back via Riksgränsen. Owing to the shortcomings of the map, which was on a scale of 1:200 000, my reckonings were ten kilometres out, and in trackless territory in Lapland one does not normally cover more than one and a half to two kilometres in the hour. Since Abisko lies 300 kilometres north of the Arctic Circle it never grows dark in summer, and we set out at three o'clock in the morning. First of all we walked for 15 kilometres along the well-marked King's Trail, which I knew already. This first stage was polished off in three hours. The remaining 15 kilometres could be done comfortably in ten hours, inclusive of halts. The route lay westwards, still along a track, although not such a good one. After a bridge the track petered out, and as foreseen we plodded on through boglands, dwarf birch and willow until the calculated ten hours were up, but without any sign of shelter. After checking our position with the compass, I pulled out the map. Suddenly the scales fell from my eyes, and I realized what a mistake I had made. There were another five hours to go! Luckily there was no nightfall, but the weather turned bad and whipped us with mixed rain and snow. In a boggy valley I had to check our course again with the compass. On account of the cloud nothing could be seen of the surrounding summits, but fortunately OE stood out of the dwarf vegetation like a lighthouse, as he is 1·93 metres tall.

As we sat down for a rest in a clearing he at last said:

"I suppose we'll be getting there soon?"

I had been waiting for the question for a long time and now admitted my mistake, feeling some trepidation about his reaction. It was not a pleasant confession to have to make. Now for it . . . but no, there was not a word of reproach; it would not have changed our situation anyway. On!

Towards midnight we reached our objective, which turned out to be a tiny cabin. Two Norwegians were snoring inside. After we had made a fire and changed into dry clothing I hauled our ample provisions out of the sack. OE fell on them ravenously like a starving man. I knew how he felt; it had happened to me after my first trip to the Dolomites. A hunger like that is impossible to master even with the best will in the world. Anything one can get one's teeth into goes straight down. As fast as I could pull things out of the sack he gobbled them, and I began to fear that he would swallow the wrappings into the bargain.

Next day OE flatly refused to cross the mountains to Riksgränsen, so there was nothing for it but to return by the same route, if you could call it that. As the weather had now turned fine again we saw something of the strange and marvellous landscape. We took our time, spent the night in a Kota—a Lapp dwelling—and finished the tour on the best of terms.

There was no doubt about it, OE had the necessary qualities of endurance and self-control for expedition life. We could now go ahead and make real plans.

The first-class passage by sea from Narvik to Rotterdam gave us a chance to relax in comfort. I turned over the question of our next goal in my mind. It would clearly be premature to aim for the Himalayas. In accordance with my principle of never exceeding the capabilities of my clients I therefore suggested Africa.

CHAPTER XVII

Africa

I REMEMBERED A tip that had been given me by Heini
Harrer after he had become a globe-trotter. His most interesting mountaineering in Africa had been the Ruwenzori, which
were relatively easy to reach by air and miscellaneous local
methods of transport. From a technical point of view they were
seemingly not too difficult; what they called for was endurance
and readiness to put up with hardships, as the rain never
stopped throughout the year. It sounded just the thing for OE!
Cautiously I began to put these ideas to him.

He seemed to have nothing against them, but if he was going
to visit Africa at all then he wanted to see Lake Chad, about
which he had heard a great deal. I on the other hand knew
little or nothing about it, so I quickly looked it up on the map
and duly discovered it on the southern borders of the Sahara.
The Ruwenzori lie on the Equator. If we were going to travel
as far as the Sahara, then I would like to see the Hoggar
mountains. This time it was OE who had never heard of them. I
described to him how in 1932 I had gazed in fascination from
the summit of Toubkal out over the unending desert, and what
a great experience it must be to cross it. In the middle of the
desert rise two ranges of mountains, the Tibesti and the Hoggar
(sometimes spelt "Ahaggar"), both over 3000 metres.

OE laconically commissioned me to work out a time schedule
and cost estimates. That was easy to say. It transpired that our
plans could only be accomplished by the use of cross-country
vehicles. The biggest problem of all is always to find the right
companions, but for this purpose I had a good choice of
"specimens" in my collection. During the war I had got to
know a doctor in Fulpmes who seemed to me thoroughly
suitable as a mountain climber, as a doctor and as a human
being. His name was Jochen Singer, and we were still loosely
in touch. A telephone call was enough. I told him what a happy
little trip I had in mind for him and suggested that he think it
over and call me back.

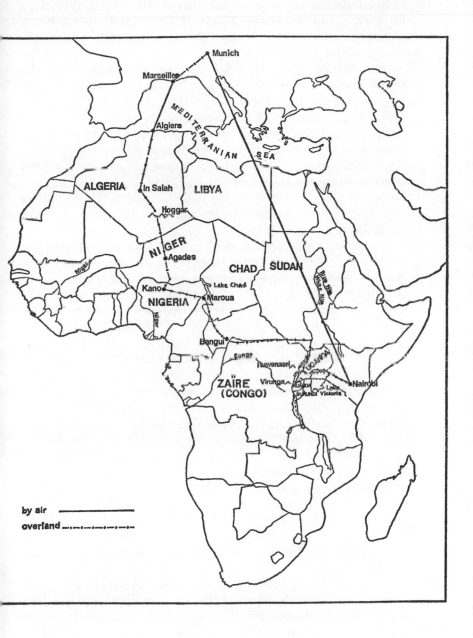

by air ————————
overland ._._._._._.

In addition, I knew a scientist with all the necessary qualities for such an undertaking. This was Dr Achim Schneider, a lecturer in geology at the University of Berlin, whose knowledge would enrich our journey.

Both agreed, although I left them in no doubt about the problems that were to be expected. The preparations took two years, but at last the time came when we could ship the vehicles and a ton of baggage off to Nairobi in advance.

In order to climb the Ruwenzori we had to take the rainy season into our calculations. We therefore settled on mid-September 1960 as our time of departure, flying towards Nairobi along the course of the Nile, which from the aircraft looked like a dribble draining down a gutter. Our vehicles and supplies were waiting for us. We collected them, and the great journey was begun.

In order to get acclimatized and for special training we first headed for Uganda in order to climb the Virunga volcanoes. We were particularly tempted by Nirogongo, which is said to possess the biggest lava-flow in the world. Unfortunately, it stands in what was then Congolese territory, and on account of the fighting and unrest going on there at that time we were unable to cross the border and had to content ourselves with the 4000er Muhawura, the "father of the lost".

Around the foot of the mountain extended a belt of bamboo forest in which gorillas were supposed to dwell. Our native guides were full of advice as to how we should behave in the event of an encounter. However, although we heard cracklings and rustlings we never saw so much as a hair. This was hardly surprising in view of the fact that the bamboo thickets grew so densely that we had to keep in physical contact in order to avoid any of the party getting lost. Without the local guides we would never have got through. One of them excitedly showed us a steaming, horribly stinking little heap that he assured us was gorilla droppings, but I was by no means sure that he had not laid it there himself for the promotion of the tourist trade.

There were also said to be snakes, as everywhere in Africa. Our doctor had an assortment of antitoxins with him, as different snakes have different venoms, and you unfortunately cannot tell in advance which kind you are going to get bitten by. Yet in the whole of our journey through Africa I saw only three snakes, two of them dead and one living. The latter was lazily sun-bathing and seemed grateful that I did not attack.

The ascent of Muhawura and the neighbouring Mgahinga, which is almost as high, gave us a foretaste of what the Ruwenzori range held in store. There were cloudbursts against which even umbrellas were ineffective, while in plastic capes we were soon soaked in our own condensed sweat owing to the warm, humid atmosphere. That is typical of mountaineering in Africa. However, nobody complained; we were all too enchanted with the change of scene.

After crossing the bamboo belt, throughout which we vainly kept an eye open for gorillas, we wanted at least to reach the summit. Our African guides could not understand this at all—I, on the other hand, could see their point of view, as we had to pass through a veritable forest of stinging nettles which were far more painful than our European ones. At last we broke out into the upper zone of groundsel, lobelia and heather, which continued all the way to the top. The most widespread plant of all was the knee-deep moss, in which it was impossible to find any firm footing. There were no views from the summit, as at high altitudes the rain takes the form of thick, drenching fog. Nevertheless, we had attained our first goal, Mgahinga.

The next objective was the nearby Muhawura. In order to reach it, we had to cross a high saddle about a kilometre wide. Our native guides were afraid of this area, claiming that it was infested with dangerous wild animals. To us it seemed more probable that they really wanted to spend the night with their wives in the village before going back up the mountain. We therefore insisted on our plan. During the march through the boggy jungle, however, we could see from their tense features and nervous bearing that they had not been pretending. In our ignorance we saw nothing dangerous. We were like beginners in the mountains standing on an avalanche slope without a suspicion of the peril they are in. The relief of our Africans was visible as we descended from the saddle on to relatively more open terrain and reached the steep flanks of Muhawura. The keeper of the next shelter assured us that the warning had been fully justified and that buffaloes and beasts of prey were constantly passing through the gap and would attack if disturbed or frightened.

The summit of Muhawura is 4600 metres above sea-level, and the 3000-metre descent was most unpleasant. We all felt the unusual effort. Nevertheless, we were in cheerful mood at having attained our first objective.

Now our way led northward along relatively good roads through the Elizabeth National Park, where we photographed an enormous elephant from disquietingly close quarters and also hippopotami, a great crocodile that looked a thousand years old, trotting giraffes, and marabou birds. The word "park" implied a preserve where all forms of hunting were forbidden. In general, the animals took no notice of cars. However, it is forbidden to get out and the rules must be observed; only then is it safe.

At last we reached the Ruwenzori, which, according to our geologist, were not volcanic in origin like almost all other African mountains, but a gigantic slab raised out of the rift valley, 5120 metres high and divided by erosion into five groups. At Fort Portal, a fair-sized town at the foot of the range, they are used to mountaineers. You go into a particular shop where the owner, an Indian, asks you:

"How many of you are there?"

"Four."

"Then you need 20 porters who will require this and that and the other."

We were dumbfounded. There was nothing to say or do but pay up.

"Where will the porters wait for us?"

"They won't be waiting for you at all. You just go down the valley and report to the chief guide. He will do the rest."

It was as easy as that. To think that we had spent so much time worrying and planning! However, it might not always turn out quite so simple. At Kampala we had paid a courtesy visit to the local mountaineering club in the hope of gathering information. It seemed that my name was known in the heart of Africa, and this smoothed our path. The club members had sent word ahead of us, which no doubt explained why everything went so easily. Climbers look after one another. A non-climber would have run into obstacles.

The walk in was extremely interesting. The route lay through house-high elephant grass. It must in fact be the most dangerous part of the expedition, as the region is full of wild animals, though there is no danger to be seen, at least until it is too late.

Elephant grass is two to three metres high, and without local guides one would never find the way through. On one occasion I remained behind in order to change a film and afterwards had no idea how to find the others, who had vanished into the sea of grass. I felt properly afraid, and was relieved to come upon a trampled-down path. Presently the guides emerged from the grass calling out and gesticulating wildly. Noticing my absence, they had come back to find me. They explained that my trodden path was not a proper track at all, but had been made by wild animals. If I had gone much farther I might have found myself face to face with an elephant, and nobody can tell how they will react. After that I kept right up with the others.

The second part of the approach march led through primaeval forest where apes swung through the tops of the trees some 40 to 50 metres above the ground. We crossed innumerable rushing streams without bridges, and trudged through swampy valleys. Then we came to a groundsel forest so strange that we would hardly have been surprised to find a brontosaurus peering at us around the corner. There was nothing new about wading in knee-deep moss, however, as we had already had plenty of that on the Virunga volcanoes.

At the end of each day's march we came to a corrugated-iron hut. The last of these was the Bujuku hut at 3800 metres, which even boasted a stove. Despite all our efforts to light it, it would only give off smoke but not burn. Our scientist then had the idea of filling the ash-scuttle with paraffin and setting fire to it. The result was a hot moment not only for the stove but for ourselves too, as we thought we were being blown up. After that everything was all right again; only the idea had not been so all right.

Our porters had found shelter in a cave and were wretchedly cold, yet they remained cheerful. I was happy to sit down in their circle and share the gruel from their pot. This gave a feeling of intimacy which we never again experienced in Africa.

The mentality of the Africans had been described to us quite differently. We had been told that they were lazy, lying and furtive. Our experience was exactly the opposite. Three days before reaching the Ruwenzori valley I lost my Rolex wrist-watch. It was sent after me by relay runners from village to village. At the Bujuku hut rain was drumming on the tin roof in the morning, and we thought that we could sleep in comfortably, as our Africans would not venture out of their cave. On the contrary, our guides and porters got us out of bed and insisted on our allocating the loads. They were right, too: a couple of hours later it was fine again.

The higher we got, the stranger the vegetation became. Vertical crags would be thickly clothed in moss, and had not Hubert Mumelter written in the *Mountaineer's Primer*: "Overhang with moss and slime, that's no place for you to climb"? Luckily we did not need to climb through the overhangs. There was always a track leading on, which at last brought us to two bivouac huts at 4400 metres on Point Helena. Here our porters deposited their loads and hastened back to their cave, as they do not go on the glacier.

It was just midday, and once again I let myself be led into a stupidity. I knew well enough from the literature that in the Ruwenzori the temperature reaches 15°C by day and sinks to −15°C by night, yet somehow I did not believe it, or at least not the second part. The first part I was forced to believe by the state of the snow on the glacier, which was just like jelly. It seemed that it could do no harm to go on right away and break the trail, so that in the morning we should have ready-made frozen steps. Thus we reached the summital icefalls, all decorated with fantastic icicles. We could have gone on to the top, but in that case would have been caught out by darkness with sopping wet feet and no bivouac equipment. It therefore seemed best to return to the bivouac hut, where we had dry things to change into.

Next day the weather was bad again, but the snow was so hard-frozen that we strapped on our crampons and were able to plod up our track without any trouble.

Suddenly a violent snowstorm blew up. It was a real blizzard. Obviously, the warm, humid air-masses from the Congo basin are cooled as they strike the mountains, and even at the Equator it does not rain at 5000 metres but snows. Now it snowed with a density greater than I had ever seen. The snow must have been mixed with supercooled humidity in the air, as a great ice bulge under which we sheltered grew a coat of rime half a metre thick. We ourselves were also completely sheathed in ice, so that after half an hour, by which time the storm had begun to abate and the air to grow lighter, we decided not to bother about Point Margherita, the highest summit, but to head for Mobius, the third highest, which we reached successfully.

Through cloud and snow, despite the fact that we were on the Equator, we fought our way back down the giant Stanley glacier to our bivouac box, where our porters were waiting for us practically frozen. Hastily we continued on down to the warmer climate of the Bujuku hut, where whisky and Toscanelli Stumpfen helped us to forget our earlier discomfort. Despite our failure to reach the highest summit we were in excellent humour, and the doctor expressed our feelings admirably by saying:

"We didn't come on this trip to be admired; we wanted to admire the sights and experiences ourselves."

There was still plenty to experience: downpours so copious that it was like walking under a showerbath that had been turned on full, and the hospitable receptions as we marched back down the valley. Out of every village rushed the wives and children of our porters with cries of delight, bringing us pineapples and bananas as tokens of welcome. These kindnesses on the part of the Africans, who were shy of strangers, were really touching, and we were correspondingly generous when the time came to pay them off. This gave rise to further celebrations with much dancing and drinking.

As we were still only at the beginning of our journey, we imagined that we should often experience the same kind of thing. In this we were mistaken, as we never again made such close contact as we had with our Ruwenzori porters.

Now our great journey across Africa really began. As it was impossible to go through the Congo (now Zaïre) on account of the troubles, we had to head north towards the Sudan and then north-west through the Central African Republic (the former French Equatorial Africa) to Cameroon, across Cameroon to Nigeria, and on up into the desert.

That does not take long to write. In places, however, there were no roads at all, and it was lucky that we had two cars, so that if one got stuck the other could haul it out. It was not possible to sleep out on account of the wild animals, but everywhere we went we either found rest-houses reserved for Europeans or else were put up by European farmers.

Our trip in the Ruwenzori had been just at the beginning of the rainy season. Now we had to pass through the rain zone as it moved southward across Africa. In places the rivers had burst their banks and flooded wide areas. As we had to cross many tributaries of the Congo, it was a matter of some suspense whether we would get through or not.

At Mboku we found an Englishman with an American car. Although it was only the beginning of October, he would be stuck until January at the earliest. We were also advised to wait, and the hospitable farmers would gladly have taken us in. With our jeeps, however, we ploughed our way across the flooded landscape. There were always a couple of local boys to go ahead of us as pilots. The roads were often flooded knee-deep, so that nothing could be seen but water. We would creep along in bottom gear behind the African boys. At the river itself there would be a whole crowd of them waiting to shove us on to the ferry with shouts of joy and then to guide us across the flooded areas many kilometres broad on the other side.

In the process we certainly learnt some geography. The Mboku flowed into the Mbomu, the Mbomu into the Ubangi, the Ubangi, after which the country was named, into the Congo. Nobody had ever told me about that at school!

It was 700 kilometres from the frontier of the Sudan to Bangassou, where the next hotel and filling-station were to be found. Even getting petrol proved difficult, as we had nothing but travellers' cheques which nobody was willing to cash. Fortunately, an American missionary appeared out of the wilderness like an angel of mercy. He had heard of our predicament and cashed the cheques for us.

Shortly before reaching Bangassou we encountered the first car we had seen for many days going the other way. Everybody jumped out and shook hands all round, asking where from, where to, what the conditions were like, and so on. Anybody who carried on like that in Europe would be taken straight off to a home.

A memorable event in the African bush was our meeting with a big-game hunter. We were getting short of petrol, and just managed to reach a French landing-strip. It was not

marked on any map, but we were directed to it when, purely
by luck, we inquired without much hope for petrol at a village.
The commanding officer was away hunting elephants and the
sergeant was unable to help us, as everything was military
property.

"When will he be back?" we asked.

"Perhaps in a couple of hours, perhaps not for a week,"
came the reply. It was a fine outlook.

It scarcely seemed worth waiting. With one jeep and all
our reserves it might just be possible to cover the 600 kilometres to Bangassou. The task fell to OE and Achim, who was
indirectly responsible for the state of affairs. The latter was
our cashier, and being short of Sudanese pounds he had not
filled up entirely at the last halt, hoping to find more petrol
at every village in the Central African Republic. Unfortunately,
there were no villages and no petrol either.

We parted with mixed feelings and made up our minds to
not seeing them again for two weeks. Jochen and I sat in the
canteen with every ground for rejoicing at our comfortable
circumstances, but somehow we were too worried about our
companions even to enjoy the beer. After two hours we were
startled out of our brooding by loud honking. Grinning all over
their faces, OE and Achim swung the jeep around to the gate
in an elegant curve. We ran out, calling:

"What's up?"

They had met the elephant-hunting commanding officer,
who had had a successful safari. He had as much petrol as we
wanted. Before long the hunters also appeared and their success
was duly toasted. Late in the afternoon the now well-oiled
Nimrod conceived a desire to go back and inspect his bag. We
were to come along; no need to change, it was only half an
hour from the road.

If hunters need only be believed with reservations, it would
seem that big-game hunters should not be believed at all. The
half hour drew out into several hours through real African
bush and bog. OE lost his shoes and as I only had sandals I
preferred to go barefoot. The hunter led on at such a pace that
OE could not keep up, and before long the former and I stood
alone together in the bush. Suddenly a bush-fire flared up
nearby and we fled into a stream. In the direction in which we
had been going I spotted a clump of trees, and headed for them.

As we drew closer we heard a general uproar, and found our friends in the midst of a band of Africans who were celebrating a meat orgy.

The body of the elephant, big as a room, had been entirely skinned. A heap of black people were tussling over the flesh, which they devoured like wolves. Men, women and children were a gruesome sight with blood smeared all over their naked bodies. Suddenly the mountain of flesh shook. I jumped: "Surely the elephant can't still be alive!"

The hunter laughed and took me around to the other side of the corpse, where I saw that there were two men in its belly, from which they were tearing out shreds of meat and throwing them to the others who, when they did not just swallow them on the spot, roasted and smoked them on grills of interwoven branches arched high over several fires, around which they danced. The rain had begun to patter down again, but could only wash part of the blood from their bodies. We were glad to have brought a few soldiers with us, for it seemed that otherwise the fear of inadvertently forming part of the feast might not have been utterly groundless.

The tusks weighed 70 kilos each. Once they had been cut out, we and the soldiers withdrew into the dusk. The feast was still in full swing, and we were assured that it could go on for another week or two.

That was Africa as no travel agency could offer it!

We travelled on out of the bush into the savannah, out of the savannah into arid plains, out of the plains into the desert. We began to see arabized negroes and then, as we went farther north, negroid Arabs. Everything was intermingled at the edges, both vegetation and races.

The land was so flooded owing to the rainy season that we were unable to reach Lake Chad. In fact we were happy to succeed in getting through to Kano in Nigeria, after which the rain zone was left behind. The closer we got to the desert, the bluer the sky stretched above our heads. Agades was the next big town on our route. Although it is really only on the southern edge of the Sahara, it seemed to us already in the middle of the desert. In former times the place lived mainly from the slave trade, but nowadays it is thronged with tourists and oil-prospectors who have flown in by aeroplane. Who would be so crazy as to drive across the Sahara?

For this purpose one was required to have a permit, which was only issued on the following conditions:

1. No vehicle was to travel alone; a convoy of two was the minimum.
2. A deposit must be paid so as to cover in advance the cost of any rescue operations that might be necessary.
3. Water, petrol, strips of matting for getting out of loose places, presents for bedouin, etc., must all be taken in prescribed quantities.
4. It was compulsory to report to the authorities at each stopping place, from which an estimated time of arrival is sent on to the next. If a party does not arrive within 36 hours of the estimated time, a rescue party is sent out.

All these are sensible measures which we had taken into our reckoning from the outset. As a consequence, one meets nobody in the desert who is not properly equipped. It would also be a good formula for the mountains, but unfortunately the Alps are too accessible and such regulations are only found in North America.

The gigantic emptiness of the desert makes a real physical impact, and the nights spent sleeping out under the unbelievably clear starry sky were among the most beautiful bivouacs of my life. We never once needed to pitch a tent, although it was now November. It was enough to spread out the groundsheet and slide into our sleeping-bags.

Our objective now was the Hoggar mountains. We had eliminated the Tibesti from our plans, feeling ourselves too inexperienced as Saharan travellers. Anybody who imagines as I did that a journey across the desert is going to be a matter of monotonous, stubborn endurance, will find that it is in fact quite the opposite.

Just as we had done in the jungle and the bush, we took turns at driving every 50 kilometres. However, the passenger has to keep just as sharp a lookout as the driver to see that the vehicle does not leave the track and run into soft sand at full speed. Nevertheless, it happens regularly. Then it becomes a matter of digging, pushing and pulling as hard as you can, all at a temperature of 40°C in the shade, which unfortunately does not exist. In the middle of the desert Achim even succeeded in finding a nail to drive over, thus producing a flat tyre. This feat must be even more difficult than finding the proverbial needle in the haystack, but Achim just would not give up trying. One is glad of every kilometre travelled without getting stuck, and as there are a lot of kilometres—over 2000 of them between Agades and Tamanrasset—one can be glad all day long.

Tamanrasset is a much-visited place with an airfield and a hotel to go with it, but unfortunately the latter was full. Unwashed and filthy, we resigned ourselves to another desert bivouac. First of all, however, we reported our arrival in the regular way to the police. As we were doing so a man in civilian clothes came into the office. From the way the clerks immediately got down to work it was clear that he must be of some importance. Taking no notice of our presence, he went over to an official, took up our papers from him and studied them. Suddenly he spun around and shot the question at me:

"Are you the Anderl Heckmair who climbed the Eigerwand?"

Astonished, I admitted that I was. He seemed overjoyed and introduced himself as the commanding officer. Being an Alsatian he spoke fluent German. Not only that, but he was a climber and well-acquainted with alpine literature. OE remarked drily:

"With you, it doesn't matter where we travel, you're as famous as a film star."

But what can I do about it?

The Hoggar range is of pure volcanic origin, formed, according to the latest theories, out of plugs forced up as out of a tube. The basalt towers rise out of the landscape here and there, all of them difficult to climb. During the 1950s Maurice Herzog, then Minister of Youth and Sport in France, had encouraged the best French climbers to go there. All the accessible summits had therefore been reached.

However, anyone who is not too worried about first ascents but nevertheless able to undertake severe climbs will find fulfilment here. There are no weather problems, and in November, when we were there, the heat was quite bearable. The only preconditions, as in any other range, are sufficient technical skill and willingness to face effort and hardship. We did a number of fine routes, among them the highest summit, the 3100 metre Ahaggar, which is in fact no more than a mountain walk. The way up lies over trackless screes among which are great lumps of petrified wood proving that in earlier times the region was afforested. There are many such curiosities in the Hoggar. Among the basalt gorges there are rock pools which, so I was informed, date from prehistoric ages. We were warned not to bathe in them, as some still contain crocodiles which, although very degenerate and no more than 50 or 60 centimetres long, are still eager to bite.

Nevertheless, some of the typical Hoggar basalt towers interested us, and we climbed one, the not too difficult Issekrem. Naturally, one does not travel across the desert merely to climb, since that can be done both better and much more simply in our home ranges. Still, when you have the ability and find yourself in front of such an obelisk, you feel a certain itching in the hands and feet. It is a special kind of fun to climb such an unusual peak and gaze out across the endless wastes on which mountains lie around like the lost toys of giants.

We did not want to leave Africa without once having ridden on camelback. Our idea of joining a caravan for a couple of days was very promptly discouraged. I could understand that, just as I myself would not have been keen to take any absolute beginners on a serious climb. However, we were able to arrange for camels at Tamanrasset. Some Tuaregs helped us into the saddle. Even that was not at all easy. The camel lies on the ground. You creep up on it from behind—the front end bites—and swing up on to the wooden saddle. Instantly the back end rises into the air. If not prepared, you hurtle head-first back on to the sand. Finally we all found ourselves in the saddle with our shoes hanging on a convenient peg in front of us. The bare feet are pressed into the camel's neck and the toes twiddled powerfully. The camel then begins to move. The more you twiddle the faster it goes, but if you doze off it stops. We rode 18 kilometres to a Tuareg colony where tea was cere-moniously prepared for us. The unveiled women were in charge while the heavily veiled men seemed to have nothing to say. In our jeeps we could have covered the distance easily in 30 minutes. By camel it had taken a good six hours, since camels walk no faster than three kilometres per hour. We began to feel a certain respect for the caravans, although they are being increasingly supplanted by motorized transport.

Finally we set out from Tamanrasset for the journey home.

At the oases of In Salah, El Golea and Ghardaia, which are linked by asphalt roads, there are comfortable hotels. The charm of the primitive and the untrodden now behind us, we headed for Algiers as fast as possible. True, it is still 2000 kilometres from Tamanrasset, but over roads that anyone could travel with an ordinary car. Although the spell of the unknown was gone, we had had plenty of it on our journey.

CHAPTER XVIII

South America

EVEN WHILE WE were travelling through Africa I began drawing OE's attention to the fact that there were a lot of worthwhile and easily accessible peaks in South America, notably in the Cordillera Blanca in Peru. As everything had gone so well in Africa it was not difficult to get him enthusiastic about this new project. Once again preparations began. They lasted two years, and by the middle of April 1963 we were ready to set off. We climbers are lucky in having interesting objectives all over the world to justify journeys across the continents.

This time OE brought his son Rudolf and the latter's friend Henno along. Besides our African team we had a very valuable addition to the party in the form of my old friend Dr Fritz März, known as "Zä" for short, who could speak Spanish and already knew Peru from an earlier expedition. There were thus seven of us, which is far too many, but each one had a job to do, and as we were all compatible there was no friction.

Nowadays one can hardly be said to travel: one flies. You go to sleep and wake up in another world. Airports, hotels and stations—and quite soon even cities—all look the same. The first thing that makes you aware of being on another continent is the sight of human beings of a different race. It is true that in Lima, where our expedition began, there are still old Spanish colonial houses, but not until we got out into the country did we sense the difference, the strangeness.

In order to reach the Santa valley we had to travel 200 kilometres and cross a pass 4000 metres high. We therefore hired an ancient truck that wheezed its way asthmatically up from sea-level and often gave us the opportunity for a little walk. As we came over the top of the pass the icy giants of the Andes rose before us.

The view up the Santa valley is dominated by the 6800 metre bulk of Huascarán. A month or so before we had set out the international press had been full of reports that an ice avalanche from Huascarán had overwhelmed a whole valley, wiping out ten villages and killing 4000 people. Nowadays the pace of life is so hectic that such news is soon forgotten. Only OE thought to ask whether we should travel to such a dangerous spot. Personally, I did not altogether believe the reports about the scale of the disaster, and replied that now the avalanche had

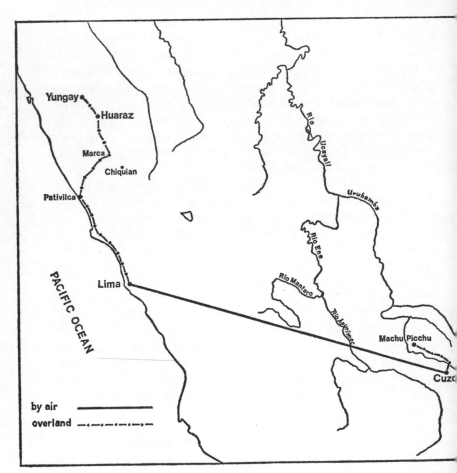

fallen there would not be another for a long time. In this I was mistaken: six years later, in 1971, a violent earthquake caused another avalanche to break loose from the mountain, almost totally annihilating Yungai and the neighbouring villages. The death-roll was 4000.

On reaching the area, we were shocked. An entire glacier

had in fact split away from the northern summit of Huascarán, poured over a rock face 1000 metres high, burst through a moraine and roared down the 20 kilometre length of the valley, rebounding from wall to wall like a toboggan and destroying everything in its path. Corpses were still being fished out of the Pacific, 400 kilometres away. Two months later, as we stood on the avalanche debris, it was already beginning to sprout green plants, for Peru is so fertile that they have a saying: "Plant your walking-stick in the ground, water it, and it will start to grow and flower." Even if it is not quite literally true, we saw the grain of truth in the proverb in that ruined valley, where life was already starting to bloom between the wooden crosses that had been placed everywhere on the avalanche rubble in memory of the victims.

The main town of the Santa valley is Huaras, which lies at over 3000 metres. We put up at the Monterrey Quarter Hotel, a little outside the built-up area. It had a swimming pool in which the water was heated to 32°C. That was enough for us; we immediately booked rooms for a month so that we could use the hotel as a base camp for our forays.

As usual, acclimatization and training tours came first. The Cordillera Negra was available for the purpose, and we hoped in this way to get a fine view of the crest of the Cordillera Blanca across the valley. However, the weather decided otherwise. This did not matter to us, as it gave us a good reason for doing some training expeditions in the main range itself. Our first trip, undertaken with the object of getting used to the height, the porters and the animals, lay past Huascarán into the Ulta valley.

The forming up of our porters with their beasts of burden in front of our hotel was observed by the other guests with some curiosity. Mountain climbers are rare enough even in our part of the world to be gaped at by the rest of humanity. Elsewhere the contrast is still greater. Among the porters was an aged man whom we indignantly told to go home. The other porters asked us to take him along, even if only at half pay. We agreed to this, and noticed that they all seemed much relieved. Some of the mules were still half wild and had a habit of leaping into the air and lashing out with all four feet as soon as the loads were placed on their backs and before the saddle-girths could be tightened up, so that bits and pieces flew in all directions.

No one could do anything with them except the old man, who only had to go near and they would fall quiet again. This phenomenon was not just an isolated occurrence; it happened every day, and in the end we gave the old fellow not half the normal rate, but double.

We rode down to the floor of the valley and then along it for several days to the "lagunas", small lakes formed against frontal moraines. On one side the glacier tongue reached into the water, on the other were thickets of rose bushes. I had never imagined such a sight. The silence was only broken by an occasional beautiful birdsong. Yet, however peaceful and marvellous these lagunas might seem, they were treacherous and much feared on account of their tendency to break down the moraine and flood the whole valley as though a dam had burst. This happened during the earthquake disaster of 1971. We decided that we had now gone far enough for a first expedition. Not only had we had wonderful impressions of flora and fauna, but the main purpose of establishing links with the porters and animals had been fully achieved.

The valley was full of white and blue lupins, while in boggy places trumpet lilies grew as thick as daisies at home. There were also masses of yellow slipperwort (calceolaria) and plants unknown to me, shrubs with red blossoms, and most amazing of all, orchids and bromeliaceae growing on box and rose trees. Only the fauna were not particularly forthcoming. We could indeed hear the birds twittering and rejoicing, but not see them. Pumas were said to be numerous, but they remained equally invisible. The porters had a panic terror of pumas and kept a fire going throughout the night.

Once we had soaked away the effects of this first tour in warm baths and the hotel bar at Monterrey we felt ready for new and more serious exploits. In high good humour and full of enterprise and resolution we rode off into the Ishinka valley, as full of flowers and blossoms as the last. This time we immediately found a goal that was within the powers of the party, a fine trapezoidal ice-peak dominating a lateral valley.

We were surprised to find a trail leading into this side valley so well trodden that we could have ridden up it. It ended before a stone-built house at the foot of a glacier. True, it had no door or windows, but it boasted a roof. There was also another laguna, artificially drained to avert flooding. As the

Mount Waddington: *right* an ice ridge; *below* the approach from the glacier

The rim of the crater, Popocatapetl

task had taken several years, the engineers had built themselves the house which now stood abandoned and available for our use. We made ourselves as comfortable as possible and climbed several 5000–6000 metre peaks. After this we felt ready to confront our chosen mountain.

All night long it snowed thickly, yet in the morning the layer was no more than ankle deep. After such a fall in the Alps it would have been up to our waists, but in the dry air of these altitudes the snow evaporates as fast as it comes down. Only in the rainy season, which is summer, such massive quantities fall that the snowcover and glaciers are built up. This is no wonder, since the moist air masses out of the Amazon basin break against the ramparts of the Andes, which in places rise up to 7000 metres. The mighty storms that result cause the formation of cornices that have been the undoing of many a mountain climber, among them Fritz Kasparek, our companion on the Eiger, who fell through one on Salcantay.

Despite cloud we found our way through the maze of crevasses as though we already knew it well. As we neared the crest we got apprehensive about cornices. Just below the top I no longer trusted the ridge and instead climbed a much harder rock buttress. Meanwhile Jochen, who had Rudolf und Henno on his rope, strolled up the snow-blade to the summit. He had heard much less about the danger of cornices and was thus less worried about them.

Presumably we were the first to climb this mountain, though it was all the same to me. I was much more interested in two majestic condors that flew past us close enough to touch.

We got back to our hut in darkness and saw the summit from which we had just returned glowing in the last light. Next morning as we set off down it was snowing again and we found the warmth of the valley very pleasant, although we camped again at 4400 metres.

It would be too blinkered to travel around the world as a climber and nothing else. As I have already suggested, the mountain objectives serve as focal points for the journey, and the experience comes from the contact with unsullied nature and lonely places. These are found above all in the mountains, and we feel them as a recompense for the innumerable hardships we undergo. Moreover, there is so much to see and hear if we consider the world with an open mind.

While still at home I had made it my business to learn something about Inca culture and had read a couple of books about Pizarro's conquest of Peru. Now that we were on the spot we were not going to miss the chance of seeing at least a couple of the world-famous cultural sites. As it was not possible to see everything, we decided to split up. Five were most interested in the Chavin civilization which was to be observed in the neighbourhood of Huaras, while Dr Schneider and I agreed to make an excursion to Cuzco.

Before leaving Huaras, however, we unexpectedly found ourselves involved in a fiesta. We were sought out at the hotel by a Peruvian whose son was studying in Germany and who wanted to meet us. He asked in passing whether we knew a place called Bad Aibling, where his son was at the Goethe Institut. It happened that Jochen Singer lived just nearby and that I had spent half my childhood there. Señor Alfonso Vega (for that was our visitor's name) was so overjoyed at this coincidence that he immediately set his whole house at our disposal. We would much rather have stayed on at the hotel with the heated swimming-pool, but to have refused the invitation would have been an insult. Four of us therefore moved over to his house, where Señor Vega enjoined us to wear a white shirt and a tie that evening, as there was going to be a little celebration. We imagined a dinner party in our honour, but it turned out quite otherwise.

Together with some señoritas we were loaded into a VW Minibus that stood before the door and driven bumpily over to Huaras. As we made the tour of the town the ladies disappeared into various houses, but we drove on through the inky night. Why we did not stop anywhere remained a mystery. Presently it began to rain, but the drive went on and on. A fine old celebration, we thought. Finally, after a good hour, Señor Vega drew up in front of one of the houses where one of the girls had vanished. Now she emerged all dressed and made up and climbed in beside us. One after another they were picked up again in all their finery.

Finally he deposited us under a projecting roof where we could shelter from the pouring rain and drove off into the night. What now? we wondered. Pressing back against the wall we waited for someone to come. Someone turned out to be Señor Vega again, this time on foot, and we followed him around to the left and through a door in single file. Inside was a patio where many people were already standing around wearing festive decorations which were now placed on us also by a young half-caste girl as pretty as a picture. Thereupon we were led into a room decorated with paper flowers and illuminated with green and pink neon tubes. The ladies sat down on one side, while the men stood on the other.

After it had been explained to us that it was the christening feast of a child which was being celebrated by the highest official in the town, we were introduced to our hostess. What we were doing there was still unclear. The others, who had a few words of Spanish, made more or less painful conversation. I sidled away into the doorway where two mulatto girls were standing. Despite their elegant dresses they seemed slightly out of place.

Some guitar players marched out, took their places, and the fiesta began with a dance. Between dances young girls brought around drinks and a veritable menu spitted on toothpicks. This went on for two or three hours, during which I cursed my social awkwardness and longed for it all to end.

Eventually I was spotted by Señor Vega as he danced by and led across to an adjoining room where there was a bar. He could have shown me that right at the beginning! After a couple of Piscos* and sangritas I began to thaw out and made my way over to the mulatto girls in the doorway. I brought them back to the bar, where we toasted each other eagerly. At this point the musicians decided to have a rest. My friends took their guitars from them and serenaded me. I had always thought that it only happened like that in dreams or films, but here it was in reality—Spanish music, Spanish singing, and with a Peruvian rhythm that went straight to my legs. I could not resist it, and began to dance. Whether it was the Pisco or the rhythm, despite the fact that I had never danced a solo in my life before the others assured me that it looked skilful and not at all ridiculous. The spell was broken; we were wallflowers no longer. Now the fiesta really got under way, and so it went on until dawn. As we made our farewells we were snowed under with invitations, all of which we unfortunately had to turn down as our private bus to Lima stood waiting.

* *Translator's note:* Pisco is a particularly excellent aniseed spirit made in the town of the same name. Sangrita is the diminutive of sangria, a punch of wine and lemon.

Achim and I were taking the expedition's baggage with us to Lima. It filled up the entire room inside. Neither driver nor bus looked especially trustworthy. Somehow we ground our way very slowly up to the top of the 4000 metre-high pass, but down the other side he began to drive like a wild man, flashing past oncoming vehicles always exactly at the stopping bays. In reply to our entreaty to drive a little slower he admitted honestly that he would be happy to do so, but that our speed was due to the brakes being out of order.

We did not stop in Lima, but flew 1000 kilometres southwards to Cuzco, passing Salcantay on the way. I got a close-up view of the icy giant on which Kasparek had fallen to his death through the cornice.

Out of necessity we dealt with a travel agency, or we would not have got seats in the plane. Moreover, it was cheaper, and all formalities were taken care of. We were met at the airport in Cuzco by a guide, the taxi was ordered and waiting to whisk us off to the feudal Grand Hotel. A whole programme was laid down. Really we did not want it at all, but it had its amenities. The other tourists followed it to the letter and obediently took the recommended rest period while we strolled straight on to the market place.

Apart from Gringos there seemed to be nobody but Indians, and the scene was correspondingly bright and scented. Strangers were ignored. Everything was still authentic, both the colourful llama-wool ponchos and the "restauración" that the Indians had set up in the street. As I am ready to try anything I sat down beside them on the kerb and had a bowl of the brew that they were offering for sale. They thoughtfully passed me a battered spoon which they first wiped on their not very clean-looking skirts, but I denied myself this achievement of civilization and ate with my fingers like the Indians. The stuff was so peppery that the water practically spurted horizontally out of my eyes. Beside me a two-year-old child was cramming the same concoction into his mouth as fast as he could. I passed him my bowl and he devoured its contents as well without changing his expression. Shaking my head, I abandoned the restaurant and returned to the hotel, where we were collected by our guide for a tour of the town and the Inca sites.

Cuzco was the last city to be destroyed by the Spanish after their invasion in 1532, but they did not succeed in razing the walls, which are composed of hewn but irregularly shaped blocks of stone fitted together without mortar. It is literally impossible to insert the tip of a knife into the joins. I knew from my readings that one twelve-cornered stone is world famous, but unfortunately I did not succeed in finding it as our guide had never heard of it.

One stands in amazement before the cyclopean constructions of Sacsahuaman. Anyone who is not moved by their evocations of the past is beyond all reach. I was lucky enough to be able to walk around on my own. The guide suggested a game of football with some urchins, and my companion joined in, so that I could give myself up undisturbed to the strange atmosphere emanating from these silent, gigantic cubes of stone.

In the short time available to us we could never have found the often very hidden-away Inca towns without guidance. In one there was an Inca bath out of which poured two streams of water, one hot, the other cold. Above it rose a wall containing trapezoidal niches in which, so the guide informed us, watchmen had stood guard. It was not necessary to take everything he said as gospel, as he also told us that the stones had been dragged hither from far away. My geologist said that this was just a load of nonsense: the stone was the same as that in the locality, from which it had certainly been quarried, but how this had been done remained a complete mystery.

The climax of our sight-seeing tour was our visit to Machu Pichu. There were only eight of us, and we did not need to take the generally overcrowded rail car, a special one having been put on for us. We set off punctually at 6.30 a.m., ascending to a pass in a series of hairpin bends, an ideal solution found by an Austrian engineer. The pass was the watershed between the Atlantic and the Pacific. Next the route went down and down into a beautiful broad valley that soon deepened and narrowed into a gorge leading into the main valley of the Rio Vilcanota. The little stream up on the pass had now developed into a torrential tributary of the Amazon, flowing into the Atlantic 6000 kilometres away.

Our little coach rattled and jolted along. The view was breath-taking. Now and again there would be an unplanned stop because of Indians driving their beasts along the track;

G

obviously there was no road. Whenever this happened a half-caste boy who was carried aboard for the purpose would jump down and clear the Indians and their herds out of the way. Suddenly we found ourselves running through gloomy primaeval forest and presently arrived at Machu Pichu "town", which consisted of a few miserable wooden shacks where a bus waits to take tourists up to the sanctuary.

In 1911 an American archaeologist who was riding through the Urubamba valley heard from an Indian that there were some ruins up on the mountain. The existence of this city had indeed been known for a long time, but nobody had yet found it. What must have been his feelings upon first seeing this mysterious ruined city, now one of the wonders of the world?

The Incas, past masters in the art of dry-stone construction, built up the city walls on extraordinarily steep slopes, thus winning one terrace after another on which they laid soil for agriculture. No irrigation was required, as Machu Pichu is in the jungle zone where it rains practically every day. In the centre are the holy temples, on which the guide gave a very thorough commentary. However, as I understood no Spanish and my companion had soon heard enough of the same old story, we set off to make our own discoveries and let the strange atmosphere work on us. In this way the experience is certainly more intense even if later it turns out that something has been missed. A short visit to such a place is always much too cursory. There is a good hotel at Machu Pichu, and it would be necessary to spend at least a week there. We always allow too little time, and then regret it for the rest of our lives. We did attempt to reach the absolute summit, on which there are more terraces and a temple, but did not quite make it on account of lack of time.

At one point I very nearly had an accident. An orchid the size of a man's fist was growing on the steep flank of the hill, and I wanted to photograph it. I could no longer be called a climbing novice, but rarely have I been so mistaken in estimating difficulty. Naturally I could see that the ground was very steep, but that neither impressed me nor prevented me from traversing across the hillside towards the flower. The layer of light humus that lay only finger-thick over the bedrock was so dry and dusty that it just crumbled away at the touch. There was no question of finding any firm hand- or foot-holds; only some thorny shrubs offered a little purchase. I had got to within a couple of metres of the orchid when suddenly a branch rose up and hissed at me. It was a snake. All of a sudden I did not care any more for the orchid, but sidled back with extreme concentration. When I reached level ground once more my knees were shaking and I think I had gone quite pale. From then on I modestly enjoyed the wild begonias that grew everywhere in an abundance such as you would scarcely find in a botanical garden in Europe.

Nature and culture could scarcely be more closely associated than they are here. With this impression we returned to Cuzco and on to Lima, where we joined up again with our companions who told us with equal enthusiasm about the Chavin culture.

Our absolutely undramatic yet thrilling "expedition" was over. Now that we had poked our noses into South America, we began to dream of the north. I therefore asked OE: "What about a trip along the 'dream-road of the world' from Canada to Mexico, striking off left and right at some of the vast number of mountain objectives?"

CHAPTER XIX

From Canada to Mexico

ONCE AGAIN TWO years went by before our "expedition" was ready, naturally under the patronage of OE, who this time brought his younger son Frederick along so that he too should undergo the test afforded by the joys and hardships of such a journey. A new member of the party was Alois Deisz, my friend and colleague as a mountain guide, who was to lose his life in an avalanche in the Ötztal in 1970. Once again Jochen Singer accompanied us as doctor. As we had learnt to our satisfaction in Africa and South America, his presence was a guarantee of good medical care.

Like naïve little Max we sought for a mountaineering goal in Canada and hit upon Mount Waddington in the Coast Range north of Vancouver. It might just as easily have been any other 4000er, of which there were plenty in the neighbourhood. By pure chance we had picked out not only the most difficult but the most inaccessible of them all. After that we wanted to climb a few peaks in the Rocky Mountains, visit Yellowstone National Park, take a look at the Grand Canyon, and then climb Popocatapetl and if possible Orizaba, the highest mountain in Mexico, while also seeing any other sights we could take in. It generally works out differently from the way you expect.

Owing to our previous experience, the means at OE's disposal and the ample time available for preparation, the whole trip went like clockwork. In any case, the great step into the unknown no longer exists—there is no time to spare for improvisation, we are constantly at the mercy of the timetable and our own objectives. Nowadays there are in practice only two ways to travel, either with plenty of money or, better, with plenty of time; best of all with both. At least we had the first on our side.

In order to recuperate from the wear and tear of preparations Alois Deisz and I set off in advance by sea on 18 August 1965 to New York, where we were to make the last arrangements. The others followed later by air. Our ulterior motive was to taste the pleasures of a first-class sea voyage just once in our lives and to see something of New York. Although the lazy life on board is marvellous, the six days from Cherbourg to New York are quite enough to weary of it. One can even have enough of eating to repletion in order to build up a hump for coming lean times.

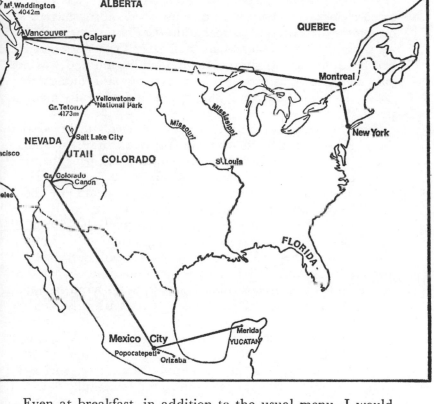

Even at breakfast, in addition to the usual menu, I would polish off some slices of leg of lamb, a veal fillet or some goulash, greatly to the disgust of Alois, who was suffering from sea-sickness. Even when he was more or less back on his feet he would suddenly go pale again over the breakfast table and rush outside to the rail. There has to be a balance of nature— one eats, another throws up.

In New York I was duly impressed by the skyscrapers. The Natural Science Museum with its unique mineral collections was surprisingly interesting, and no less so a visit to a bar in Harlem. There had just been a bout of racial disturbances, and we were warned off the negro quarter. In fact we saw nothing of any danger. Probably much simply depends on how one behaves.

Next day we almost missed the aeroplane. We returned home at 3 a.m. and had to get up again two hours later in order to be at the airport by seven o'clock. It was exactly seven o'clock when we woke up! Unwashed and unshaven, we caught the aircraft to Montreal at the very last moment. There we were met by the world-famous climber Fritz Wiessner. He had been the first to climb Mount Waddington and was not only able to give us precise information but also contacts that greatly facilitated our undertaking and indeed really made it possible.

From Stowe, his home in Vermont, he telephoned God and the world on our behalf, which in America is no light undertaking on account of the time differences. It happens that one calls up a friend 5000 kilometres away on the west coast at eight o'clock in the morning only to hear him grumbling about being hauled out of his bed at 3 a.m. If friendship is international, mountaineering friendship is particularly so. We all serve the same ideal, and in the case of anyone whose reputation is known beyond his own home ground everybody is aware of what he has done and—more important—what kind of a person he is. Recognition and esteem go hand in hand, friendship is immediate, and each one does what he can for the other.

Thus Canadian climbers were waiting for us at Vancouver airport ready to take us into their homes and show us with justified pride around the wonderful Pacific city, ringed in with mountains. It contained the most beautifully laid-out parks I had ever seen.

Fips Broda, president of the Vancouver mountaineers, had been born in Salzburg and knew every climber in the place. Some had been to Mount Waddington and showed us photographs, dwelling on the peculiarities of the mountain. For the first time we began to understand what we had bitten off. There was no reason to fear the technical difficulties, although they were around Grades 5 and 6. The difficulties of access are also less than they were in Wiessner's day. He had been obliged to fight his way for weeks and months through trackless country even to reach the mountain. Nowadays one takes an aeroplane and finally a helicopter and is simply set down at the foot of the peak. This was only one aspect of the arrangements in which we received every kind of help. Nobody would fly in a non-climber. It was necessary to have a handwritten recommendation from well-known people, of whom luckily we were not in short supply. The great danger is that if the weather breaks the thermometer can plummet in an hour from zero to $-40°C$. The supercooled humid air masses drive in from the ocean and condense on the mountain as ice. This can happen in the Western Alps too, as I knew from the Eiger and the Grandes Jorasses, but whereas there the layer of verglas may be 10–20 centimetres thick at the most, on Mount Waddington it can reach over a metre.

The summit of Mount Waddington is just over 4000 metres high, while the place where the helicopter set us down was at about 2000 metres. It was already September, the month in which these sudden storms occur most frequently. We had to promise solemnly to remain where we were even if it snowed for weeks. Good weather was bound to come in the end, and then they would get us out. We therefore purchased enough food for three weeks and an equivalent amount of fuel for melting snow; after all, we did not have to carry it all. Our doctor had explained to us that theoretically one could go a whole month without solid food, but only three days without water.

Two seaplanes carried us and our baggage to Ghost Lake, a tarn in the mountains, where we were picked up by the helicopter and transported in relays to our starting point amid ice and snow. Here we set up a base camp.

As the helicopter chugged away after bringing in the last loads we began to realize the solitude in which we had had ourselves set down. There was no way back under our own steam, and if things came to the worst we should just have to dig into the snow and wait for three weeks. For the time being, however, the weather could not have been finer. Before long the tents were up and the cookers purring. After an ample meal and a good swig of Canadian whiskey my Toscanelli tasted as satisfying as always. Everything is relative, and no comfort in a Grand Hotel could compensate for the romantic scene around us. The following day we made a faint-hearted attempt to reconnoitre the notorious Bravo glacier.

Some Japanese climbers had been here shortly before us. Owing to bad weather they had failed to reach the summit, returning with reports of very rotten ice. And in fact the glacier did not look particularly inviting. It was seamed with crevasses and séracs that loured apparently ready to fall at any moment. On the right of the glacier was a rocky spur that we thought climbable and up which we made our way for a couple of pitches. Only we kept wondering how we were going to get back on to the glacier.

Despite this uncertainty, the following day the whole party climbed the spur, which turned out to be not so simple. Our doubts proved groundless, as we were able to reach the upper glacier easily and without any great loss of height. Thus we circumvented the Bravo glacier, in which on one occasion a whole expedition had come to grief.

The way forward was plain to see. Less plain was how we were going to get past an almost horizontal stretch of ice ridge. There was no other solution but to sit astride it and work our way along for an hour and a half, not a very agreeable pastime on ice. I knew how suddenly such a thin rind of ice could crack off, and took good care to keep the pressure of my thighs equal on both sides—no doubt under the influence of a healthy fear—for the entire time, so that as a result I had cramps in my legs throughout the following night. Next came a steep but compact stretch of glacier up which we also climbed despite signs of growing fatigue due to our heavy sacks. Just as dusk was falling we reached a level place where we could pitch our high-altitude tents.

The following day we were supposed to go back down again in order to carry up further supplies of food, but somehow the idea gave us the shivers. We therefore seized on the excuse that not a single day of fine weather should be wasted and decided to go straight for the summit. It was true that we had no food, but had not our doctor told us that it was possible to go without for 30 days? While it was still dark next morning we kicked our way up breakable crust for some hours to the upper rock-buttresses. It was a real treat to lay hand on the warm, dry rock.

From a gap on the ridge we could see the summit towering above us. Now that we were sure of getting there I wanted to enjoy the climbing to the full (as if I could not get any amount of it around home) and got rid of all unnecessary ballast. Even my two cameras remained in the sack which I left in the gap, an action which I have never stopped regretting to this day, as nowhere else have I seen such strange ice formations on a vertical face. We had been told that in these parts ice could form metres thick on perpendicular rock walls, but I had not really taken it literally. This layer is then eroded by the warm air, so that transparent, tattered banners of ice are left projecting as much as five metres, looking as though they have been attacked with a pair of scissors. Beautiful as they look when illuminated by the sun, they were in reality extremely dangerous, since a single one might weigh several hundred tons and they were ready to fall at any moment. On this occa- sion I was climbing last on the rope and would have had time to take photographs. But there it was, the cameras were back in that accursed gap, for which I have never forgiven myself. The technical difficulties were considerable, but gave us pleasure rather than trouble. We pulled up on to the summit with real Bavarian whoops of joy.

The descent consisted of abseils as far as the glacier, down which we then rushed towards the tents. When we reached them, we got a shock like an icy shower: the surface on which they were pitched now formed part of a bridge over a vast crevasse. We shuddered to think what might have happened during the night.

Since it was now necessary to strike camp in any case, we continued to descend while the daylight lasted, and so reached the narrow ice ridge. We had no desire whatever to ride our way along it again, so I investigated the edge of rock on which it rested 50 or 100 metres below. To our stupefaction it went without any difficulty at all, and we came upon a perfect little bivouac site.

The sun had set and the full moon was rising over the glacier as we spread out our bivouac gear on a granite slab. There was not a breath of wind; we had plenty of warm, dry things; only there was nothing to eat, so we made do without. We knew that the fleshpots were waiting for us in base camp, from which no serious obstacle now separated us. The nylon high-altitude tent served me as groundsheet, and before long I was blissfully asleep.

In the middle of the night I awoke out of a profound slumber. For no reason that I could think of I was wide awake and admired the fantastic view. The full moon stood above an icy peak that shone with reflected light. Entranced with the sight, I wondered why I had not noticed this mountain before going to sleep. Suddenly the realization shot through me that I had gradually slid down the smooth nylon under-surface until my head had passed the rock flake which had previously blocked the view. My feet were already dangling over space. Cautiously I wriggled back until I could sit up and anchor myself with piton and rope. Then I lay down again behind the flake and went back to dreaming of the beautiful view.

The remainder of the descent next day was protracted but not particularly difficult, and we reached our well-supplied base camp towards evening. Only someone who has experienced such a healthy hunger can imagine how that food tasted, although so primitively cooked. Then we called up Vancouver on the radio transmitter that we had been left with for all eventualities, duly obtaining a connection and an answer; we were to be picked up next day. The following morning we joyously struck camp, packed all the kit up in its travelling crates, gobbled all the food that we really liked, sat down on the crates and waited. Every time there was a noise we jumped up, but it always turned out to be a distant icefall rumbling down. No helicopter appeared. As the shadows grew longer so did our faces, but we sat where we were and did not abandon our posts. At last twilight gathered and it grew cold. We grumpily unpacked again, pitched the tents and crawled inside.

In the night the Canadian wind began to howl and before long hail began to fall. Presently its drumming changed to the rustle of snow. A shock of fear ran through me. Could this be the great snowfall that might last three weeks? Nobody could sleep any more, yet as day dawned we all lay where we were. Nobody spoke a word. At about ten o'clock there was a sudden humming in the air; it could not be another avalanche. We tore out of the tents, and there was a helicopter sweeping towards us like a hornet. The evacuation and the liaison between the helicopter and the seaplane that picked us up at

Ghost Lake went like clockwork. The press and the television were already there, but we were feeling too happy to be upset by that and just let it all flow over our heads.

The real jubilation took place in Vancouver, where our mountain friends were waiting for us. We had to tell our story over and over again, and I think that if we had failed to climb the mountain our friends would have been far more disappointed than ourselves. We were fully aware of how lucky we had been with regard to weather and conditions and of how much we owed to all those who had helped us in our adventure.

In the Glacier National Park in British Columbia there are many fine mountains, and we had picked out Eagle Peak as our next goal. It is neither particularly high nor particularly difficult, and so not the kind of mountain for name-dropping. What it does call for is endurance, a quality it shares with most of the peaks in the Rocky Mountains. The trek takes ten or twelve hours and has the peculiarity that the place is swarming with bears. Though very strong, the brown bears are not particularly aggressive, but the grizzlies are irritable and very dangerous. The park warden told us some real horror stories. It is no good carrying a gun, as you do not get a chance to shoot when you are having a rumpus with a bear. The best thing is to make a lot of noise as you go along, shouting and banging, which we were able to do with our pitons and kara-biners. The ideal solution would have been a cow bell to hang around our necks, but unfortunately we had neglected to bring one with us. Warned thus, the animals have time to move out of the way before one reaches the danger zone. At high altitude we saw a lot of fresh bear tracks in the new snow. The bears withdraw to high altitude in order to hibernate and there dig themselves in. Perhaps luckily for us, we never encountered one.

After our ascent of Eagle Peak, a park warden took me in his car to a rubbish dump which was carefully fenced off, and where there were bears busily rooting around. They are omnivorous, and if they find nothing better will devour cartons, packing and all. We had hardly been there a minute when he suddenly stopped and listened. "There's a grizzly growling!" he said. I could hear nothing and wanted to get out of the car to photograph the bears, but the warden hauled me back at once. Apparently the beasts move so fast that I would not have had time to jump back in. When one is completely new to a thing one just has to rely on the experience of others, and so once again I missed seeing one of these feared creatures.

We now travelled by Canadian Pacific express across the Rocky Mountains to Calgary via famous places such as Golden, Lake Louise and Banff. The mountains resemble our central Alps but are not so excessively developed, and are unlikely to become so in a hurry, mountaineering being a much less popular pastime in America than in Europe. Anybody who goes climbing has to be self-sufficient, as there are no villages and huts to depend on. Almost all mountain ranges are national parks. The park wardens, who are held responsible for seeing that nothing goes wrong and that the regulations are observed, take good care that nobody undertakes mountain adventures beyond his powers. For mountaineering a special pass is required, and this is only issued to those who can show a certificate from a mountaineering club or a well-known climber. We had such a certificate, and as the wardens were mainly Austrians, Swiss or Germans they nearly all knew my name, which often helped to clear obstacles from our path.

Our minds were not only set on mountain climbing. Yellowstone Park lay on our route and, as already planned, we were able to pay it a visit. We therefore travelled by Greyhound coach from Calgary to Livingstone, where we hired a car to continue the journey and drove up via Gardiner to the park. Nowhere in the world are there so many natural marvels all gathered together in one place and easily accessible. The ground steams and puffs; there are not just hundreds but thousands of geysers, whole valleys full of them. The biggest and most famous is Old Faithful, right in front of a big hotel built in a trashy turn-of-the-century rustic style.

Yellowstone Park has a lot to offer quite apart from geysers. Upon entry you receive a prospectus and a map on which everything is clearly indicated, among other things a petrified forest which interested me particularly. This was reached by a fine macadamed road that ran past lakes and over a pass 3000 metres high. It was snowing, but as we sat in a car with the heating turned on that did not worry us particularly. At the viewpoint at the top stood a warning notice about bears which, being perfectly used to traffic, make a beeline for the cars and beg. Immediately afterwards we saw bears on the road and halted. A big one with two young came lumbering towards us. We took a couple of quick snapshots and dived back into the car. Although they looked as comical and harmless as a rough-haired dachshund at home, nevertheless they were slightly bigger. Forgetting this is the mistake which a lot of tourists make in spite of all the warnings. Naturally one feeds them whatever one has brought along for the purpose. Thus an American held a carrot out of the window; the bear gobbled down not only the carrot but also the fingers which held it. How is a bear supposed to know the difference? I am sure it intended no offence. In Yellowstone Park there are two hospitals that are full throughout the season with patients mauled by wild animals.

The petrified forest turned out to consist of a single petrified tree around which an iron paling had been erected in order to save it from tourists with an appetite for souvenirs. A notice stated that the tree was 40 million years old.

Only a few miles south of Yellowstone Park lies Grand Teton Park, which was another of our objectives. There we had a very special introduction. At Trail Creek Ranch near Jackson Hole lived Mrs Woolsey, captain of the American women's ski team at the 1936 Olympic Games and an internationally renowned mountain climber into the bargain. In 1937 she had been with Fritz Wiessner on the first ascent of Mount Waddington, so we were welcome guests. Fritz Wiessner had also promised to come and join us in an ascent of the 3800 metre Grand Teton.

While waiting for him to appear, we toured the area. There were 70 horses on the ranch, and for the first time I began to enjoy riding. Up to now I had always sat astride old nags, but never a real horse.

Jackson itself was an original kind of place, probably a genuine old cowboy town. Apart from the barrack-like houses there remains from those days a Silver Dollar Bar where we refreshed ourselves with whisky. All around us lounged people looking like characters out of a cowboy film, but real. One of them with a deeply weathered face was the father-in-law of the King of Siam. When a cattleman stands up you can see that he can ride better than walk, which is not surprising in view of the fact that they spend ten hours in the saddle almost every day. Despite the very "high" atmosphere they were all pleasant to one another and to us. We found it amazing that such a milieu should still exist. Not to be outdone, we stood a couple of rounds ourselves, though it was purely a gesture of politeness as by our standards these farmers are immensely rich. Apart from a fleet of cars and their own used-car dump most of them have their own aircraft and landing-strip. The unit of trade is not the steer but the herd. A farm is generally so big that it takes days to ride around it. We in our turn were something special for them: not just the ordinary run of rubber-necking tourists but mountain climbers. No doubt because of living near the Grand Teton they were well grounded in mountaineering and knew all about the north face of the Eiger.

The following day Wiessner turned up and we packed our sacks for the ascent of the Grand Teton. It is possible to drive up to the foot of the mountain in a car. We were expected and had no difficulties at the park entrance, which has a building and a barrier just like a customs post. One of the wardens joined our party, which proved to be a great advantage as he had access to a hut strictly reserved for wardens just below the start of the final difficulties.

A path led up through the woodland zone and ended at the point where the going became more difficult. Half a metre of new snow had fallen, filling in the holes between the blocks in the boulder field. We had to be extremely careful not to break a leg. It took us a full eight hours up to the hut, which was just a Nissen hut of corrugated iron, although a very roomy one. We undressed and lay down in our sleeping-bags, covering up with damp hut-blankets. The saddle on which the hut was built was at 3500 metres, so it got quite cold. In the night a storm of such violence blew up that I was expecting the whole box of tricks to be blown away at any moment. The thought of standing there in the fresh air, clad in nothing but a shirt, was not inviting. Next morning everything was deeply buried in snow and the rocks completely iced up. As we were not abso-lutely obsessed with the idea of fighting our way to the top at any price we decided to give up and descend.

Despite not reaching the summit we were all entirely satisfied with this tour. Making a trail downhill in thigh-deep snow is no problem. The American park warden slid down most of the snow gullies on the seat of his pants at the speed of an express train. In Germany this method of descent is strongly disapproved of, as it has led to too many accidents, but in spite of that I was finally unable to resist the temptation. Back on the woodland path we could wander along at our pleasure, enjoying the wonderful atmosphere of the place through the intermittent cloud as we strode back down to the valley, passing elks and huge deer, called wapiti, at very close quarters. If the weather had broken like that while we were on Mount Waddington we would have been in a fine pickle. This thought lent wings to our happy mood in spite of not reaching the summit. We handed back the hire-car at Jackson airport and flew off over Salt Lake City towards the Grand Canyon.

In this greatest gorge on earth there are places to climb, but they were not the main source of attraction for us. We just wanted to take a look at them by the way if everything went well, which it certainly did not.

Near the southern edge of the canyon there is a regular forest of hotels populated with troops of tourists from all over the world who are content with a view into the depths. It is in fact impossible to see right down to the bed of the canyon, but most of them do not care about that as you can buy post-cards of it in the hotel. Anyone who wants to penetrate into the gorge has to go to the "Indian Garden", which is generally done on mule-back and takes a whole day. Only a few press on right down to the bottom. We climbers went on foot. The mule-track is broad and well trodden, so there is little need to take care and one can concentrate on the strange, impressive landscape.

The plateau lies at over 2000 metres and is covered with pine and juniper. The deeper you go, the more the vegetation changes; in fact one passes through practically all zones of vegetation from evergreens to cacti. The most remarkable phenomenon of all is the 2000 metre-deep incision in the earth's crust, which the geologists ascribe to a rising of the land over millions of years during which the already existing river had time to carve its way through. The upper levels consist of sandstone and limestone in horizontal strata, but below a certain depth one comes upon crystalline rocks, gneiss and granite. The dark coloration of the crystalline rock streaked with pale veins of quartz is striking in the extreme; one of us remarked: "That looks just like a well-larded petrified meat-loaf!" The Colorado river is far from being the poor little brooklet that had been described to me, but a full-grown river over 2000 kilometres long quite powerful enough to perform the mighty work of erosion.

There is an iron bridge over the river. The poor mules that carried down the materials for it deserve a monument. A few kilometres farther on, on the other bank, is the Phantom Ranch, swimming-pool and all. As we were out of season the ranch was closed and the pool unfortunately empty of water. A little notice saying "Open from 6 p.m." hung on the door.

It was noon. We had set off much too early, although the eight-hour march was only half as hard as it would have been later. Nevertheless, the heat on the valley floor was such that our tongues stuck to the roofs of our mouths, and the sight of the empty pool did nothing to help matters. Everybody looked for a patch of shade, but I was seized with a desire to reconnoitre one of the peaks that we might be able to climb next day.

"Peaks" is really a funny word to use for these cones formed by erosion. They also have strange names such as Shiva's Temple, the Pyramid of Cheops, Zoroaster's Temple and so on. The latter attracted me and I wanted to climb it.

As soon as you take one step off the beaten track you are in the virgin wilderness. Carefully making my way around the cactus bushes, I sought out the rocky steps where I got some exciting climbing. In between them were flatter terraces covered with thorny scrub. Everything had spines, not only the cacti. There was a little wall about four metres high where I enjoyed the bright-red rock and the plentiful holds. Just as I was about to pull out over the top there was a horrible rattling noise so that I let go out of fright and dropped to the bottom. We had been warned about rattlesnakes everywhere we went. Probably this was one, but I did not get time to see it. The fall would not have been so bad if I had not landed seat-first in a cactus. After that I made my way down, finding the descent quite a thorny problem. It was a full three days before the doctor succeeded in extracting all the prickles.

Following this adventure, for which everybody naturally made fun of me, I no longer had quite the same enthusiasm to climb another such peak. We therefore decided to go back via the Kaibab Trail. By contrast with the luxury hotels on the southern edge of the canyon, the Phantom Ranch turned out to be quite a simple place where the service was personal and friendly.

Next day we set off early, well supplied with tins of beer. Naïvely, the Americans only quote the distance of 6·8 miles without a word about the height difference of 1600 metres, which must have caused trouble to many a person inexperienced in mountain matters. We were able to work out for ourselves how long it would take us. The trail was a real walkers' path, and the rock scenery almost more impressive than along the Angel Trail by which we had descended.

All of a sudden we encountered a youth group, first of all the fresh and cheery, then the ones with red faces, then the ones with their tongues hanging out, and last of all two guides, probably teachers, one of whom should have been in front setting the pace. At least, that is how it is done where I come from. But it is also worth mentioning another episode in which the credit is on their side. A chewing-gum wrapper was lying on the path: I simply glanced at it, but one of the youngsters picked it up, put it in his pocket and walked on. I pondered whether we could ever educate our people to this point.

Higher up I began to suffer from thirst and remembered the beer in the rucksack. After enjoying every delicious drop I flipped the empty tin in a high arc into a gully below. At that moment a group on horseback came around the corner and heard the noise of the tin rattling downhill. They all looked at me indignantly, while the accursed can clattered on. It is taboo to throw away any kind of rubbish in the nature reserves, but somehow I had not really absorbed the point until I received that annihilating stare. The damned tin rattled and tinkled down and down as though wanting to accuse me in its turn and unable to find any rest. To think that I had to travel to America to learn that lesson!

The Grand Canyon is far from being the only thing to see and wonder at in Arizona. The centre is Flagstaff, where we stayed. It is a country which never ceases to surprise. Deserts, mountains and gorges all exist in close proximity to each other and to unique natural phenomena like the giant meteor crater which is still a puzzle to scientists. The most interesting to me was the petrified forest, which here really does consist of an entire wood of petrified trees. Naturally, it is closely guarded. The buildings of the park management stand at the entrance like customs posts. Tourists are given precise indications as to where they may drive and walk, and it is strictly forbidden to leave the track. The reason is that there are hundreds of trees which have turned into a semi-precious stone, agate, and are thus worth a lot of money. They are not allowed to be taken away or used industrially. Everything must remain just as it is. Millions of years ago mighty floods covered the forest with mud and pressed it thousands of metres deep into the earth. The wood could neither carbonize nor perish. The cells were pervaded with silica, so that the entire trunk turned to stone. Later the sunken strata rose again; the hard-caked mud turned to dust and was eroded by the wind. The petrified trunks, some of them a metre thick, were left scattered around an area of several square kilometres. Agate splinters of all colours lie around in heaps, but it is forbidden even to pick them up. This is a sensible precaution, as if all the generations of visitors took their pick even the most abundant supply would soon be cleaned out. Outside the protected zone, stones the size of a side plate were being traded for two to four dollars, though guaranteed not from the petrified wood. On the way out we once again had to stop at a house with a barrier to be questioned about stones as though at the customs, and both cars and passengers were thoroughly searched.

Once again we turned in our hire-car at the airport and flew direct to Mexico, the terminus of our dream journey. What mountaineer would not wish to stand just once on the 5300 metre summit of Popocatapetl? Orizaba, which at 5700 metres is the highest mountain in Mexico, is also tempting. Naturally we also wanted to see the city and the centres of Aztec and perhaps Mayan culture. It was rather a big programme for one visit, but none of us knew if he would ever get a chance to return.

It is said that Popocatapetl can be seen from the city, but if so I did not see it. Even the approaches to the mountain are not at all easy. Mexican roads are good, but as soon as you get off them—and mountains are never on them—there are only rough tracks. Signposts also are only found on highroads. It was thus hardly surprising that we immediately got lost amid the fields of maize. The Mexicans we asked were friendly and indicated the way with voluble gestures which, however, were all wrong. Finally we succeeded in finding the right road, which brought us up into a park-like landscape at 4000 metres, where we found a lodging house. It was none too clean and a bit annoyingly primitive, but the owners were friendly. Anybody who is hypersensitive in this respect would do better to stay at home anyway. A little dirt does one no harm, especially in the pure air at high altitudes.

We set off before dawn, following an indefinite path through a gigantic lava field. The whole time our lungs suffered from an irritating, constricting pressure that made us want to cough. Later I was to read that this was caused by the volcanic dust, but at the time we did not see it on account of the darkness. By daybreak we were already up on the snow slopes which ascended at a steady angle of about 40° to the edge of the crater, and it was just a case of drawing our heads in and kicking our way upwards step by step. The important thing was to avoid hurried movements. The rarer air at 5000 metres makes itself felt, but only if you break the most elementary rules of mountaineering and go too fast.

There is really nothing more boring than plodding up a featureless, giant snowfield. One asks oneself, and rightly, what pleasure there is in it. In the last resort it is not a question of pleasure but just of getting on with it.

It looked as though we could reach out and touch the edge of the crater, and yet we never seemed to get any nearer. The air was so thin and crystal clear that distance was impossible to judge. It is not always like that; it depends on the air pressure, the time of year and all sorts of factors. Anyway, although I had often felt more worn out on other climbs, I had rarely felt so sour. My mood changed magically as we reached the crater. The edge was decorated with two crosses fashioned out of iron cable that had benevolently been placed here rather than on the true summit a further two hours away, which few bother to visit. We saw no reason to out-Herod Herod. The distant view was enormous in its expanse, while the view straight down, not only towards the valley but into the mountain, was fascinating. Out of every crack issued steam, as in Yellowstone Park. In the floor of the crater, 400 metres below, lay a small emerald-green lake that sparkled like a jewel whenever it was not obscured with a cloud of vapour.

When our hunger and thirst had been satisfied and the Toscanelli smoke was mingling with the puffs of steam from the crater, my happiness knew no bounds. It was not the first time that the feeling of achievement had produced this sense of rapture, but on Popocatapetl, perhaps on account of these vapour clouds, it was particularly intense. That in itself is a reward for our pains, and one feels ashamed to have been peevish even for a moment.

Meanwhile the snow had softened more than ankle deep; too deep already for walking down in comfort. Thinking of my glissade on the Grand Teton I sat down on the seat of my smooth nylon overtrousers and whizzed downhill at breakneck speed for well over 1000 metres. Although my companions were all appreciably younger they were no longer childish enough to get so much pleasure from sliding on their bottoms, so they dutifully stamped their way down as one should. I was well aware of the danger and braked to a stop before shooting on to the lava slopes. Everything went well, and there was even time for my spread-out clothes to dry before the others arrived. The track that I had scooped out with my popo* led like a ruled line to the summit of Popocatapetl.

After this it was child's play to run down through the whirling dust to the lodging house. On the way we were able to collect specimens of volcanic glass, which lay all around.

The car that had brought us was ready waiting to whisk us back to the city, only 50 kilometres away. The luxuries of civilized life—for by this time we felt all comforts as luxuries, even a hot bath—were now restored again to their proper perspective, and we enjoyed them to the utmost. An evening with the Mariachis, the Mexican musicians, where the mescal flowed freely, left our memories of the mountain somewhat hazier but none the less beautiful.

After a rest day, needed not so much because of our efforts on the mountain as on account of the celebration that had followed, we felt ready for the next adventure. Our last goal was Orizaba. This time the journey was somewhat longer, eastwards past Pueblo. In one little place it was market day, and buses were parked anywhere and anyhow. It looked as though we would never get through. One of us was seized with panic and insisted that we should reach our objective via a short diversion. As nobody had any better suggestion to

* *Translator's note:* In German, Popo = bottom. The name of this mountain is therefore a source of high delight and frequent punning.

offer, we did just that; but instead of 35 kilometres the diversion turned out to be 200. It gave us a chance to see something of the country, yucca woods, lonely pueblos and a pool that had brimmed out into an extensive lake. It was the time of transition from the rains to the dry season, which we judged the best for our purpose.

The point of departure for Orizaba was a village with the (to us) strange-sounding name of Tlaquichuga, where they are all prepared to cope with the needs of those wanting to climb the mountain. There is only one store, but it has everything from boot-laces to a cross-country vehicle. The latter had just left to work in the fields and we had to wait until it got back in the evening. It turned out to be an ancient four-wheel-drive Dodge that groaned and rattled its way up the fearful tracks leading towards the mountain so that we thought it was about to fall apart at any moment. The driver's name was Primitivo, but he could drive nevertheless. It was dark by the time we reached the hut, a simple corrugated-iron shack once again, but roomy and relatively clean.

We were up and away before 3 a.m. The wind was howling and the snowflakes whirled so thickly around us that we could not tell which way to go. Uphill, of course. That much was clear, but nothing else was.

In the course of a lifetime of mountain climbing one somehow develops a kind of sixth sense. I had often relied on it when there was nothing else to go on; only it is important that it should not be called into question, since no one can be that confident and I immediately get led astray. On this occasion nobody did so, as it was impossible to see or recognize anything at all. We hit off the glacier at precisely the right point. The Mexicans are very proud of the Orizaba glacier, and we had been warned about the danger of crevasses. However, we had no intention of dropping into a letter-box of that kind in Mexico of all places, so we just kept away to the right of them.

The snowstorm had increased rather than decreased. It was bitterly cold into the bargain, and I had to pull on my wind-proofs, promptly freezing my fingers in the process. In the few minutes in which I had not worn mittens my hands had turned as white as a linen sheet and my fingers a yellowy hue, but by immediate friction with a woollen garment one can

bring them back to life. Next I wanted to make up for lost
time by setting a faster pace, which I hoped would also enable
us to warm up. I might have saved myself the trouble, as the
net effect was to make me out of breath. Not until I had settled
back into my usual rhythm did I recover. The wind drove
away the cloud and the sun began to warm us, although it
remained cold all the way to the summit.

By contrast with Popocatapetl, Orizaba has a proper
summit, not just a highest point on a crater. The crater itself
is still deeper and wider, but extinct. It would not have been
difficult to climb down into it, but there seemed no particular
point. The summit was much more interesting. From it you can
see two oceans, the Atlantic in the east and the Pacific away
to the west. In fact all we saw was two silvery lines but almost
persuaded ourselves that they were the sea. The summit cross
consists only of lengths of piping screwed together, some of
which was missing. In spite of the cold it was beautiful, but
we did not hold out for long.

This time there was no question of glissading down as on
Popocatapetl, although I had been looking forward to it. We
had to stamp our way step by step down the icy, wind-blasted
slope with crampons on our feet, giving the "terrible" crevasses
a wide berth. The slopes were less monotonous than on other
volcanoes. It would seem that it has been extinct long enough
for erosion to take effect.

By the time we returned Primitivo was waiting for us
practically frozen. In Tlaquichuga the greengrocer solemnly
decorated us with medals for our successful ascent of Orizaba.

Although we almost regretted that our mountaineering
programme was now completed, it left us free to concentrate on
the night-life of Mexico City. This really had something to
offer, as the Mariachis are incomparable. As we said goodbye
two bands played us into the car, one on each side, both playing different tunes and trying to drown each other out.

I never miss an opportunity of seeing a market. The one in
Mexico was something quite special, a kind of flea-market of
gigantic size. Fruit, flowers, vegetables and above all pottery
are traded in the neighbouring streets and halls, where there is
already plenty to keep the visitor interested for days. But the
real surprises are to be found in the flea-market. Under piles
of junk one comes upon strange treasures. Under Mexican

rule the Indians continue to fashion figures and figurines in the same style as in the days of Montezuma. Silverware and precious stones, both rough and polished, are offered for sale beside nylon tights and spare parts for bicycles. In between may be a wooden crucifix on which Christ is represented in wire, probably for lack of any other material. Our modern artists and op-artists could find plenty of stimulation there.

The greatest surprise of all was to run into a man from Oberstdorf. Before I had set off on the trip he had told me that we might meet in Mexico. I had not taken this in the least bit seriously, as he had no money. However, he did have special talents. By the time he had been in a country two weeks he could not only get by in the language but would also have picked up its customs to such an extent that you could hardly tell him from a native. Although he had climbed no higher than the flocks of sheep he had already been to the Himalayas. Penniless he might be, but time also played no part in his calculations. Whom should I meet in the market, then, but this fanatical globetrotter, whose name was Pit. Our greetings attracted attention even in the hubbub of the market. Already he could show us the most hidden corners of the city. No doubt he was fully acquainted with the underworld, which is quite extensive.

He insisted that we should not leave Mexico without seeing a bull-fight, so one afternoon we went along with him. The atmosphere of the arena was fascinating, but it was an effort to try to enjoy the spectacle itself. Perhaps the best matadors were not present that day; also one needs to understand the rules and rituals in order to appreciate the finer points of a corrida. For me it was just slaughter dressed up in a lot of hocus pocus. When one of the bulls was stubbornly unwilling to lose its life, Pit bellowed in Spanish—freely translated— "Give him a gun, somebody", and the entire arena roared with delight. Personally, I had seen enough, and we slunk out feeling queasy.

In the course of this journey we had received powerful impressions, overcome the inevitable mutual tensions, and enriched our lives with indelible experiences. This is of the essence of mountaineering, so often misunderstood. It enables us to travel away from the beaten track and to find satisfactions unsuspected by or simply unavailable to the plainsman.

What followed was just the usual kind of travelling in high style—a flight to Yucatan, visits to the Mayan sites of Chichen Itza and Uxmal, and finally a swim in the Caribbean, warm as a bath. There were scarcely any breakers, only smooth swell as high as a room on which I drifted far out, rising and falling, revolving in memory all the wonderful experiences we had been through. It was such a perfect pleasure that I was pervaded with a sense of peace with the whole beautiful world.

Yet such a vision of peace is only fantasy. Barely ten metres away from me a huge fish broke the surface, and I remembered that we had been warned that this bay was infested with sharks. After that the green waves, blue sky and deceptive silence no longer entranced me so much, and I made for shore as fast as I could. A hole was yawning in my dream of a world of peace.

On the shore stood a pair of refreshment stalls, almost incomparably hideous corrugated-iron shanties. In each of them a gramophone was turned up to the maximum. The full moon was beginning to climb out of the sea behind the wind-dishevelled palms, a farewell picture to bear away.

Each of us bought a huge coconut from a pedlar. The man peeled them, punched a hole in the shell and placed a drinking-straw in it. We sucked up the ice-cold milk, some with expressions of bliss, the others with a grimace. Then we had the nuts split open; ours were marvellously white and delicious, the others brown and stinking. From outside no difference had been perceptible.

So it is with life and with journeys: outwardly the same for all, yet so different.

Index

Compiled by H. E. Crowe